Inclusive Education Learners and Learning Contexts

The companion volume in this series is:

Inclusive Education: Diverse Perspectives
Edited by: Melanie Nind, Jonathan Rix, Kieron Sheehy and Katy Simmons

Both of these volumes are part of the second level Open University course E243 *Inclusive Education: Learning from each other* which can be studied on its own or as part of an Open University undergraduate degree.

How to apply

If you would like to register for this course, or simply to find out more information about available courses, details can be obtained from the Course Reservations Centre, PO Box 724, The Open University, Walton Hall, Milton Keynes, MK7 6ZW, UK (Telephone 0 (0 44) 1908 653231). Details can also be viewed on our web page http://www.open.ac.uk.

Inclusive Education: Learners and Learning Contexts

Edited by Melanie Nind,
Kieron Sheehy and Katy Simmons

 **David Fulton** Publishers

The Open
University

in association with

David Fulton Publishers Ltd
The Chiswick Centre, 414 Chiswick High Road, London W4 5TF

www.fultonpublishers.co.uk

First published in 2003 by David Fulton Publishers

10 9 8 7 6 5 4 3 2 1

Note: The right of the individual contributors to be identified as the authors of their work has been asserted by them in accordance with the Copyright, Designs and Patents Act 1988.

David Fulton Publishers is a division of Granada Learning Limited, part of Granada plc.

British Library Cataloguing in Publication Data
A catalogue record for this book is available from the British Library.

ISBN 1 84312 066 6

Typeset by Pantek Arts Ltd, Maidstone, Kent
Printed and bound in Great Britain

Contents

About the Editors

Melanie Nind is best known for her work on Intensive Interaction, an interactive approach to teaching children and adults with severe learning difficulties (*Access to Communication; Interaction in Action; Implementing Intensive Interaction in Schools*, David Fulton Publishers). She has taught in special schools and coordinated learning support in further education colleges before teaching in higher education. Her research interests include, alongside teaching and learning, inclusive school cultures, mental health and profound learning difficulties, and the politics of special education movements and interventions. She is a senior lecturer in inclusive and special education in the Faculty for Education and Language Studies at The Open University.

Jonathan Rix has worked as a language learning support teacher in a London comprehensive, and as a writer and facilitator in a wide variety of community, educational and theatrical settings. He has written over 50 basic language audio tours for people with learning difficulties. He is a parent representative on the National Portage Association Executive, and on the steering committee of his local playgroup. His current research is on the use of simplified materials and on access to cultural sites for people with learning disabilities. He is a lecturer in inclusive education in the Faculty for Education and Language Studies at The Open University.

Kieron Sheehy has worked in both education and health settings as a teacher, psychologist and lecturer. He has published in the areas of child development, learning and technology. His research is concerned with developing inclusive classroom practice through new technology and promoting mental health in people with profound learning difficulties. He is a lecturer in inclusive and special education in the Faculty for Education and Language Studies at The Open University.

Katy Simmons has taught in schools and higher education in the UK, USA and Australia, working with migrant groups, disadvantaged pupils and pupils with learning difficulties. She has acted as an advocate for parents and a campaigner on legal rights issues for young people with disabilities. She is a Trustee of the Advisory Centre for Education and chair of governors of a large secondary school. She has published on policy issues and is a lecturer in inclusive and special education in the Faculty for Education and Language Studies at The Open University.

Acknowledgements

We would like to thank all those who have contributed chapters to this Reader or who have approved their reprinting from other publications. Grateful acknowledgement is made to the following sources for permission to reproduce material in this book (chapters not listed have been newly written):

Chapter 2: McConkey, R. (2002) 'Reciprocal working by education, health and social services: lessons for a less-travelled road', *British Journal of Special Education* **29**(1). Reproduced by permission of Blackwell Publishing Ltd.

Chapter 3: Norris, C. and Closs, A. (1999) 'Child and parent relationships with teachers in schools responsible for the education of children with serious medical conditions', *British Journal of Special Education* **26**(1). Reproduced by permission of Blackwell Publishing Ltd.

Chapter 4: Brodie, I. (2000) 'Children's homes and school exclusion: redefining the problem', *Support for Learning* **15**(1). Reproduced by permission of Blackwell Publishing Ltd.

Chapter 5: Visser, J., Cole, T. and Daniels, H. (2002) 'Inclusion for the difficult to include', *Support for Learning* **17**(1). Reproduced by permission of Blackwell Publishing Ltd.

Chapter 6: Cooper, P. and Lovey, J. (1999) 'Early intervention in emotional and behavioural difficulties: the role of nurture groups', *European Journal of Special Needs Education* **14**(2), 122–31. Reproduced by permission of Taylor & Francis Ltd, http://www.tandf.co.uk/journals

Chapter 8: Alderson, P. and Goodey, C. (1999) 'Autism in special and inclusive schools: "there has to be a point to their being there"', *Disability and Society* **14**(2), 249–61. Reproduced by permission of Taylor & Francis Ltd, http://www.tandf.co.uk/journals

Chapter 9: Clough, P. and Nutbrown, C. (2002) 'The index for inclusion: personal perspectives from early years educators', *Early Education* **36**, Spring.

Chapter 10: Bannister, C., Sharland, V., Thomas, G., Upton, V. and Walker, D. (1998) 'Changing from a special school to an inclusion service', *British Journal of Special Education* **25**(2). Reproduced by permission of Blackwell Publishing Ltd.

Chapter 11: Cook, T., Swain, J. and French, S. (2001) 'Voices from segregated schooling: towards an inclusive education system', *Disability and Society* **16**(2), 293–310. Reproduced by permission of Taylor & Francis Ltd, http://www.tandf.co.uk/journals

Chapter 12: Hamill, P. and Boyd, B. (2002) 'Equality, fairness and rights – the young person's voice', *British Journal of Special Education* **29**(3). Reproduced by permission of Blackwell Publishing Ltd.

Chapter 13: Fazil, Q., Bywaters, P., Ali, Z., Wallace, L. and Singh, G. (2002) 'Disadvantage and discrimination compounded: the experience of Pakistani and Bangladeshi parents of disabled children in the UK', *Disability and Society* **17**(3), 237–53. Reproduced by permission of Taylor & Francis Ltd, http://www.tandf.co.uk/journals

Chapter 14: Lloyd, G., Stead, J., Jordan, E. and Norris, C. (1999) 'Teachers and Gypsy Travellers', *Scottish Educational Review* **31**(1).

Chapter 15: Crowley, C., Hallam, S., Harré, R. and Lunt, I. (2001) 'Study support for young peole with same-sex attraction – views and experiences from a pioneering peer support initiative in the north of England', *Educational and Child Psychology* **18**(1).

Chapter 16: Nind, M. and Cochrane, S. (2002) 'Inclusive curricula? Pupils on the margins of special schools', *International Journal of Inclusive Education* **6**(2), 185–98. Reproduced by permission of Taylor & Francis Ltd, http://www.tandf.co.uk/journals

Chapter 17: Collins, J. (2000) 'Exclusion: A Silent Protest', *Combating Social Exclusion Through Education: Laissez-faire, Authoritarianism or Third Way?*, ed. G. Walraven, C. Parsons, D. van Veen and C. Day. Antwerp: Garant.

Chapter 21: Gregory, E. (2000) 'Recognizing differences: reinterpreting family involvement in early literacy', *Combating Educational Disadvantage: Meeting the Needs of Vulnerable Children*, ed. T. Cox. Reproduced by permission of Taylor and Francis Books Ltd, London (Falmer Press).

Every effort has been made to contact all the copyright holders of material included in the book. If any material has been included without permission, the publishers offer their apologies and will be happy to make acknowledgement in any future edition of the book.

CHAPTER 1

Introduction

Melanie Nind, Katy Simmons, Kieron Sheehy and Jonathan Rix

The thinking behind this collection

Inclusive Education: Learners and Learning Contexts and its partner book *Inclusive Education: Diverse Perspectives* are readers/set books for the Open University course Inclusive Education: Learning from Each Other (E243). They contain a mixture of challenging new material and a compilation of some of the best (in our view) pre-published material. The chapters offer a rich resource for any student of inclusive education, interested educational professional or person whose life has been affected by the issues raised in the book. Many of the chapters reflect the direct experience of people who have themselves been marginalised or excluded; we know that some readers will have shared those experiences. *Inclusive Education: Learners and Learning Contexts* is a collection of diverse material intended to support the study of inclusive education across the phases of *starting out, thinking it through, listening to others, working it out* and *making it happen.*

These readers are part of a bigger story that began at the Open University in the 1980s when Tony Booth, Patricia Potts, Will Swann and colleagues asked searching questions of the education system and the professionals working in it and paused to study it. Their thinking was fundamentally shaped by the experiences of the adult disability movement and by a commitment to social justice. Learning for All (1992-2003) and the set books, *Curricula for All* (Booth *et al*. 1992a) and *Policies for All* (Booth *et al*. 1992b), crusaded for change in the creation of an education system responsive to all learners. The story continues here in the context of (apparent) national and international support for inclusive education and a wider social inclusion agenda.

This is not a book in which authors debate the pros and cons of inclusive education. We believe the case for inclusive education has been made. As Richard Rieser (2003) has said, it is a case based on the principles of equality and human rights. We have made a commitment to the development of 'regular schools' as 'the most effective means of combating discriminatory attitudes, creating welcoming communities, building an inclusive society and achieving education for all' (Salamanca Statement, paragraph 2, UNESCO 1994). Our starting point is that inclusive education is a matter of human rights and social justice. We share the Centre for Studies in Inclusive Education's view that:

> Familiarity and tolerance reduces fear and rejection. Inclusive education contributes to a greater equality of opportunities for all members of society. The benefits also include relationships and creativity that were not possible in the past.
>
> (CSIE 2003)

While the human rights position is an obvious starting point we acknowledge the need to build from here. The position is based on an ethical critique of the oppression and exclusion in traditional schooling but we need to understand this in more than abstract terms (Armstrong *et al.* 2002).

The form that inclusive education takes, in responding to the human rights agenda, is contested territory. Is this about the right to attend one's local school, or to be an active participant in broader educational decision-making, or much more about one's classroom experiences? We find ourselves asking what it is we actually mean by inclusive education. What does the official 'inclusion' of government policy documents have in common with the unofficial, lived experience of inclusion/exclusion in schools and communities?

With complex concepts like this it can be an over-simplification to talk about inclusion as a single entity. There may be key principles inherent in the concept – like valuing diversity, being responsive, listening to everyone, and enabling active participation – that hold it together in some way. But the concept is enacted in a diversity of ways. As academics working together to prepare the course and edit the set books we have shared values in common. But as teachers, parents or advocates, we have different visions – different 'inclusions'. These volumes get to the heart of some of these inclusions.

An assumption underpinning this book, then, is that our notions of inclusion and inclusive education are not fixed. This is a fluid concept. While working on this project over three years our individual views of what inclusive education means to us have moved. Similarly, the people we have worked with who actively seek to make inclusion happen have developed their ideas based on their own evolving inclusion/exclusion experiences.

Inclusion is also a contextual concept. We have seen, read about and been involved with many different versions of inclusion in practice. In each different context people strive for inclusion in a range of ways and sometimes reproduce exclusion through familiar or new processes. A common theme is bringing down barriers to participation and learning but, as we see in this volume, these barriers take many different forms.

Another theoretical position that informs our choice of material for these books is that there is nothing inevitable about excluding others. Common-sense discourses may mean we have internalised oppressive and discriminatory notions, so that we see it as natural to place ourselves in hierarchies – to see who is cleverer than us, better looking than us and so on – and to treat people who are different from us with suspicion. The context in which we work may be one in which certain qualities (such as literacy, physical prowess) are valued above others (such as sensitivity, creativity). We may have to operate within certain contexts and parameters (the educational market-place and league tables, for example). But common-sense notions are open to question and to change. Internationally, we have seen political regimes transformed; attitudes to disability challenged; marginalised people claim power for themselves. It is not, therefore, beyond the imagination that we can re-build education systems to reflect a different set of values. The education environment does not have to be built on competitiveness, success for a few, and sorting people into those who achieve and those who do not. It can alternatively value different kinds of participation, collaborative effort and communal success. In this volume we see examples of these alternative values in action.

A common thread in the literature about inclusive education is that it is about more than 'special educational needs' (Booth 2003). Indeed, if the concept is to survive and grow, separate from the history of concepts of integration, we need to recognise the diversity of learners who face barriers to learning and participation. OFSTED do this by listing 'inclusion groups':

'any or all of': girls and boys; minority ethnic and faith groups, Travellers, asylum seekers and refugees; pupils who need support to learn English as an additional language (EAL); pupils with special educational needs; gifted and talented pupils; children 'looked after' by the local authority; other children, such as sick children; young carers; those children from families under stress; pregnant school girls and teenage mothers; and any pupils who are at risk of disaffection and exclusion.

(OFSTED 2000)

This, however, risks being another way of labelling young people, and a way of categorising and pathologising some learners as 'other'. We are concerned with all learners, and what we can learn from others by listening to different learners' experiences of inclusion/exclusion in different contexts. We are also conscious of the way in which learners are all multidimensional, each with a gender, ethnicity, cultural background, sexuality, possible impairments, physical, cultural and material resources and so on (Benjamin, this volume).

So many books about inclusive education focus on disabled pupils and pupils with learning difficulties. This often reflects the history of the authors and editors and their involvement as professionals or survivors of special educational provision, caught up both in questioning and maintaining concepts of special educational need. We have been acutely aware of our own tendency to draw on the examples that we are most familiar with and to limit ourselves in this way. In this volume though, we bring together material on a much richer diversity of learners and learning contexts. And we look at the way indices of difference, such as being a Traveller and a girl, disabled and Bangladeshi and poor, come together to shape people's experiences of inclusion/exclusion.

The contents

The chapters are organised into sections to enable thematic clustering of material on the diverse learners and learning contexts. Thus, we have the structure of *More than just the three 'R's, Transitions, On the margins, Inside classrooms* and *Beyond classrooms*. Each chapter is preceded by a brief introduction and summary and followed by editorial comment. These interludes offer the coherence of our voice as editors, threaded through the rich diversity of other voices, to draw out themes of significance to us.

In the first section, *More than just the three 'R's,* we are invited to consider the way that our experience of learning is about much more than life in the classroom. We see learners as complex wholes with diverse characteristics. We also see that responding to these learners requires different professionals working together and working with the learners themselves. Roy McConkey sets the scene by showing how the decline of the 'deficit' model of disability might lead to new ways of working. Professionals who once saw themselves working in isolation are re-defining themselves to work collaboratively with colleagues from different backgrounds, with families and within local communities. The following chapters each have a particular community of learners in mind, whether these be learners with serious medical conditions (Norris and Closs), children and young people 'looked after' in children's homes by local authorities (Brodie) or children with 'emotional and behavioural difficulties' (Visser *et al.* and Cooper and Lovey). They share in common, however, a concern with addressing the learning context to make this more supportive and responsive, rather than seeking to 'fix' the learners in some way to make them fit in. The authors share insights into the processes that help to keep these learners included in the education system and also the more subtle processes that lead to them being included (or not) in a more meaningful sense. The chapters show the centrality of listening to what children and families have to say.

In the next section, *Transitions,* we look at a range of learning contexts and ask questions of particular versions of inclusion (see particularly Alderson and Goodey). Each version or setting might be seen as at a different stage of a journey towards inclusive education. Indeed, the staff involved with the inner city Bangabandhu school (Phillips and Jenner) reflect on their own journey as a school, in which they have developed understandings and practices to enable them to respond with confidence to an increasingly diverse school population. Likewise, we are given insights into the decisive moments of transition for the Somerset Inclusion Project (Bannister *et al*.). Thus, we see learning contexts not just as diverse but as ever changing.

The chapters bring together a range of different voices on the theme of educational provision in transition. We hear from educational managers, teachers and support staff, early years educators (Clough and Nutbrown), and crucially, pupils themselves (Cook *et al*.). Indeed, it is the pupils' accounts of the transition about to happen in their lives, as they move from a segregated school to mainstream provision, that illustrate the real complexities and subtleties at work in inclusion/exclusion.

Overall we can see both the strengths and limitations of the metaphor of inclusion as a journey. There are dangers in over-simplifying this journey. Certainly not all schools start from the same place. They may not even be headed to the same destination and they most definitely do not seem to be following the same map. Whilst these chapters illustrate some of the ways in which schools working to enhance their inclusivity are addressing broader issues of school improvement, they also illustrate more variation and contradiction than a simple improvement or journey model might imply.

The chapters in the next section, *On the margins,* once again cover a diverse range of learners. This includes those learners whose behaviour is challenging (Hamill and Boyd; Nind and Cochrane), those learners whose behaviour allows their non-participation to go unnoticed (Collins), and those who experience intensive disadvantage and/or discrimination (Fazil *et al*.; Lloyd *et al*.; Crowley *et al*.). By bringing together the stories of disaffected pupils, lesbian and gay young people, minority ethnic families, pupils with profound and complex learning difficulties and quiet children, we see resonance between them. As a whole, the group of stories makes an even more valuable contribution to understandings of inclusion than they can do individually. Together, the chapters in this section demonstrate the kinds of exclusion that can happen when people make assumptions about other people and when they fail to listen and to make adjustments for each other. They tell of the embedded, systemic nature of some discriminatory practices. But they also tell of the simplicity of some of the solutions as barriers are taken down and opportunities opened up. We see the difference that can be made by individuals who find time for people, who act as mentors for others, and who enable people to find their way to much needed support and resources.

A common experience of the diverse learners is that they are often on the margins of school life. The chapters often illustrate tough challenges to inclusive provision and a pushing at the boundaries of school placements. Some of them illustrate clashes of values between learners and their families and educators. The call for learning from each other is rarely more pertinent. In these chapters we not only see learners taking an active role in shaping their own experiences of inclusion/exclusion at school but also learners' experiences being limited by attitudes, systems and resources. The contradiction here is evident both in these chapters and across the volume. Moments of inclusion take place in contexts, some of which are more supportive of inclusion than others (Benjamin, this volume).

The volume continues with a more detailed look at teacher–pupil and pupil–pupil interactions. This is an under-researched area of inclusive education and in the next section three new and challenging chapters examine the processes by which inclusion is negotiated *Inside classrooms*. Susan Hart takes us beyond ideas about differentiating the curriculum for learners of different abilities, articulating the limitations of such thinking. She shows instead, through a discussion of the choices made by one teacher, how learning experiences can be made to be meaningful for all. Similarly, Susan Simmons explains how her work in classrooms moved on from its original focus on technical resources to aid curriculum access. She began to engage instead, in a process of reflective and reciprocal learning, in which the prime resources were the learners involved and their experiences. Shereen Benjamin takes us back to the interactions of various aspects of diversity and how these affect classroom experience.

In the final section, we look *Beyond classrooms* at the relationship between active participation as a learner and active participation in a community. The chapters by Margy Whalley and Eve Gregory address 'head on' the issue of cultural difference between home and school. Central to our notions of inclusion, they show how inclusive education has to do something fundamentally different from teaching pupils and their families how to fit in to, or accept, school cultures and norms. Instead, inclusive education has to empower learners and their families to use their personal and community resources to be active agents in building a future for themselves that they want and value. This can only happen when learners are themselves respected and valued for what they contribute to their learning setting. Only then can inclusive education meet our expectations as a vehicle for, and inherent part of, social justice.

If we see inclusive education as an ongoing process, then it is not surprising that we end this introduction thinking about what might be in a further, not yet written, next volume. Maybe that virtual volume will be even more a celebration of difference, positioning the experiences of previously marginalised people more centrally as simply 'an ordinary human variation' (Giangreco 2003) or to be affirmed (Swain and French 2003). Or maybe it will reflect the way in which increasing inclusion in mainstream has diminished that sense of community and bonding that sometimes occurs when people are marginalised. Fleischer and Zames (2001) cite Susan Scheer's observation that young people with disabilities, for example, tend to forget the struggle of a previous generation:

> They don't realize that if they're not vigilant, they can lose what they've got. Clearly, the disability rights movement is not as visible, not as entrenched, as other civil rights movements. So, as a fringe movement, it's more vulnerable than the other movements . . .
>
> (Fleischer and Zames 2001: 213)

Editors of inclusive education readers of the near future would not be able to be complacent. The case for inclusion may be made, but the backlash is alive and well (e.g. Wilson 1999; 2000). Proud assertions of difference cannot be made just once but, like 'coming out' as lesbian or gay, have to be made over and over again in each new context where a set of assumptions predominate. We suggest we need to keep sharing stories of schools changing, attitudes changing, practices developing. We need to keep sharing accounts of how different groups have addressed the challenge of bringing down barriers to participation and what they have learned along the way. Currently, 'common sense' discourse might be: 'but their needs are better met in a more specialised environment'. It can, however, become 'what "everybody" must have the opportunity to do, learn and experience' (Hart, this volume). It may take a lot of stories of doing things differently, and starting from a different mindset, to change the dominant narrative, but a paradigm shift is happening.

When John Tomlinson (1996: 11) advocated inclusive learning in further education he was keen to stress:

> Everything we propose is within the grasp of the system if we all want it enough, because its full growth or its seeds are already present somewhere: we are not recommending an idealistic dream, but the reality of extending widely the high quality which already exists in pockets, locked in the minds and actions of the few who must become the many.

Some 'pockets' of inclusive education are shared in this volume, even if it is not all rosy reading and some of the chapters tell of how much more there is to be done. Certainly the vision or motivation to bring about change is shared or generated by the contributions. In some ways, perhaps, our virtual next volume might not need to be very different. There is scope for plenty more stories of shifting from exclusion to inclusion in our thinking and our practice.

References

Armstrong, D., Armstrong, F. and Barton, L. (2002) Introduction. In Armstrong, D., Armstrong, F. and Barton, L. (eds) *Inclusive Education: Policy, Contexts and Comparative Perspectives*. London: David Fulton.

Booth, T., Swann, W., Masterton, M. and Potts, P. (eds) (1992a) *Curricula for Diversity in Education*. London and New York: Routledge in association with The Open University.

Booth, T., Swann, W., Masterton, M. and Potts, P. (eds) (1992b) *Policies for Diversity in Education*. London and New York: Routledge in association with The Open University.

Booth, T. (2003) Viewing inclusion from a distance. In Nind, M., Rix, J., Sheehy, K. and Simmons, K. (eds) *Inclusive Education: Diverse Perspectives*. London: David Fulton Publishers in association with The Open University.

CSIE (Centre for Studies in Inclusive Education) (2003). www.inclusion.uwe.ac.uk/csie/csiehome.htm (accessed 24 March).

Fleischer, D. Z. and Zames, F. (2001) *The Disability Rights Movement: From Charity to Confrontation*. Philadelphia: Temple University Press.

Giangreco, M. F. (2003) The stairs don't go anywhere: A self-advocate's reflections. In Nind, M., Rix, J., Sheehy, K. and Simmons, K. (eds) *Inclusive Education: Diverse Perspectives*. London: David Fulton Publishers in association with The Open University.

Ofsted (Office for Standards in Education) (2000) http://www.ofsted.gov.uk/public/docs00/inclusion.pdf (accessed 5 October 2002).

Rieser, R. (2003) The struggle for inclusion. In Nind, M., Rix, J., Sheehy, K. and Simmons, K. (eds) *Inclusive Education: Diverse Perspectives*. London: David Fulton Publishers in association with The Open University.

Swain, J. and French, S. (2003) Towards an affirmation model of disability. In Nind, M., Rix, J., Sheehy, K. and Simmons, K. (eds) *Inclusive Education: Diverse Perspectives*. London: David Fulton Publishers in association with The Open University.

Tomlinson, J. (1996) Introduction. In The Further Education Funding Council, *Inclusive Learning: Report of the Learning Difficulties and/or Disabilities Committee*. Coventry: FEFC.

UNESCO (United Nations Educational, Scientific and Cultural Organisation (1994) *The Salamanca Statement and Framework for Action on Special Educational Needs*. Paris: UNESCO.

Wilson, J. (1999) Some conceptual difficulties about inclusion. *Support for Learning*, **14**(3), 110–12.

Wilson, J. (2000) 'Doing justice to inclusion'. *European Journal of Special Needs Education*, **15**(3), 297–304.

Part 1

More than just the three 'R's

Reciprocal working by education, health and social services: lessons for a less-travelled road

Roy McConkey

In this chapter Roy McConkey reflects on some of the themes from work in the 1960s by Ron Gulliford which retain relevance today. He focuses, in particular, on collaboration between practitioners from different professional backgrounds. He invites the reader to reflect on some of the strengths of current practice and to consider the ways in which these initiatives might be taken forward. The chapter closes with a set of strategies that could be used to develop innovative, holistic, inter-agency approaches in the future.

'Intellectual disability is a social as well as an educational problem. It is both inefficient and uneconomical to tackle one aspect and ignore the other.'

Another road

These wise words could have been written by a disabled activist promoting a social model of disability. In fact they were written over 40 years ago by Ron Gulliford and his longstanding colleague A. E. Tansley in their landmark text on the education of slow learning children (Tansley and Gulliford 1960).

It is a tribute to Ron's foresight and incisiveness that these words are still as true today. There is wider acceptance of the first part of the statement but my generation of educationalists, health professionals and social service staff have done little to tackle both the educational and social dimensions of disability in any coherent way. It truly has been a road 'less travelled' as each service system has forged its own highway in trying to reduce the disabling effects of an intellectual impairment and the inevitable social consequences that it brings. Worse still, at times they have worked competitively rather than cooperatively, blaming one another for perceived shortcomings. And perhaps most seriously of all, they have worked in ignorance of one another's values, priorities and achievements. Yet, as Robert Frost reminded us in the poem from which this phrase is taken, the less-travelled road can make all the difference. [. . .]

The social consequences of disability

Let us begin by considering these facts (Emerson *et al.* 2001) about the lives of people with an intellectual disability in Britain today:

- most (91 %) attend day centres for people with learning disabilities;
- most (92%) live in congregated settings of five plus persons who are not related to them and with whom they have not chosen to live;
- most (95%) never marry or have a sexual partner;
- most (60%) have few friends whom they see regularly and fewer still have non-disabled friends.

These data stand in marked contrast to the aspirations for greater social inclusion contained in recent Government reviews of learning disability services in these islands (Scottish Executive 2000; Department of Health 2001). [. . .] Educationalists clearly have a major role to play in ameliorating the learning problems young people encounter but, as Tansley and Gulliford (1960) wisely noted and the above data amply demonstrate, the impact of education or therapy on the social consequences of their disabilities has been very limited. In many ways, their life chances in this new century appear little different from those of their counterparts of a decade and more ago.

Similarly our social and community services, preoccupied as they have been with scarce resources and an emphasis on the social care of people who are viewed as being unable to learn and likely to be forever dependent on others, have struggled to overcome the social exclusion of these young people when they leave school. [. . .]

A change of direction

The 'old road' treated intellectual disability – and indeed many other handicapping conditions – solely as an impairment of the individual which needs to be put right. Traditional folklore invoked explanations of possession by evil spirits that needed to be exorcised while today medical science tries to identify the genes that may account for children's deficiencies and impairments such as autism, speech and language problems. Psychologists and therapists have invented a battery of tests to identify a myriad of deficits in 'problem' children and created many therapeutic approaches – often contradictory in their aims and methods – to remediate these diagnosed faults.

Educationalists too have taken to this deficit view with alacrity, labeling pupils as having attention deficits, dyslexia or poor sensory integration and creating all sorts of remedial programmes aimed at correcting the faults in the child. [. . .]

In recent years, this deficit view of disability has been challenged by developmental psychologists who espouse a transactional view of children's acquisition of social and cognitive skills.

In this view language acquisition, numerical competence and reading skills – to name but three important intellectual functions – will be influenced by the experiences to which young children are exposed, primarily in their daily interactions with more competent humans. Deprive children of these nurturing opportunities and their development invariably suffers. The effects of institutionalisation are well documented, as is the superior performance of children from more affluent families on tests of academic attainment from pre-school years through to A levels.

Likewise, disabled activists have argued that their disabilities are compounded by the denial of opportunities which are readily available to their able-bodied peers. These opportunities include:

- having access to a suitable means of communication if you have hearing impairments or learning disabilities;
- being socially included in family and community events from the pre-school years onwards;
- having the chance for suitable vocational training and employment.

Activists argue that it is the denial of such opportunities, rather than any biological impairment, that subverts their intellectual, social and emotional development.

To my mind, the transactional view of development underpins all our endeavours in the field of special educational needs. It is the learning opportunities that we offer children, both in school and beyond, that will overcome some of the potentially disabling impairments that children are born with or those they acquire through childhood illnesses or accidents. [. . .]

Successes of education

The new road will also take more account of the successes that educationalists have had in facilitating the learning of children whom past generations would have dismissed as ineducable [. . .] Education has evolved a number of strategies that have proved highly effective in overcoming children's learning disabilities. These include:

- *functional assessments*, which rely on devising means of ascertaining what the children can do in terms of everyday, observable skills rather than relying on assessments of abstract concepts such as intelligence;
- *learning goals*, which entail the identification of clearly stated learning targets that are appropriate to the child's present level of competence and provide the focus for teaching in school and at home;
- *learning methods*, which include teaching strategies such as breaking tasks into small steps, the use of prompts, positive reinforcement and modelling, all of which have proved effective in helping children acquire new skills and in managing challenging behaviours;

- *evaluating progress,* which involves monitoring learners' progress through careful observation and recording these findings to enable even small changes to be identified;
- *accredited learning,* which entails developing new means for accrediting students' learning so that nearly all may leave school having attained some form of externally recognised competencies.

Sad to say, many of these approaches are not widely applied outside of the school and classrooms. In residential homes provided by health or social services, there is growing interest in the concept of care staff providing 'active support' to residents so that they can acquire the skills that will enable them to live more independently and to manage problem behaviours more effectively (Jones *et al.* 1999). But active support is but another name for the learning approaches developed and applied by many teachers in special needs education.

Likewise the increased emphasis on supported employment as an alternative to attending day centres became possible as trainees were given 'systematic instruction' in the skills needed to do the job (Beyer and Kilsby 1997). Once again, teachers would recognise these methods as being closely akin to their practice.

Yet we still have a long road to travel until the majority of adult persons with a learning disability are living in their own accommodation or have part-time paid employment. One can but wonder whether these targets might be more attainable if the skills and strategies of teachers were made more available to staff in social services. This process will need to go beyond extending access for these students to further education, excellent though that development has been. It is my experience in Northern Ireland – and I suspect this is true for many other parts of the United Kingdom – that social service staff in day centres or residences are often ignorant as to what happens in colleges and vice versa. The road to partnership working is largely untrodden but before we get too despondent let us remember that new avenues have opened for joint working.

New avenues

I want to highlight three avenues, starting with early intervention services. Many disabling conditions are identified at birth or within the first 12 months. Yet it has only been in recent years that health and social services have developed support services for families, often offering home-based support to parents and giving guidance on activities that can be used at home to promote the child's development. Many of these schemes also involve educational personnel as peripatetic or home teachers. Such services consistently receive high ratings from parents for their helpfulness and many epitomise the best attributes of trans-disciplinary working as they focus on common goals for the child and family (Carpenter 2000).

A second avenue that has opened for bringing together professionals from different disciplines is that of statutory assessments and issuing Statements of Special Educational Needs. I realise there is much that is imperfect in the way the system works and the wide variation that exists across the country, yet at the heart is a brave attempt to take a more holistic view of each child's needs. In this, I am echoing the views of a parent quoted by Jones and Swain (2001):

> Education is not the three 'R's'. To educate our children you have to educate the whole child. It's their health needs, it's their social needs and it's their education, the whole child has to be seen to.
>
> (p. 61)

Likewise the annual review process is another avenue for pooling expertise and setting common agendas.

The third avenue of opportunity is transition planning. Legislation makes it mandatory for the career service and social services to join with educational personnel in developing a transition plan that will take the young person and the family through the final years of his or her schooling into some form of post-school provision in a planned and, hopefully, seamless way. It is perhaps too soon to judge the efficacy of these procedures as their full implementation is still patchy but in other countries there is clear evidence that they do result in wider choices for the young people and families and that new forms of provision have been developed in response to their needs (Phelps and Hanley-Maxwell 1997).

I want to draw two lessons from these new avenues. They have all occurred within the last 20 years; often in response to parental and professional dissatisfaction with what was on offer. Hence it is possible for education, health and social services to work together more closely, albeit within a relationship enforced by legislation.

Thus it is worth pondering on what new avenues for partnership need to be opened. Among those that I would nominate are:

- helping children who have been excluded from schools because of their behaviours;
- managing the risks involved when students use community facilities such as public transport;
- the provision of lifelong learning opportunities.

However, the second lesson to be drawn from these new initiatives comes from the cynic who dismisses many of them as 'window-dressing' and doubts whether joint working really occurs in practice. I fear there is much truth in these claims but this is only a reminder of the lack of bridges on these new roads.

Roads but no bridges

Here are some examples of the lack of bridges that presently beset our services. Health professionals deliver therapeutic programmes in clinics that take little cognisance of the social circumstances faced by families or the practical application of the child's skills into daily life. Such therapy may even be done separately from the education provided by the child's teachers whose work is open to similar criticisms of being isolated from the child's life outside of school. Indeed the world beyond the clinic and classrooms is seen as the domain of social and community services with teachers and therapists having little or no responsibilities or influence.

Such dichotomies of functions are bolstered by the different management and funding structures of education, health and social services. They have become ever more entrenched with the growth of professional training and career structures that emphasise uni-disciplinary pathways.

But perhaps the main justification for the continuing separation of functions follows from the demands already placed on the various professionals by their own systems. Therapists are under pressure to get the waiting lists down; for social workers, the management of families in crisis is a priority; and teachers have recently been preoccupied with a myriad of tasks from the implementation of the National Curriculum to school attainment tests. There is little spare energy or enthusiasm for building bridges across agency boundaries.

Building bridges

Fortunately we have some blueprints for building bridges across service systems. The following paragraphs summarise some of the tested designs. [...]

Individual family plans

In the United States, legislation mandates early intervention services to create plans that embrace the family's needs and not just those of the child. At worst, this at least keeps all the diverse professionals informed about the family's needs and aspirations. At best, it can create the milieu around which joint working unfolds as teachers, therapists and social workers interlink their efforts towards common outcomes.

Out-of-school learning

Schools are limited in the 'real-life' experiences they can offer learners. Hence schools and services need to mobilise and utilise the resources that all communities can offer by way of facilities and personnel to further students' learning. Indeed this is the ethos that underpins the work experience opportunities many schools make for pupils in senior classes. This approach could be extended to other spheres of community life – leisure, public transport, voluntary service and political activity.

Merging staff roles

In the British system we have clearly demarcated the roles of teachers from those of therapists and social workers. Other European countries have developed more integrative training for staff whom they call 'pedagogists' and other countries have experimented with joint training for nurses and social workers. Similar calls have been made in this country for increased collaborative working between teachers and speech and language therapists (Law *et al*. 2001). [. . .] In all these examples, there is a realisation that the staff will work within a specialism defined by the needs of the people they serve. The British model is predicated on the notion that staff will follow career paths within their own discipline. Perhaps the time has come to rethink this presumption?

Reorganising services

Another radical response to the challenge of building bridges between services might lead us to question the wisdom of administering education services separately from the health and social services offered to children and families. Might there be a case for an integrated child and family service that brings teachers, therapists and social workers under a common management and finance structure? Some local authorities in Scotland and England are making moves in that direction following on from the recent reorganisation into unitary authorities (Walters 2001).

Creating new freeways

The American expression 'freeway' is so much more expressive than the British term 'motorway'. Building a road free of obstacles may seem to be a pipe dream now but 30 years ago, the idea that children with severe mental handicap (as it was then called) could be educated also seemed to most commentators to be a pipe dream. Today, that freeway is well established, so much so that it takes learners into mainstream schools as well as special schools.

I can think of three examples of freeways that might appear in the future to support the development of joined-up services for the benefit of children and families.

The school as a community resource with varied functions

The trend towards using the school as a community resource has already begun, with pre-school playgroups meeting in vacant classrooms or public libraries sharing the building. But this concept could develop much further. Child health and ante-natal clinics could take place in the same building. Social workers and community workers might also be based there. These community facilities could be open at evenings and weekends so that opportunities for lifelong learning could be extended to young people and their parents. Such 'one-stop' facilities could be owned by the community they serve, rather than be the property of a health trust or an education authority as happens at present.

Multi-skilled personnel

Providing a common context in which people work will not in itself provide a freeway to joint working among people from different professions. More opportunities are needed for joint training at both a pre-service and in-service level (Law *et al.* 2001). Some of these may take the form of one or two-day courses on specific topics while others may lead to postgraduate qualifications that recruit students from a range of professions to equip them with the multidisciplinary skills needed to focus on certain client needs, such as early intervention services; adolescent and young adult services; supported employment; or supported living. Training courses of this sort are starting to be offered and I predict we will see many more in the future.

Common management

Shared buildings and shared staffing will invariably lead to common management structures or, conversely, common management is required to produce these two outcomes. Either way, it will not come without courage and pain as the last bastion of a uni-disciplinary service is the power that comes from directing others and allocating money. Even so, there are already local authorities that have merged their education and children's social services and the Government is encouraging health authorities to develop jointly funded initiatives with social services departments for adult persons with learning disabilities (Department of Health 2001). This trend towards merging money and management has the potential to address the cost-effectiveness arguments raised by Ron Gulliford some 40 years ago.

Research and evaluation

If you have journeyed with me thus far, then it is only fair that I confess some doubts about whether these new freeways will take us to where we want to go. Human beings have a wonderful capacity to subvert the best of intentions to their own ends. One safeguard is to have open and objective feedback systems that demonstrate whether or not the goals are being achieved and identify the most effective means of producing them. In short we need to research and evaluate partnership working. There are three broad strategies for doing this.

Developing model projects

The experiences gained in setting up a 'model' project at a local level, by even a small group of innovators, will provide many learning experiences that, if documented and shared, will make it easier to repeat similar operations elsewhere. [. . .]

Evaluating new styles of services

The literature is replete with many studies investigating the efficacy of various educational and therapeutic interventions for disabling conditions. Far fewer multidisciplinary evaluations of services have been published. We have much to learn about how to obtain funding for such studies, as well as about the skills required by the evaluators and how they might meet the challenges of this new style of research in the measures and methods they use with a diversity of stakeholders.

Longitudinal studies

More ambitiously, we need to follow the progress of children and families over time and across service systems. For example, the data on social inclusion that I presented at the outset could be replicated within each local authority on these islands if schools (or some other body) were charged with following up the young people. [...]

Ironically, these research and evaluation initiatives will probably only occur when there is a culture that values and nurtures partnership working. Evaluation can inform us about how to do better the job we are committed to doing. It will not get us started on making the change.

The end of the road

[...] Our vision today is more clearly stated than ever before. It focuses upon inclusion within society and the right to a full and decent life. In order to achieve this, education must join forces with other services for, as Tansley and Gulliford (1960) asserted, it is both inefficient and uneconomical to be travelling on our own road when there is another one we should be taking that could make all the difference.

References

Beyer, S. and Kilsby, M. (1997) Supported employment in Britain. *Tizard Learning Disability Review*, **2** (2), 6–14.

Carpenter, B. (2000) Sustaining the family: meeting the needs of families of children with disabilities. *British Journal of Special Education*, **27**(3), 135–44.

Department of Health (2001) *Valuing People: a new strategy for learning disability for the 21st century*. London: Department of Health.

Emerson, E., Hatton, C., Felce, D. and Murphy, G. (2001) *Learning Disabilities: the fundamental facts*. London: Foundation for People with Learning Disabilities.

Jones, E., Perry, J. and Lowe, K. (1999) Opportunity and the promotion of activity among adults with severe intellectual disability living in community residences: the impact of training staff in active support. *Journal of Intellectual Disability Research*, **43**, 164–78.

Jones, P. and Swain, J. (2001) Parents reviewing annual reviews. *British Journal of Special Education*, **28**(2),60–4.

Law, J., Lindsay, G., Peacey, N., Gascoigne, M., Soloff, N., Radford, J. and Band, S. (2001) Facilitating communication between education and health services: the provision for children with speech and language needs. *British Journal of Special Education*, **28** (3), 133–7.

Phelps, L. A. and Hanley-Maxwell, C. (1997) School-to-work transitions for youth with disabilities: a review of outcomes and practices. *Review of Educational Research*, **67**, 197–226.

Scottish Executive (2000) *The Same As You? A review of services for people with learning disabilities*. Edinburgh: Scottish Executive.

Tansley, A. E. and Gulliford, R. (1960) *The Education of Slow Learning Children*. London: Routledge and Kegan Paul.

Walters, B. (2001) Does size matter? Is small beautiful? *British Journal of Special Education*, **28**(1), 35–43.

The metaphor of the journey, used by Roy McConkey in this chapter, is one that recurs in much writing about inclusion. It conveys a sense, which we also find elsewhere, of an unfolding process that encompasses much more than school. This chapter gives directions for a collaborative, holistic way of working that brings together professionals and addresses shared problems. It prompts us, as does the next chapter, to consider what such new ways of working might mean for professionals and for their established ways of working.

CHAPTER 3

Child and parent relationships with teachers in schools responsible for the education of children with serious medical conditions

Claire Norris and Alison Closs

In this chapter, Claire Norris and Alison Closs describe a small study of the interpersonal relationships between children with chronic and/or deteriorating conditions and their parents and teachers. This was one aspect of a wider study (Closs and Norris 1997) which sought ways of enabling the mainstream education of such children in Scotland.

The research population

Terminology is problematic in areas of overlap between illness and disability (Barnes & Mercer 1996) but prior discussion with families, voluntary organisations, educational and other professionals indicated that *uncertainties* about the future health and abilities of children might be a key issue in educational responses. Therefore the research was limited to concerns about children whose conditions were not 'static' but were fluctuating or deteriorating, both physically and cognitively.

As the experience of illness is both highly individual and subjective, it was not thought advisable to establish a 'hierarchy' of conditions, but to select children whose state of health was of sufficient severity and duration to disrupt significantly (in their own, their parents' and their schools' view) patterns of school attendance and educational progress. Illustrative examples of conditions experienced by the children were cancers including leukaemia; ME (myalgic encephalomyelitis); chronic heart, kidney and other organ malfunctions; cystic fibrosis; muscular dystrophy; rheumatic and mucopolysaccharide conditions; Niemann Pick syndrome; severe asthma; eczema; psoriasis; and some forms of epilepsy. Disabilities which were, debatably, more *static* such as cerebral palsy, visual and hearing impairments were not included, nor were mental health conditions, infectious diseases, injuries or conditions requiring routine surgery. Children who required a series of extended surgical interventions (such as orthopaedic conditions or plastic surgery following burns), however, were included in the general study, although none were profiled.

Many of the issues in education facing these children, and those involved in making educational provision for them, are shared by other groups of children whose education may be constantly disrupted. Nevertheless, children with chronic and deteriorating conditions are likely to experience an identifiable *constellation* of difficulties (including absence and fatigue) in attempting to maintain access to, and progress within, education. The risk of pathologising these children and their families was recognised (Eiser 1993) and it was salutary to be frequently reminded by the children interviewed of the wide range of experiences, interests and aspirations which they *did* share with other children, as well as their dislike of 'difference' and their wish to be 'the same'. Scott, a ten-year-old with Friedrich's ataxia, described his PE lesson:

> . . . they usually play things like shots and victories at basketball and I can't do all of that, so sometimes I just get to shout orders or just to shoot for the basket, and I don't like it then because I'm different and people make fun of me . . .

Sources of data

In order to understand how school education was experienced by all those involved, 18 authority-based personnel in two demographically contrasting authorities were interviewed: education officers responsible for mainstream schooling and for pupil support services; special education 'support for learning advisers'; access officers; education welfare officers; and educational psychologists. In addition 21 staff from a primary and a secondary school in each of the two authorities: headteachers; class and subject teachers; learning support and guidance staff; and auxiliary assistants; in addition to school doctors and nurses. Eighteen children across Scotland, from 6 to 18 years of age, were profiled, using in-depth interviews, follow-up meetings and telephone conversations with one or both parents and (when informed consent could be obtained and health allowed) with the children themselves. The children can therefore only be viewed as illustrative of a large and extremely heterogeneous population, and the British Paediatric Association (1995) reports that just under 10 per cent of children under the age of 15 have an illness which chronically reduces their functional capacity.

Some children in our sample, despite sometimes extensive absences and poor prognosis, were fully included in their school community but about two thirds of them and their parents felt that they were marginalised or excluded. There was no clear relationship between the severity of the condition or the extent of absence and feelings of inclusion or exclusion. Not surprisingly, we found that good relationships between teachers and pupils and teachers and parents were perceived as fundamental to positive, inclusive educational experiences. There were, however, a number of issues relating to pupils with serious medical conditions, their families and their teachers, which could enhance or impede these relationships.

Teacher–pupil relationship

We recognised the difficulties in maintaining what might be considered 'normal' teacher–pupil relationships with children who were often absent. As one headteacher in the study remarked, 'Schools are busy places, and once a child is not there you tend to forget about them.' Some seriously or terminally ill children continue to attend school as do others with less dramatic but still debilitating and irritating conditions. Yet even when children were attending school regularly, it was found that teacher–pupil relationships could be negatively affected by teacher perceptions of pupils' medical conditions.

Teachers were sometimes unsure whether or not to treat their pupils with medical conditions in the same way as their peers. Some of the parents interviewed, described teachers' 'softness', 'lowered expectations' and 'over-protectiveness' arising from anxiety. One learning support teacher commented that her colleagues had asked about an under-challenged abler pupil with a physically deteriorating condition, 'Should I push him? Should I make him do this?'

A parent described the fearful response of her daughter's reception class teacher on being told that the child had nocturnal epilepsy. The mother volunteered to stay in the class with her daughter and later an auxiliary helper was employed on the insistence of the teacher. This arrangement effectively separated the child physically and socially from her peers since both teacher and auxiliary were happy for the auxiliary to 'care for' the child at the far end of the classroom. The matter was only resolved in the following year when a more confident teacher took over and included the child fully in school activities.

Another teacher described a colleague's refusal to take a pupil with a physically deteriorating condition to school camp, listing the activities in which the boy could *not* participate. The interviewee said that thinking about the boy's condition 'gutted' his colleague, such were his own inhibitions about disability and death; this attitude impeded his constructive responses.

The examples given above show how ignorance, fear and inhibitions about death and illness (Leaman 1995) can impede positive relationships and experiences. In contrast, the class teacher of a child with a recurrence of acute lymphoblastic leukaemia tried to discriminate positively in relation to the boy's behaviour. She described her feelings and responses:

> My relationship with him is different from that with other children, and when I don't know what his prognosis is, it alters the stance I take with him. There are times when he can be a bit naughty and cheeky and a little bit forward, and in other children you would reprimand that behaviour, but with him you don't because you don't want him to have any negative experiences, and you want your relationship with him to be almost like a fun relationship . . . I'm conscious of the fact that over the next two or three years everything might be over for him, so you want everything to be good for him . . .

23

Her responses arose therefore not from fear or ignorance of his condition but from her own wish to give him happiness. Not surprisingly, this led to some peer rejection.

Teachers' capacity to empathise and relate positively with children, whether arising from personal experiences or simply from greater interpersonal skills, enhanced teacher-child relationships and also contributed positively to peer relationships. One girl with Hurler's syndrome described how her class teacher had explained in class circle-time that he (the teacher) had diabetes, got very tired and therefore could understand how she and 'any other child who felt poorly' might not always be able to do perfect work, but that trying hard was the most important thing in life. The class then all discussed the times when they felt tired or unwell and agreed to support each other.

The children in the sample were *in tune* with our professional interviewees on what was effective teaching for them (Cooper & McIntyre 1993). They appreciated well-organised teachers who accepted their difficulties, and who helped them to learn by being clear and going over missed work or offering lesson notes. They liked classes to be orderly and good-humoured, but made a clear distinction between good humour and the kind of cruel, insensitive remarks disguised as 'jokes' which were sometimes made by their peers and even occasionally by their teachers. These children had much to lose if teachers did not model positive acceptance and respect.

Brown and McIntyre (1986) found that teachers describe their work in terms of their pupils' progress and behaviour. Leaman (1995) argued:

> The structure of teaching and learning itself, the notion of a curriculum with its grades and hierarchy, with its ranks and promotions, encourages the idea that life consists of a series of stages and obstacles which must be met and surmounted if one is to be successful.

(p.22)

If one adds to this the multiple pressures on teachers in the drive towards raising school achievements, it is perhaps not surprising that some come to view pupils with chronic illness, who fall behind in their work, as problematic or even 'bad' pupils, rather than pupils of equal value who require additional support.

Class and guidance teachers were key communication links when children were absent. Packages of homework might enable 'keeping up' but the more personal contact of letters, cards and phone calls, sometimes initiated and less frequently maintained by teachers, facilitated social continuity. Larcombe (1995) noted the importance of social contact with friends and teachers for absent children in preventing the onset of school phobic-type symptoms at the thought of returning to school, also noted by some of the interviewees. Few absent children were visited by teachers, even when their condition was serious and long-standing. Those who were visited, however, were positive. Jenny commented:

It was kind of embarrassing, I suppose, but I did feel really pleased she came. I mean, I think it showed she cared . . . and she said they hadn't forgotten me and would be pleased to see me back. I won't forget it.

Parent–teacher relationships

Parents described how some school staff had facilitated their children's education. They appreciated staff who listened to them, understood that their worries about health or educational progress were real, and accepted and used the information that they gave. One mother described how her son's headteacher had not only read leaflets she had brought into school but had also bought a book for the children's library and another for the staff. It seemed, however, from parent and teacher interviews, that schools did not find it easy to accept all parents as knowledgeable about their own children, far less medically authoritative about their condition. A headteacher's comment about one mother was revealing in its implications for other 'non-professional' parents, 'Of course, she really does know what she's on about. She's a properly qualified nurse.'

Headteachers have considerable influence on a school's ethos and attitudes towards potentially disadvantaged children. Parents also perceived headteachers, particularly in primary schools, as both establishing, and ensuring the continuity of, supportive systems. Mark's parents had been very agitated about his progress after he developed learning difficulties as a result of treatment for leukaemia. They had tense relations with the school and 'officialdom', although neither teachers nor educational psychologist had been aware that irradiation could cause cognitive impairments in children and had consequently offered no additional help. The arrival of a headteacher, whom they felt to be more knowledgeable and active on their behalf, enabled the school and the family to form better relationships even when Mark's leukaemia recurred. In such tense situations, the skills and attitudes of staff are vital.

Several parents described how medical crises or inappropriate school responses to a medical need had resulted in conflict. Sally, who has Hurler's syndrome, was sent by a new teacher on a school cross-country run in cold weather although she was only supposed to take limited exercise in the gym. Her mother had phoned the headteacher to ask why this had happened and, since she was already angry, added that she was upset that a change of teacher had only been notified to the children the day before the transition, and not to the parents. The headteacher had apologised but had followed up the call with a four-page letter detailing what the school was doing for Sally. Her parents felt that the letter was both a defensive action and also a reprimand for their complaint:

It would have been much better if we could just have sat down together informally for a chat. I'm sure we would all have felt better because really we were not making a general complaint.

Although secondary headteachers were also perceived by parents as being very important, the direct parental contact was often dispersed across guidance, learning support or registration staff. This scattering of contact was confusing and worrying to parents, and a single influential and reliable contact was thought necessary. Rick's mother had expected to be in contact frequently when her son went to secondary school as his condition was deteriorating and he had been bullied at primary school. Her anxiety, however, had abated because she had confidence in Rick's guidance teacher: 'He's really vigilant, he phones regularly and I can go up at any time.'

Any mismatch in values and in aims for children's education between school staff and parents could be exacerbated by issues related to the child's condition. Although rarely made explicit, some teachers seemed to expect families' compliance with school values and practices 'in exchange' for the extra effort it took to meet children's needs. Time spent by parents and school staff getting to understand each other's concerns and in initial shared planning, was fundamental to subsequent positive experiences. A guidance teacher described how she, '. . . spent two hours at the beginning to *save* 22 later'.

One mother described the last year of her daughter's life when Rae still very much wanted to be in school with her friends despite failing health and the need for piped oxygen. The headteacher and other staff also wanted Rae to be there but were conscious of her physical vulnerability:

> They (the school staff) were cautious. They not only had the home number, they had the office number and the car phone number, I had that for the last 18 months of Rae's life, so the headteacher could get me at any time, and she would let me know if she had concerns about Rae's breathing or if she had bad colour. On the other hand she didn't just phone me always or panic, they were cautious but not excessively.

Not all accounts were so satisfactory. Beth had been absent intermittently for nearly two terms with glandular fever, during which time her mother had regularly sent in medical certificates and requests for homework. Her mother only received one phone call from the guidance teacher and one package of homework, and felt that there should have been more contact and,

> They could have made a wee bit more effort. Compared to what they used to be, I mean, it's gone down hill',

referring to the school in the time of the previous headteacher who

> paid attention to things like that.

The educational welfare officer involved thought that Beth's mother was less able socially to assert her real concerns to the school and described the school's attitude to her family as 'negative'. 'Beth has the odd time off even when she's well,' was the guidance teacher's response to the welfare officer's enquiry. The school had made value judgements in relation to its own resource allocation and also failed to refer Beth to the home-visiting teacher service. In Scottish education authorities, unlike England and Wales, the provision of education for children not attending school is a 'permitted action' but not a 'mandatory requirement'. A consultation document (SOEID 1998), however, asked whether this situation should be changed.

For many parents, optimising their child's educational progress and ensuring that they 'kept up' were matters of deep concern. While parents of children who had had periods of acute illness recognised that there were times when education was irrelevant, a poor prognosis in itself was not seen as a reason for not attending school. For some parents, regardless of their children's ability, educational achievement at their own level was a marker of children's existence and in some cases it was also perceived as a compensation for their physical limitations. Attendance, however irregular, at local mainstream schools was seen as 'normalising' and offering the best chance for children to find friendship (Closs and Burnett 1995). Some school staff did not see such parental aims for their children as 'strictly educational' and were critical of the resource implications for schools.

Parents of children with serious medical conditions (especially their mothers) are under multiple pressures, not all of which are readily perceived by school staff or easily communicated by parents. For example, many families in the study faced increased expenditure associated with their child's diet, heating and transport, but did so on a single income because of the need for one parent to be available for care duties. Others were deeply concerned about siblings' well-being. Eiser (1993) suggests that life can never be truly 'normal' for a family with a child with a very serious condition. Nonetheless, many aspire to normality and achieve it to a remarkable degree, and a mother in our study described the process:

> The way I see it, we have two lives, the one that's like everyone else's where we eat and sleep and communicate and see friends and go on holiday, and the other that's tied to this condition with hospital and hospice visits, and lifting, and phoning and waiting for the special this, that and the next thing and waiting for all the professionals . . . and so on, a real struggle. I suppose what I try to do is to ensure that the second world doesn't take over the first. Sometimes, amazingly, I succeed.

In such circumstances, however, it would be surprising if home–school relationships were not occasionally fraught. Gordon's mother described how she felt when she discovered that the school had not told her how far behind Gordon was in his maths:

> They said he caught up quite quickly, but what's been happening is that he's caught up on what they are doing then, but there's a space left behind and it shows later. I can't be up at the school every day seeing if that's happening. You

just assume that the teacher's doing that . . . It's his education and I feel time is very important. They don't know how long he's going to be all right this time, the specialist said maybe six to nine months, so we're nearly up to seven months so if he relapses in another couple of months who knows how often or how long he will be off then, so when he's well I want every minute to count for his education and I don't want somebody else being lax about it when I'm doing my damnedest to make sure everything is going right.

Teacher training and information

As Ainscow (1997) has argued, if we are to recognise fully the implications of inclusion, we need to begin by assuming that all children have the right to attend their local school:

> Therefore, the task becomes one of developing the work of the school in response to pupil diversity . . . this has to include a consideration of overall organisation, curriculum and classroom practice, support for learning and staff development.
>
> (p.5)

The great majority of children with a medical condition attend mainstream schools and it became clear during the research that schools could indeed 'develop the work of the school in response to pupil diversity'; in this case the specific, and sometimes complicated, needs of the research group. Rae's mother, after her daughter's death, was able to say of the local primary school, 'I have a great admiration for this school. They have done everything they possibly could to help us.'

However, the teachers in our study acknowledged their need for more staff development. Training teachers in the special needs of children with serious medical conditions is a neglected area, both in initial teacher training and in-service courses. Eiser and Town (1987) and Eiser (1990) have noted how poorly trained and ill-informed many teachers are in terms of childhood disease, and how they tend to overestimate the likelihood of medical emergencies arising in school. Leaman (1995) notes that most teachers respond to illness and death as lay people rather than as trained professionals.

Official guidance on duties and good practice in schools in relation to pupils with medical needs issued jointly by the DfEE and DoH (1996a; 1996b) in England and Wales (which have as yet not been matched in Scotland or Ireland) address meeting the medical needs of pupils in school. It is good to record that all 18 pupils profiled in the study were, in their own and their parents' opinions, having their medical needs fully met even though these had sometimes required extended negotiations between parents and community child health officers, and the school. The good practice guide is useful as it is important for a member of a school staff to be trained and willing, for example, to give rectal valium to counteract an epileptic seizure or to use a 'histostab' to reduce anaphylactic responses to acute allergies. However, the general and special needs of many more children would be met more effectively by a general awareness raising of a practical kind, opening up issues and raising questions, developing positive attitudes and laying foundations of good policy and practice on which training in relation to individual children can successfully be based.

Part of the awareness raising could also include the opportunity for teachers to examine their own preconceptions, attitudes and fears about illness and death, which are important factors in relationships between pupils and their teachers. Several teachers in the study described feelings of initial fear and repulsion over a child's illness. Death as a topic for discussion, especially when raised by a child in relation to her or himself, can be so distressing to a badly prepared teacher as to incapacitate him or her:

> When he said he wanted to die because he was so unhappy about what the others had said but that he would be dying anyway, I didn't know what to say . . . I wanted to cry or to hug him but I think I just said to get on with his work.

Conclusion

There is an urgent need for more initial and in-service staff development to enable the inclusive education of children with serious medical conditions. Above all there would appear to be a need for staff to develop their interpersonal skills, useful in all aspects of their professional and personal lives, but absolutely *essential* when working with children with serious medical conditions and their families.

References

Ainscow, M. (1997) Towards inclusive schooling. *British Journal of Special Education*, **24**(1), 3–6.

Barnes, C. and Mercer, G. (1996) *Exploring the Divide: Illness and Disability*. Leeds: The Disability Press.

British Paediatric Association (1995) *Health Needs of School Age Children*. London: BPA.

Brown, S. and McIntyre, D. (1986) How do teachers think about their craft?. In M. Ben Peretz, R. Bromine and R. Halkes (eds) *Advances in Research on Teacher Thinking*. Berwyn, IL: Liss, Swets and Zeitlinger.

Closs, A. and Burnett, A. (1995) Education for children with a poor prognosis: reflections on parental wishes and on an appropriate curriculum. *Child: Care, Health and Development*, **21**(6), 387–94.

Closs, A. and Norris, C. (1997) *Outlook Uncertain: Enabling the Education of Children with Chronic and Deteriorating Conditions* (Research Report). Edinburgh: Moray House Institute of Education.

Cooper, P. and McIntyre, D. (1993) Commonality in teachers' and pupils' perceptions of effective classroom learning. *British Journal of Educational Psychology*, **63**, 381–99.

Department for Education and Employment and Department of Health (1996a) *Circular 14/96, Supporting Pupils with Medical Needs in School*. London: DfEE/DoH.

Department for Education and Employment and Department of Health (1996b) *Supporting Pupils with Medical Needs: a Good Practice Guide*. London: DfEE/DoH.

Eiser, C. (1990) *Chronic Childhood Disease: an Introduction to Psychological Theory and Research*. Cambridge: Cambridge University Press.

Eiser, C. (1993) *Growing Up with a Chronic Disease*. London: Jessica Kingsley Publishers.

Eiser, C. and Town, C. (1987) Teachers' concerns about chronically sick children: implications for paediatricians. *Developmental Medicine and Child Neurology*, **29**, 56–63.

Larcombe, I. (1995) *Reintegration to School after Hospital Treatment*. Aldershot: Avebury.

Leaman, O. (1995) *Death and Loss: Compassionate Approaches in the Classroom*. London: Cassell.

SOEID (1998) *Special Educational Needs in Scotland: a Discussion Paper*. Edinburgh: Scottish Office.

This chapter, like many in this volume, goes beyond school and looks at how inclusive practice can extend to relationships with homes and families. This reaching beyond school demands new responses from professionals. To work effectively in more inclusive ways, teachers are likely to need more broadly based training as well as insight into their own attitudes and perspectives.

CHAPTER 4

Children's homes and school exclusion: redefining the problem

Isabelle Brodie

This chapter focuses on one group of children and young people 'on the margins' – those who are 'looked after' by local authorities, often referred to as 'in care'. The author, Isabelle Brodie, argues that we need a more complex understanding of exclusion that goes beyond formal official exclusion from school. She shows a range of routes through which 'looked after' young people come to be out of school in what can be a de-motivating process for all concerned.

The education of children looked after by local authorities ('in care') is currently high on the professional and political agenda. Moreover, there is generally a consensus on the nature and seriousness of the issues which need to be addressed. Few would contradict the view of the House of Commons Health Committee (1998) that 'It is clear that SSDs [Social Services Departments], LEAs and schools are failing to work effectively together to promote educational opportunities for children in their care' (p. lxii).

In the light of the criticisms of numerous reports, the government has now sought to respond to these issues through a range of policy initiatives, most notably through the 'Quality Protects' programme (Department of Health 1998a). Most recently draft guidance has been issued on the education of children 'looked after'. This will eventually replace the current guidance contained in Circular 13/94 (Department for Education 1994) and is generally more comprehensive, seeking to improve information gathering and planning at all levels of policy and practice in the local authority (Department for Education and Employment 1999).

This chapter is concerned with the exclusion from school of children looked after by local authorities. Available evidence suggests that children 'looked after' are more likely to be excluded or not to attend school, but relatively little consideration has taken place of the processes through which children 'looked after' come to be excluded from school, and the ways in which this is managed by the professionals involved.

The discussion will begin by examining the evidence concerning the exclusion from school of children 'looked after'. It will then consider in greater detail the ways in which children 'looked after' come to be excluded or 'out of school', arguing that formal official exclusion is not always the issue and that a more complex understanding of what constitutes exclusion needs to be developed if appropriate professional interventions are to be made. This part of the discussion will draw on evidence from an intensive study of the exclusion from school of a group of young people looked after in residential accommodation in England (Brodie 1999).

Background

In England and Wales on 31 March 1998 there were 53,000 children looked after by local authorities (Department of Health 1999). Of these, just over 35,000 were living in foster care, with a much smaller number – 4,900 – looked after in local authority children's homes. Another 770 lived in privately registered homes. The remainder either remained at home with social work support, or were resident in, for example, secure units. It is important to remember that these statistics refer to the number of children 'looked after' on one day, and do not take account of the larger group which move in and out of the care system during the course of a year. The majority of children looked after in residential accommodation are adolescents, though many local authorities do make provision for younger children. Many young people will be resident in a placement for only a few weeks or months, though many will experience more than one placement during their time 'looked after' (Department of Health 1998b).

There are no nationally collected data on the kind of schools attended by children 'looked after' or on their educational attainment. There is equally a lack of national research data, with most studies that focus on the education of 'looked after' children being local or regional (see Borland *et al.* 1998). Additionally, much more is known about the educational experiences of children living in residential accommodation than about those in foster care, despite the fact that the latter is a significantly larger group.

The most recent national studies show that most children looked after in residential accommodation who are not disabled are registered in mainstream schools, with some 10 per cent registered in special school provision (Social Services Inspectorate (SSI)/Office for Standards in Education (Ofsted) 1995; see also Department of Health 1998b and Borland *et al.* 1998). The research evidence suggests, therefore, that children 'looked after' will usually represent only a tiny minority in any one school and may not, in fact, be perceived as a distinct group or expected to present problems (Berridge *et al.* 1997).

The exclusion from school of children looked after by local authorities

In regard to non-attendance and exclusion, the Audit Commission (1994) reported that 40 per cent of 'looked after' children were not in school for reasons other than illness. A joint inspection by the SSI and Ofsted (1995) of residential and foster care in four authorities found that this problem was most concentrated at secondary school, with 25 per cent of the 14- to 16-year-olds in their sample out of school. These findings are reflected in smaller studies. Berridge and Brodie (1998), in a follow-up study of residential care in three local authorities (Berridge 1985), found that of 21 adolescents of school age living in five children's homes, only three were attending school regularly. Of the 18 non-attenders, seven were formally permanently excluded. On the other hand, in the three homes for younger children studied, all the children resident were attending school. A survey in Strathclyde (Lockhart *et al.* 1996, cited in Borland *et al.* 1998) found that one in five children's home residents were not registered at any school, employment or college and almost 40 per cent were absent from school on the day of the survey. Among those of school age, 16 per cent were not registered at any school. It is fair to conclude, then, that non-attendance and exclusion constitute a significant problem for the 'looked after' population.

The educational difficulties of children 'looked after' are not confined to exclusion and non-attendance, but are inevitably linked to other problems. Research into the educational attainment of children 'looked after' has shown that a disproportionate number fail to achieve the standards of their peers. The SSI/Ofsted study found evidence of widespread underachievement. This was most pronounced at secondary school level, where none of the sixty children studied were judged by their teachers to be likely to achieve five subjects at Grades A–C in national examinations at age 16. This compares poorly with the general school population; Biehal, Clayden, Stein and Wade (1995) found that two-thirds of their sample left care with no qualifications, whereas the proportion in the general population is 16 per cent. Similarly, studies of young people leaving care have found that few obtain any recognised qualifications, a fact which bears negatively on their future employment prospects (Biehal *et al.* 1995).

The educational difficulties experienced by children 'looked after' are generally thought to result from a combination of factors. The experiences of children prior to entering the care system are clearly important. Recent research has emphasised the fact that the group entering residential accommodation presents more complex and challenging problems than in the past (Berridge and Brodie 1998, Department of Health 1998b). These include higher levels of previous emotional, physical and sexual abuse. That said, it has rightly been argued that to plead past experience can be 'an extremely lame and convenient excuse' for the often poor quality of educational experience within the care system (Firth and Horrocks 1996). Depressingly, research continues to highlight the unstimulating educational environment, poor recording of educational information and low priority given to education by carers and social workers (Berridge *et al.* 1997, Department of Health 1998b). Poor planning and lack of liaison and communication between education and social work professionals also continue to stand in the way of the educational welfare of the children concerned.

'Redefining' school exclusion

While existing research evidence is fairly conclusive in showing that children 'looked after' frequently do not attend or are excluded from school, much less is known about how their experience of exclusion – and when and why this occurs – relates to their experience of the care system. The rest of this paper will be devoted to a more detailed discussion of what exclusion means in relation to children looked after in residential care, based on findings from an intensive qualitative study of 17 boys aged 6–16 living in residential accommodation in three local authorities.

Some information about the group studied is necessary. All seventeen had extremely troubled backgrounds. Ten were known to have experienced some kind of abuse or neglect. Other research has shown a strong statistical association between experience of abuse and educational difficulties, including exclusion (Farmer and Pollock 1998, Department of Health 1995). The group also had unusually lengthy histories of care, with 14 of them 'looked after' for a year or more, and seven for four years or more. This is atypical of the care population as a whole, but perhaps provides the opportunity for a better understanding of the relationship between the care system and exclusion.

Eleven of the boys had experienced a previous exclusion from school on either a fixed-term or permanent basis. In three cases, the exclusion had taken place from a special school for children with emotional and behavioural difficulties. Seven of the group had statements of special educational need at the time of their exclusion, and in a further case a statement had been pending. However, while by most standards this group presented significant challenges in respect to their education, this did not make their permanent exclusion from school inevitable.

This research was initiated in response to concerns voiced by residential staff regarding the problem of exclusion. However, during the initial fieldwork for the research, it frequently became apparent that children described as 'excluded' were in fact not attending school for other reasons or had been excluded by informal processes. Staff were not always aware of the precise educational status of the young people in their care and were consequently not always able to respond appropriately. An important question for the research therefore became what was meant by 'exclusion' and how this affected the experiences of the young people and professionals involved.

Legislation makes provision for two types of exclusion: fixed-term, which can take place for up to 45 days across the school year, and permanent. Most research has, understandably, focused on exclusion which corresponds to these statutory definitions. Reference has also been made, however, to 'unofficial' or 'informal' exclusion. Stirling (1992) found that of a sample of 60 children living in seven children's homes, 32 were not attending school. Only two of these were officially excluded. Stirling therefore argued that informal exclusion represented a means by which schools could circumvent reporting exclusions to the local education authority. The Department for Education (1994) also noted, on the basis of anecdotal evidence only, that schools were more likely to exclude informally children 'looked after' on the grounds that they had access to full-time day care. The research was therefore interested to learn more about how formal exclusion, when the official procedures contained in Circular 13/94 were invoked, related to informal exclusion.

An alternative framework

Through in-depth interviews with young people and the professionals involved in the case, including teachers, social workers, carers and others such as educational psychologists, the research identified four ways in which children looked after in residential accommodation were excluded. While the numbers are small, these four 'routes' or 'pathways' are helpful in developing understanding of how children come to be out of school and how this relates to different patterns of professional response.

Exclusion by non-admission

For three young people in the sample, their 'exclusion' had arisen from the fact that they did not have a school place. All presented serious behavioural problems, but the disruption of their education had also occurred for other reasons, including changes of placement. All the children in this category had arrived at the residential placement without prior arrangements being made for their education. The difficulties which then emerged concerned persuading schools to admit the young people. It was difficult to discern how far these problems were due to the fact that a child was 'looked after'. Care staff in particular felt strongly that the children in their care were stigmatised and examples were given where schools had explicitly refused admission on the grounds that they were 'looked after'. The consequence of this view was that children's homes tended to target schools which had the reputation of being amenable, or those which were undersubscribed and would find it more difficult to refuse admission. However, negotiations tended to be lengthy and the time the young people spent out of school considerable.

In one case, considerable efforts were made to encourage a school to admit a 10-year-old. The headteacher visited the children's home and a part-time timetable was worked out as a starting point. This proved successful and had the merit of ensuring that when the child did start attending the school on a full-time basis, all those involved were aware of the level of support likely to be required.

Exclusion on admission

This group involved young people who were officially or unofficially excluded very quickly after their entry to a school, usually within a few days or a few weeks. Two issues seemed especially important in relation to this group. As with other young people whose educational careers are characterised by transience, these young people had arrived with little information about their backgrounds and previous schooling. This made it difficult for the new school to assess their situation, and made dealing with their behaviour more difficult when problems arose, as they soon did.

Furthermore, young people in this group tended to be unprepared for entry to a new school and lacked the knowledge of school systems and culture which would have enabled them to integrate. In some cases, indeed, they had not even wanted to attend the new school.

Nicki's case is a good example of these problems. Nicki was 13 and was living in a private children's home some distance from his own local authority. Scarcely anything seemed to be known about either his educational or care background; he was last known to have attended a junior school for a few weeks aged 8. He began attending the education unit attached to the private children's home, but the local authority withdrew funding for this part of the placement, and a school place had to be found elsewhere. The children's home had weak links with schools in the area, but eventually found a school willing to accept Nicki. He was excluded after only two days after punching another boy during a games lesson.

In these cases, neither the children, carers or schools indicated a strong commitment to the young person attending the school. Indeed exclusion, when it came, was generally welcomed. The lack of information and prior preparation on the part of all those concerned made it unlikely that the placement would succeed, and the episode, however short, appeared only to add to the young person's educational problems.

Graduated exclusion

This group consisted of five adolescents, all of whom had a school place. In accordance with other research findings, exclusion occurred via a fairly lengthy process. In all the cases, exclusion was predicted by at least one – and usually all – of the professionals involved, who felt that the young person could not remain within the school unless significant improvements in his/her behaviour were made.

Teachers and social workers also emphasised that attempts had been made to prevent the exclusion. This contrasts with the category of 'exclusion on admission', above, where such efforts were not perceived to be worthwhile. Thus, for young people who experienced a graduated exclusion, classroom support and consultation with external professionals such as educational psychologists did take place. The children's homes also offered support, usually by removing the young person when requested for 'cooling off' time.

Such support was valued by the school, but obviously further reduced the amount of time spent by the young person in the classroom. Indeed, the exclusion process in these cases was characterised by the progressive isolation of the young person from his/her peers and teachers. While time out did appear helpful in containing the situation, in these cases it sometimes seemed questionable whether this was realistically a long-term measure by which exclusion could be prevented.

Planned exclusion

For two of the young people involved, exclusion was not only anticipated but was also 'planned'. As problems escalated, professionals sought to minimise the consequences of the exclusion by making alternative plans. These were generally intended to reduce the amount of time the young person would be left without education in the event of exclusion taking place. In one case, this involved the negotiation of an alternative care placement with education attached, and in another preparing a report recommending placement at a Pupil Referral Unit.

These cases were characterised by at least one professional taking responsibility for the young person's education and making considerable efforts on their behalf. This links to other research into the care process, particularly as it is experienced by adolescents, which has commented on the fragmented nature of professional involvement and the absence of any one individual to advocate on the young person's behalf (Department of Health 1996). The professionals who performed the active role in cases of planned exclusion also had good informal links with other key individuals, and were supported by colleagues in the young person's school and children's home. Significantly, they also perceived the young person to have the ability to respond positively to education, if this was provided in an appropriate context.

Exclusion from school and professional intervention

The four categories outlined above are unlikely to be exhaustive, but draw attention to the different ways in which 'exclusion' can take place. It is important to point out that when exclusion took place in all these categories, this occurred through both formal and informal mechanisms.

A striking feature in all categories was the unevenness in professionals' understanding of the educational needs of the children concerned and in the action taken. Consequently, while considerable efforts were made on behalf of some young people, other cases were allowed to drift for unacceptably long periods of time, making a return to education increasingly remote. The educational prospects for the children concerned were therefore often a matter of chance.

Within these categories there are, regrettably, many familiar themes concerning continuity of care and the need for careful planning. No matter how committed certain teachers, social workers or residential carers might be to the education of the young person, they were often struggling to deal with a problem which had been allowed to fester for many years and had been subject to the attentions of numerous other professionals.

Overall, however, it seemed that greater differentiation was required in terms of understanding the nature of educational problems presented by young people 'looked after'. The reasons why children are out of school when living in residential accommodation are inadequately described by the term 'exclusion'. Greater attention is required both to the care and educational careers of individuals and also to the context of residential care. Specific types of care placement may have important implications for the 'route' to exclusion that is taken. For example, in this research, children living in private homes were more vulnerable to 'exclusion on admission' due to such factors as the weaker links between the home and local schools.

More generally, however, and as a smaller number of children are looked after in residential accommodation, it is clear that they often present acute problems which will require expert help (Department of Health and Others 1998). While it should not be assumed that children 'looked after' will have difficulties at school, it is essential that the professionals concerned have sufficient information with which to work and know how best to obtain help from others.

Conclusion

Children 'looked after' share many of the characteristics of other children excluded from school, most obviously in terms of their troubled backgrounds at home and at school. Being 'looked after' is, nevertheless, an additional complication which can have significant implications for the way in which the exclusion process unfolds. It is therefore important that research into exclusion, and the development of good practice in this area, takes account of this specific context when seeking to address the problems associated with school exclusion generally.

References

Audit commission (1994) *Seen but not Heard: Co-ordinating community child health and social services for children in need.* London: HMSO.

Berridge, D. (1985) *Children's Homes.* Oxford: Blackwell.

Berridge, D. and Brodie, I. (1998) *Children's Homes Revisited.* London: Jessica Kingsley.

Berridge, D., Brodie, I., Ayre, P., Barrett, D., Henderson, B. and Wenman, H. (1997) *Hello – Is Anybody Listening? The education of young people in residential care.* University of Warwick: Social Care Association.

Biehal, N., Clayden, J., Stein, M. and Wade, J. (1995) *Moving On: Young people and leaving care schemes.* London: HMSO.

Borland, M., Pearson, C., Hill, M., Tisdall, K. and Bloomfield, I. (1998) *Education and Care away from Home.* Edinburgh: Scottish Council for Research in Education.

Brodie, I. (1999) *Redefining School Exclusion: Children's homes and the educational process.* PhD thesis, University of Luton.

Department for Education (1994) *Pupils with Problems* (Circulars 8–13/94). London: DFE.

Department for Education and Employment (1999) *Draft Guidance on the Education of Children Looked After by Local Authorities.* London: DfEE.

Department of Health (1995) *Child Protection: Messages from research*. London: HMSO.

Department of Health (1996) *Focus on Teenagers*. London: HMSO.

Department of Health (1998a) *Quality Protects: Framework for action*. London: Department of Health.

Department of Health (1998b) *Caring for Children Looked After away from Home*. Chichester: Wiley.

Department of Health (1999) *Children Looked After in England, 1998/99*. London: Department of Health.

Department of Health and Others (1998) *The Government's Response to the Children's Safeguards Review* (Cmnd 4105). London: HMSO.

Farmer, E. and Pollock, S. (1998) *Caring for Sexually Abused and Abusing Children away from Home*. Chichester: Wiley.

Firth, H. and Horrocks, C. (1996) No home, no school, no future: Exclusions and children who are 'looked after'. In E. Blyth and J. Milner (eds) *Exclusion from School: Inter-professional issues for policy and practice*. London: Routledge.

House of Commons Health Committee (1998) *Children Looked After by Local Authorities*. Vol. 1. *Report and Proceedings of the Committee*. London: HMSO.

Social Services Inspectorate and Ofsted (1995) *The Education of Children Looked After By Local Authorities*. London: Ofsted.

Stirling, M. (1992) How many pupils are being excluded? *British Journal of Special Education*, **19**, 128–30.

Isabelle Brodie has demonstrated here the importance of recent initiatives aimed at preventing young people in care from falling through the net of potential support. Like other pupils 'on the margins' these young people can be invisible and vulnerable to subtle as well as explicit exclusion; and like others they can also be resilient. The chapter is important because we need to understand exclusion in order to promote inclusion.

CHAPTER 5

Inclusion for the difficult to include

John Visser, Ted Cole and Harry Daniels

This chapter reports on the findings from a DfEE funded study of mainstream schools' practice in relation to 'pupils with emotional and behavioural difficulties'. The authors outline some key features of school which cater successfully for many of these pupils. They suggest that schools that foster a culture of caring, sharing and learning are more effective in achieving inclusion for those pupils who are regarded as the most difficult to include.

Introduction

The consultation Special Educational Needs Green Paper (DfEE 1997) and resultant Programme of Action (DfEE 1998) show the current Government's commitment to the increased inclusion of pupils with SEN in mainstream schools. [. . .] The Government suggests that inclusion should be seen as a 'process' rather than merely as 'placement' of pupils in a mainstream school. However, it is clear in these documents that some pupils are seen as more problematic than most when it comes to the achievement of inclusion. These pupils are generally perceived as those whose special educational needs fall into the area of emotional and behavioural difficulties (EBD). Both documents (DfEE 1997; DfEE 1998) highlighted pupils with EBD as constituting a greater challenge for inclusion than all other areas of SEN.

Pupils with EBD have always presented a challenge to schools and teachers, and yet some schools have a much better record of meeting these pupils' needs without recourse to permanent exclusion or a statement requiring the pupil to be educated in a special school or placed in a Pupil Referral Unit. In 1997 we (the Bimingham EBD research team) were awarded a grant by the DfEE to establish the features to be found in such mainstream schools. The details of this research were published by the DfEE (Daniels *et al*. 1998).

Methodology

The research used a three-phase nested design, where the main purpose of each phase was the clarification and refining of an understanding of good practice and how it is achieved. In Phase One, criteria associated with meeting the needs of pupils with EBD were taken from relevant reports, research and reviews. These criteria were distilled into a draft model whose validity was probed in interviews with key professionals within the field, and included DfEE, Ofsted, SCAA (now QCA), LEAs, social services and staff in schools. A refined model was then examined at a one day conference with sub-groups using nominal group techniques as well as plenary discussions. The research team used this data to further refine the model.

Phase Two identified, in consultation with others (Ofsted, LEA officers, DfEE), 30 mainstream schools representing a range of social and economic contexts, maintained and grant maintained status and the full range of Key Stage configurations. Each school was visited and the model used as the reference point for interviews with key personnel in the areas of management, special educational needs and pastoral care.

Five primary and five secondary schools were chosen, on the basis of their practice, their willingness to cooperate and their locational spread from the Phase Two group for Phase Three. This last phase examined policy, provision and practice in depth and related this data back to the model which underwent further modification.

Two other studies contributed to the development of the model. The first was a national study of special school provision for pupils with EBD (Cole, Visser and Upton 1998). The second was a study of one LEA's provision and practice in relation to pupils with EBD which has remained confidential to that authority. [. . .]

Non-prescriptive features

The key features of the model described below are not put forward as prescriptive. The research took us into a wide variety of secondary and primary schools, where differing policies, practices and provision were observed. We did not find one dominant approach which, if transplanted to all schools, would meet all the needs of every pupil with EBD. There is not a single, 'one size fits all' approach to the different needs of pupils with EBD. Like MacGilchrist, Myers and Reed (1997), in their work on school improvement, we found no blueprint in terms of systems or particular approaches (such as 'assertive discipline') for the effective inclusion of pupils with EBD in every mainstream school.

Rather, the features we describe provide teachers and schools with a way of examining their policy, practice and provision against some key principles which interact with each other. These interactions are governed by factors intrinsic and extrinsic to the school, and are underpinned by the values, attitudes and beliefs held by teaching staff and governors. The outcomes of these interactions make up the unique features of each school's approach to meeting the needs of its pupils.[. . .]

Finally we do not think that the features we outline are a surprise. The features we found resonate with much of the literature on effective schooling (for example, Sammons, Hillman and Mortimore 1995). What we do emphasise is that good practice in meeting the needs of pupils with EBD is derivative of good practice in meeting the learning needs of all pupils.

Key features

The key features found in schools which demonstrate inclusive practice in relation to pupils who are difficult to include were:

- effective leadership which generates direction for all staff
- a 'critical mass' of staff committed to inclusive values
- senior management (SMT) who are committed to the development of good quality teaching which matches the learning styles and abilities of pupils including those with EBD
- a willingness and ability to access outside agencies to help develop and sustain inclusive practice.

These features formed the basis for an ongoing dialogue between key staff, in particular the school's leadership, and a critical mass of other staff. This dialogue was based upon values which espoused caring, sharing and learning. These values enabled schools to maintain and sustain the ethos and processes which enable pupils with EBD to be included.

Leadership

Creating, maintaining and sustaining effective leadership is seen by a wide range of sources as a major feature in any discussion of good practice. These sources (for example, Davies 1997; Prince 1997; DfE 1994) often list the features which create effective schools but are less explicit about those which sustain and maintain good practice. The maintenance of good practice lies in ensuring that the structures remain appropriate and meet the needs of all concerned. To sustain good practice the morale and commitment of staff has to be nurtured and acknowledged. Structures, systems and organisations need maintenance to remain effective. Relationships, values, beliefs and attitudes need sustaining – they are key aspects of inclusion in meeting the needs of pupils with EBD.

We found that these aspects of creating, sustaining and maintaining good practice were found in leadership patterns which sought to consult and seek consensus while giving a 'clear sense of direction'. This sense of direction was built upon a collegiate approach providing consensus, consistency and cohesion. Staff in good practice schools showed an awareness of the need for consensus in arriving at decisions and policies, consistency in their application, and cohesion of purpose of schooling implicit in their policy, practice and provision. These three 'Cs' enabled schools to be more flexible and transparent in meeting the needs of pupils. This is of particular importance for inclusive practice where the valuing of diversity is high on the daily agenda of staff.

Teachers and schools meet the educational needs of pupils with emotional and behavioural difficulties, through the relationships they develop and the organisational strategies they employ (DES 1989; Gleeson 1992; Mortimore *et al.* 1988; Ayers, Clark and Murray 1995; HMI 1987; Smith and Laslett 1993). We found considerable variation between teachers and schools in these relationships. A variety of styles of teaching, ways of motivating pupils and responses to behaviour found challenging were observed. Common strands in these observations were the fostering of a climate of praise, with a high level of expectations in behaviour and academic progress, together with 'understanding' when these were not achieved by individual pupils.

The practice of these staff was enhanced when they had an understanding of EBD, where they were able to differentiate this from general 'naughtiness' and the transient misbehaviour most pupils engage in. The practice exhibited by staff was characterised by attributes and beliefs which showed a professional commitment which engendered a consistency in approach, allowing for flexibility in their skilled responsiveness to an individual pupil's needs. They offered constructive support to colleagues. They had a problem-sharing and solving approach to issues which encouraged an open discussion of classroom management issues. Above all they *believed* in the inclusion of pupils with SEN in their mainstream school.

These effective leaders and staff formed a 'critical mass' in the schools we examined. In some schools this critical mass consisted of a majority of the staff while in others it was a smaller number of staff. These critical mass groups contained those who were perceived of as key players in the school. The importance of this 'critical mass' lay in the creation and ownership of the school's behaviour policy. They understood the emotional components of pupils' EBD and the sometimes fractured lives outside school of pupils with EBD. The 'E' in EBD was not swamped by an over-concentration on the 'B'. They also sustained a belief that pupils could alter their behaviour to an extent. Of importance in achieving the 'alteration' was the provision of an orderly, controlled, yet relaxed atmosphere underpinned by a positive whole school behaviour policy. These policies were integral parts of the school's overarching aims. They were linked naturally to the school's mission statement or corporate aims, rather than separately established and bolted to them. They flowed from the aims, values and beliefs espoused by the critical mass of staff. These behaviour policies matched criteria outlined as good practice by a number of sources (see, for example, Clarke and Murray 1996; Ofsted 1993; DES 1989).

These schools' behaviour policies were linked to a concern for educational progress; pupils with EBD were seen as pupils whose special educational needs did not preclude them from needing to, or wanting to, achieve academically. The sample schools had staff with a wide range of classroom management techniques, where teaching and learning was viewed as important, and thus the curriculum being followed and accreditation achieved was given equal status, or at least was not accorded a lower status than that followed by other pupils (see Visser 2000 for an exposition of these factors). The emphasis was upon the learning needs of the pupil being met.

The need for multi-agency work in meeting the often complex range of needs which pupils with EBD have has been advocated over a long period of time and by many authors (Cole *et al.* 1998). However, the evidence suggests that formidable obstacles (a mixture of finance, time and inclination) face schools in achieving or taking part in a multi-agency approach. Even within education (intra-agency approaches) some of the sample schools struggled to achieve the services of support teachers and educational psychologists. Where this was achieved it was largely on the basis of local factors such as personal professional relationships rather than systems and structures which promoted collaboration in identification, assessment and provision for pupils with EBD.

These features and others, such as teacher characteristics, discussed more fully in our report (Daniels *et al*. 1998) were found to varying degrees in all the schools within the study. They were also apparent in an earlier study of provision within special schools (Cole *et al*. 1998). A further analysis of these features gave rise to three descriptive terms which identify common themes in the schools we studied. They were all, to varying degrees, caring, sharing and learning schools.

Caring schools

The schools cared about their pupils. The rhetoric of inclusion was borne out in practice. Pupils were seen as part of a community which the school served; as such they were valued by staff in all their diversity and individuality. Their emotional needs were recognised and addressed, often by staff spending time listening to what pupils had to say. Staff cared by setting achievable high standards in behaviour and learning, while being tolerant and forgiving of lapses by pupils. Caring was not a soft option, misbehaviour was confronted, but it was the 'deed' which was condemned, not the person. These schools did permanently exclude the occasional pupil, but rarely, and always reluctantly. Their systems of rewards and sanctions were applied to meet individual needs whilst upholding widely agreed standards. They understood the need to provide pupils with 'cooling off space' when issues got out of hand, and modelled ways of coping with the strains and stresses of school life.

Sharing schools

These were schools where staff, pupils and parents were able to discuss openly between themselves, and with each other, issues of behaviour. In particular, staff could discuss their concerns over incidents where pupils had been challenging. Staff would collaborate in seeking positive ways forward to enhance their own skills as well as in meeting an individual pupil's needs. They focused on learning and teaching skills rather than upon difficulties perceived as being intrinsic to the child. They acknowledged that the solution to many emotional and behavioural difficulties lay outside of the school's ability to address fully. However, they were equally confident of schools' and teachers' ability to make a significant difference to the lives of their pupils with EBD.

Learning schools

We found that Dennison and Kirk's (1990) model of a do-review-learn-apply cycle was in evidence in all the schools. These were institutions where staff frequently reflected upon their actions, decisions and organisation. Importantly these reflections were taken into account in the planning of their subsequent actions. These were not schools which proceeded in a linear fashion to plan-do-review where the review does not feed back into the planning. There was a genuine circularity to their educational activities, where their reviews were an active part of their planning. Also these actions were not seen as separate entities, where separate incidents or processes were examined as if they had no wider consequence within the institution. Each action by pupil and staff, while seen as important within its own context, was also reviewed to ascertain its wider implications for staff, teachers, pupils, parents and SMT in the context of the whole school. Meeting the needs of pupils with EBD was not seen as separate from meeting the needs of all pupils. What was found to be effective in a given situation was used to inform policy, practice and provision more widely.

Conclusions

The lessons which we believe schools can draw from these findings to become more effective in meeting the needs of pupils with EBD echo the work of Thomas, Walker and Webb (1998) and the Elton Report (DES 1989). Schools need to be communities that are open, positive and diverse, not selective, exclusive or rejecting. They need to ensure they are 'barrier free' for pupils with EBD. The development of a collaborative ethos is a key feature. This entails collaboration within school, between staff and between staff and pupils, as well as with outside agencies. Lastly, schools need to develop a sense of equity in promoting every pupil's rights and responsibilities in all aspects of school life. These lessons from our research are easy to state, but we appreciate from this DfEE study and subsequent research (for example, Cole, Daniels and Visser 1999) just how difficult it is for schools to achieve the challenges they pose.

References

Ayers, M., Clark, D. and Murray, A. (1995) *Perspectives on Behaviour: A Practical Guide to Effective Interventions for Teachers*. London: David Fulton.

Clarke, C. and Murray, A. (1996) *Developing a Whole School Behaviour Policy: A Practical Approach*. London: David Fulton.

Cole, T, Daniels, H. and Visser, J. (1999) *Patterns of Educational Provision Maintained by Local Education Authorities for Pupils with Behaviour Problems*. A report for the Nuffield Foundation, The University of Birmingham.

Cole, T., Visser, J. and Upton, G. (1998) *Effective Schooling for Pupils with Emotional and Behavioural Difficulties*. London: David Fulton.

Daniels, H., Visser, L., Cole, T. and De Reybekill, N. (1998) *Emotional and Behavioural Difficulties in Mainstream Schools*. Research report RR90. London: DfEE.

Davies, L. (1997) *Beyond Authoritarian School Management: The Challenge of Transparency*. Ticknall: Education Now.

Dennison, B. and Kirk, B. (1990) *Do Review Learn Apply: A Simple Guide to Experiential Learning*. Oxford: Blackwell.

DES (1989) *Discipline in Schools* (The Elton Report). London: HMSO.

DfE (1994) *The Education of Children with Emotional and Behavioural Difficulties*. Circular (9/94). London: DfE.

DfEE (1997) *Excellence for All Children: Meeting Special Educational Needs*. (Green Paper). London: DfEE.

DfEE (1998) *Programme for Action*. London: DfEE.

Gleeson, D. (1992) School attendance and truancy – a socio-historical account. *Sociological Review*, **40**(3), 437–90.

HMI (1987) *Good Behaviour and Discipline in Schools*. Education Observed Series. London: Routledge.

MacGilchrist, B., Myers, K. and Reed, J. (1997) *The Intelligent School*. London: Paul Chapman.

Mortimore, P., Sammons, L. and Ecob, R. (1988) *School Matters*. Wells: Open Books.

Ofsted (1993) *Achieving Good Behaviour in Schools*. London: HMSO.

Prince, L. P. (1997) The neglected rules of leadership: leadership and dissent. In Coulson, A. and Baddeley, S. (eds) *Trust in the Public Service*. New York: Policy Press.

Sammons, P., Hillman, J. and Mortimore, P. (1995) *Key Characteristics of Effective Schools: A Review of School Effectiveness Research*. Report Commission by Ofsted.

Smith, C. and Laslett, R. (1993) *Effective Classroom Management: A Teacher's Guide*. London: Routledge.

Thomas, G., Walker, D. and Webb, J. (1998) *The Making of the Inclusive School*. London: Routledge.

Visser, J. (2000) *Managing Behaviour in Classrooms*. London: David Fulton.

This chapter shows how inclusive schools extend beyond classroom boundaries. Like other authors in this volume, John Visser, Ted Cole and Harry Daniels see inclusion as a process based on clear principles. It involves professionals in reflection that may challenge their existing assumptions and in willingness to work across existing boundaries. Such new ways of working may well be challenging and difficult.

CHAPTER 6

Early intervention in emotional and behavioural difficulties: the role of nurture groups

Paul Cooper and Jane Lovey

In this chapter Paul Cooper and Jane Lovey describe nurture groups and discuss their effectiveness as a way of intervening early in the education of young children with emotional and behavioural difficulties. The findings from their research show how staff familiar with nurture groups view them as an inclusive and positive approach to retaining challenging children in mainstream schools.

Background

Nurture groups (NGs) were first established by the Inner London Education Authority (ILEA) in the 1970s, by Marjorie Boxall, an ILEA Educational Psychologist (Bennathan and Boxall 1996). They take the form of discrete classes, located in mainstream primary schools, for approximately 12 students, staffed by a teacher and a specially trained learning support assistant (LSA). They were set up in response to what was seen as the alarming prevalence of emotional and behavioural difficulties (EBDs) among children entering mainstream primary schools, the effect of which was to disrupt the education of children in mainstream classes. Boxall's analysis highlighted the importance of attachment theory (Bowlby 1971–80) in understanding the causes of these problems, and it is this theoretical position that underpins NG philosophy.

Stated briefly, attachment theory deals with the dynamic interactions that occur between dependent young children and their care-takers (i.e. parent or substitute carer). The theory suggests that young children engage in 'proximity-seeking attachment behaviour', usually in the form of emotionally charged demands for attention (e.g. screaming, tantrums) or severely withdrawn behaviour. When these demands are met with the appropriate form of 'care-taking' behaviour, the child experiences a sense of well-being and security that enables him or her to engage in the 'exploratory' behaviours that are so important to normal child development. Appropriate care-taking involves behaviour that is neither neglectful nor over-protective. Failure to experience such appropriate care-taking may lead the child to become stuck at an early developmental stage, or to regress to that earlier stage, when his or her needs were last met most satisfactorily (Tyrer and Steinberg 1993). This will often take the form of developmentally inappropriate proximity-seeking attachment behaviour.

The UK government has identified NGs as a promising intervention for children with EBDs, against the background of increasing concern about the high level of EBDs among early years children (DfEE 1997), as well as the massive rise in school exclusion over recent years and its apparent association with unmet special educational needs (Castle and Parsons 1997; Hayden 1997). In support of this view, the present authors present NGs as an important approach to meeting the needs of young children with EBDs, and stress that this should be seen in the context of mainstream, whole-school approaches to EBDs, towards the development of which, it is suggested, NGs may contribute.

The nurture group philosophy

The essence of the NG philosophy is that children who exhibit emotional and behavioural difficulties are often experiencing emotions and exhibiting behaviours that are inappropriate to the developmental stage of the majority of their same-age peers. Normal infant behaviour, for example, is characterized by extreme egocentrism and disregard for the needs and feelings of others. In order to progress from this state to the level of social competence that is required in the standard infant school classroom, the individual has to go through a set of experiences to see her/himself as distinct from other people. This process is essential to healthy psychological development in general, since without such progress individuals will be severely impaired in their ability to understand and regulate their behaviour, form relationships and to communicate with others. The process is also vital in laying the social and psychological foundations for learning. [. . .]

Thus, while NGs derive much of their theoretical justification from theories of emotional and social development, their central thrust is educational. The core feature of the NG approach is that teachers employ teaching approaches which are directed at students' developmental rather than their age levels. Thus important aspects of the NG curriculum will include opportunities for pupils to engage in learning experiences that most children experience at the pre-school phase: a focus on early language development, and the development of early mathematical concepts. The task of the NG's staff is to facilitate pupil engagement with the curriculum through careful attention to pupils' needs for positive recognition and the experience of genuine social and academic success. The intensive small-group experience is designed to be relatively short-lived (on average, less than one school year), with gradually increasing periods of partial reintegration into mainstream classes.

Nurture groups in practice

The practical arrangements to be found in NGs have been described elsewhere (Bennathan and Boxall 1996; Bennathan 1997; Iszatt and Wasilewska 1997). What follows is a summary of their firsthand accounts.

NGs usually cater for between 10 and 12 students in a discrete class group. The children are of infant age (usually 4 or 5 years of age). The class is staffed by a teacher and specially trained NG learning support assistant, and is located in a mainstream primary or infant school.

Because the central aim of the NG is to provide children with the kinds of experience that they would receive in a normal nurturing home environment, the form and routines of NGs tend to incorporate some of the qualities that one would normally associate with a family situation rather than an educational institution. Thus, along with the usual furniture of the classroom (desks, chairs, etc.), NG classrooms strive for an atmosphere of comfort and conviviality through the use of soft furnishings, including decorative curtains, lounge chairs and couches. The classrooms also contain a kitchen and dining-area, where breakfast and other meals are eaten daily.

The NG is an educational facility, in which the term 'education' is defined in its widest sense to include the cognitive content that is central to curriculum for all children, along with social and emotional content. Thus the spaces before and in between formal lesson-time, such as 'breakfast', lunch and break times, as well as lesson-time itself, are seen as times when important social and emotional (as well as cognitive) learning takes place. A central aim of the NG is to enable children to learn to value themselves through the experience of being valued and cared for by others. NG staff are trained to use mealtimes and other periods of social contact with pupils to help build pupils' sense of being valued and cared for. Similarly, their interactions with pupils during more formal learning situations are marked by staff warmth towards pupils, and willingness to listen to pupils, and a concern to make learning and social interaction, in general, rewarding and affirming. This means that children are encouraged to express their personal views and concerns with others (staff and/or other pupils), both in relation to the formal curriculum and in terms of their personal social and emotional functioning. Opportunities will usually be created several times during the day for staff and pupils to interact in a group or subgroups, as a means of sharing ideas and understandings, and in order to promote group cohesion and personal validation.

Children in NGs are encouraged to develop initiative, and to be confident in introducing ideas, as well as to initiate conversation and activities. Rules of conduct are developed in consultation with pupils, and behavioural problems are dealt with therapeutically rather than through the use of coercive strategies. Emphasis is always placed on enabling the pupils to learn about the meaning of their own and others' behaviour. By coming to an awareness of the meaning and consequences of behaviour, in relation to others and the self, the child becomes increasingly aware of the behavioural choices that he or she has, and through this is able to develop internal controls. This kind of understanding can only be developed through regular opportunities to explore and discuss feelings and behaviour, both within the formal curriculum and through 'informal' interactions. A key aim of these groups is to help children to develop a sense of being a valued member of the class community, and to learn that personal reward (in the form of self-esteem and recognition) can result from active and constructive participation in community life.

One of the places where the formal and informal are most closely interrelated is in the area of language development. A particular focus of the NG curriculum is the development of pupils' expressive language.

The effectiveness of nurture groups

Although evidence from systematic evaluation studies is rare, a recent study carried out by the London Borough of Enfield (Iszatt and Wasilewska 1997; Bennathan 1997) found that of 308 children placed in six NGs since the 1980s, 87 per cent were able after an average placement of less than one year to return to mainstream classrooms. Eighty-three per cent required no additional SEN help, while only 4 per cent required stage 3 (DfEE SEN Code of Practice) support (i.e. requiring additional resources and expertise outside the school's normal range of resources). Thirteen per cent of the NG students went on to require statements, including 11 per cent of the original cohort who required placement in special schools. Comparison between this group and a second group of 20 children who had been assessed as having the level of difficulty to justify NG placement, but for whom no placements were available, found much higher levels of persistent difficulties, with 35 per cent being placed in special schools and only 55 per cent managing to cope in mainstream schools without additional help. The Enfield study also compared the cost of NG placement with other forms of provision. It was found that the cost of NG placement was between 10 and 30 times less than residential school placement, and less than a quarter of the average costs attracted by statements for EBD pupils. A further interesting, but unresearched, aspect of NGs is the claim attributed to headteachers and class teachers (*ibid.*) that NGs can have a significant impact on whole-school approaches to dealing with learning and behaviour, whereby through liaison between NG and mainstream staff aspects of NG philosophy and practice become integrated into mainstream teachers' classroom practice (Bennathan and Boxall 1996).

The Boxall Profile

A major tool which has been developed to be used in conjunction with NGs is *The Boxall Profile* (Bennathan and Boxall 1998). This is a rigorously trialled diagnostic instrument, which can be used to measure a child's level of emotional and behavioural functioning, as well as to highlight specific targets for intervention within a child's individual functioning. The Profile is divided into two main parts. The first deals with developmental factors underpinning the individual's ability to engage effectively in the learning process. Section two of the Profile deals with the child's behavioural characteristics that may inhibit or interfere with the child's social and academic performance. Once the full Profile is completed, a representation emerges of the child's characteristics (as defined by the teacher) across the range of emotional and behavioural factors. The Profile also enables staff to define target areas and, through repeated use of the Profile, measure progress and development. [. . .]

Practitioners' perceptions of nurture groups

The opportunity to research the views of practitioners with expertise in relation to NGs was presented during a national meeting that was held at the University of Cambridge in April 1998. The majority of attendees at the meeting were invited because of their knowledge and expertise in relation to NGs, and their commitment to the future development of NGs. The delegates included:

- teachers who are currently working in NGs
- headteachers of schools where NGs are situated
- headteachers and teachers from schools where they were planning to establish an NG
- educational psychologists in authorities with NGs
- a nurse-therapist interested in the links between emotion and learning
- a consultant psychiatrist
- a DfEE representative.

The 35 delegates were presented with a questionnaire which contained the following four questions:

1. How do NGs differ from other support for children with special needs?
2. How would you describe the child who would benefit from time in an NG?
3. What would you expect this child to gain from the group?
4. How do you think the school is affected by having an NG?

Findings

1. How do NGs differ from other support for children with special needs?

Answers to the above question tended to highlight the focus and precision of the NG approach, with its emphasis on the child's emotional needs:

The support is immediate, educationally focused, accessible when needed and flexible.

NGs start from the true recognition of where the child is at – and valued as such; and enable children to reach where they should be.

There are opportunities for 'containing' and 'holding' the characteristics of individuals in one's mind to support development and respond on all levels to the needs of the child.

The group allows each child to start at the level of early development and work through the levels until they are able to go back to mainstream class – and not only cope, but have success. It works from where the child is and allows the growing-up process to be accelerated.

The positive, therapeutic approach encouraged by the NG ethos was contrasted to the control focus that was perceived to dominate some more conventional approaches to dealing with early emotional and behavioural difficulties:

> It tackles the child's need, not the needs of the providers.

> An NG offers a child help on many levels. There are parallels with therapy – emotional holding, developing a real sense of self and experience of a good parental relationship.

Of particular concern to several respondents was the power of NGs to enable pupils to develop the emotional resources which will enable them to survive and thrive in mainstream classrooms:

> NGs are aimed at enabling children to re-experience early nurture, gain self-esteem and learn to use their curiosity constructively, so that they can go on to benefit from all mainstream opportunities.

There was widely shared enthusiasm for the positive, non-pathological emphasis of NGs, as well as their potential for helping mainstream staff and whole schools to recognize and meet the emotional needs of children, and in so doing become more effective as educators:

> They meet early nurturing needs alongside the curriculum, and they require a good relationship between two staffs, between the NG staff and the rest of the school, and between the school and the parents. It can be a full-time provision.

> It provides a multi-stranded emotional, social and cognitive learning experience and is thus educational, with the focus on growth and not on pathology. It affects the orientation of the whole school and leads it to energizing commitment. It gives primary importance to the total self of teachers and their assistants in their interactions with the children. It is energizing and gives confidence and self-esteem and is a learning experience for the teachers and assistants. No one is seen as an expert; the work belongs to everyone.

> An NG re-parents the child. He or she learns to relate, share, express him/herself.

2. How would you describe the child who would benefit from time in an NG?

In many responses to this question, there was an emphasis on the developmental theories of childhood underpinning NGs, and a recognition of the fact that schools are organized on the basis of a notion of 'normal' age-related development. The NG approach encourages schools and staff to address the serious mismatch that sometimes exists between the demands of schools and the capabilities of students who have yet to achieve the developmental level most appropriate to their age-group. Some respondents placed emphasis on the likelihood that pupils with the kinds of need catered for by NGs may have experienced inadequate early nurturing in their family situations, such as the following:

A child with emotional/cognitive delay due to confused environment/attachment experience.

One who demonstrated pre-school need/behaviour and was unable to adapt to school routine without support.

One from a very disrupted family, or in care . . . who has experienced many moves, etc.

One who has, for whatever reason, missed out on those nurturing experiences that enable learning and responding in a normal way.

One who has experienced a disturbed early development between the ages of 1 and 3 years.

Such attributions are, however, by no means universally expressed, as the following quotations illustrate; for example:

Any child who is failing to thrive in the educational climate provided by the school.

One who needs a lot of containment and some pre-school needs met in order to have a good enough 'internalised parent'.

One with significant emotional and behavioural difficulties . . . struggling with relationship/peer difficulties.

These observations might be taken to support the view that it is possible to identify a child's needs without making assumptions about the causes of those needs. This is a particularly important issue when we consider the potential for using the NG concept as a tool for blaming parents for their inadequacies. Blame of this kind is unlikely to help parents to become more effective. It is also far from always being an accurate assumption to attribute a child's emotional needs to parental incompetence. Finally, such blame is likely to be counter-productive, producing resistance/ uncooperative behaviour and/or a lack of self-confidence in 'blamed' parents.

3. What would you expect this child to gain from the group?

In answer to this question, there was a wide consensus that NGs are effective. Respondents tend to fall into two groups. The first group refers to the personal benefits that pupils are likely to accrue from placement in an NG:

Self-worth and self-confidence to meet life's challenges.

The knowledge and assurance to he happy with who they are.

Successful experiences at any level; good self-image; and an ability to make and sustain peer/adult relationships.

Trust in adults and self-esteem.

Growth and development in all areas, confidence to be at ease with themselves and in their relationships with others.

Successful experiences at whatever level.

Ability to make trusting relationships with interested adults, and learn to feel secure enough to take risks and learn through experiment. The opportunity to regress in order to experience early learning opportunities which may have been missed.

Marked increase in general competence and autonomous functioning, improved social relationships, concern for others, greater self-awareness and self-esteem, emergence of reflective behaviour and self-regulation.

The second group of respondents refer to educational and other 'performance' factors:

A sense of themselves, how to negotiate physically (body space) and emotionally with peers and adults. A fundamental basis for learning and development.

To re-attain capacity and internal stability to resume emotional and cognitive development.

Ability to function in a mainstream class.

The capacity to relate to normal educational opportunities, to peers and to adults in order to benefit his/her own needs and aspirations.

4. How do you think the school is affected by having an NG?

This is an important question, given the current international concern over the issues of inclusion in and exclusion from mainstream educational provision. It is important to emphasize that the literature on NGs (e.g. Bennathan and Boxall 1996) stresses the need for children from the NGs to be also members of mainstream classes. It is also seen as important that they share playtimes with their peers from mainstream classes. It is stressed that the transfer from NG to the full-time placement in mainstream class should be a gradual process, with mainstream and NG staff teachers working in close harmony. It is therefore reassuring to note that NGs are seen by respondents as integrally related to the mainstream school in which they operate. It is seen to be important that an NG should have a beneficial effect on the whole school, and its pupils be seen as members of the mainstream school community. First, respondents saw the NG as contributing to the overall ethos of the school:

The whole ethos is altered.

The whole school must have a nurturing approach . . . focus on children's emotional and social experience in learning filters throughout the school.

Whole-school policies which change the culture, so that ideas and concern for children permeate through all the staff.

The school is sensitized to the needs of pupils and alerted to the possibility of change.

It deepens the professional stance and approach of all concerned with the children (provided they can take the concept an board) and thereby benefits all children's learning environment.

The school becomes a nurturing school. Teachers in class take on nurturing strategies. Individual classes learn to accept and help children having difficulties.

There are opportunities to consider all children's nurturing needs and gain insight into children's learning and development.

Staff can feel supported by one another in the quest for meeting individual needs, and find a positive way of managing the impact of working with children who may be distressed.

Everyone, with few exceptions, is highly motivated and energized and working relationships improve.

Details of school organization come under scrutiny and the changes made make the total school situation more manageable for the underdeveloped nurture child. These changes reflect the 'attachment and supported separation' principles underpinning nurture work, and extend to arrival at school, assembly, playtime and dinner-time.

Of particular importance is the way in which NGs are perceived to give school staff a way of dealing with difficult situations in a constructive manner:

Work in the NG is stressful, but it is a constructive stress, not frustrating stress.

In the school as a whole, optimism and constructive attitudes replace negativism and rejection of the children.

A great deal of emphasis is placed on the way in which the NG can contribute to improved relationships between school staff and pupils' parents:

Parents feel they have been given support and full recognition of the child's needs without exclusion from mainstream.

Helps to build home–school links and makes parents feel supported.

There was confidence that it was possible for the NGs to make a major difference to schools that were, at the same time, committed to all the policy developments and 'innovations' that have assailed schools in England and Wales over the past decade and a half. These include a compulsory core curriculum, the national programme of end of key stage testing and the introduction of 'league tables' by which the public, especially parents, can judge which school shows most evidence of being successful in teaching children.

The importance of the relationship between the NG and its host school is illustrated by the case of one NG, which was described as facing problems in establishing itself in an appropriate form. This group encountered problems from the start as it was based in one school, but was intended to cater for a wider catchment area, with the possibility of reintegrating the NG children into schools without their own NG. The key seems to be the indissoluble link between the mainstream school and its own, on-site, NG.

Conclusion

It is clear that for some children there is a need for the experience of nurturing that we normally relate to the pre-school years at home. Without this experience, some children, unable to cope with the demands of the classroom, suffer constant negative feedback from their teachers and peers and experience ongoing problems as they progress through school. It seems likely that, at its best, a school with a fully integral NG not only benefits its most vulnerable children, but provides for all an ethos of caring and nurturing.

References

Bennathan, M. and Boxall, M. (1996). *Effective Intervention in Primary Schools: Nurture Groups.* London: David Fulton.

Bennathan, M, and Boxall, M. (1998). *The Boxall Profile: A Guide to Effective Intervention of Pupils with Emotional and Behavioural Difficulties.* East Sutton: Association of Workers for Children with Emotional and Behavioural Difficulties.

Bennathan, M. (1997). Effective intervention in primary schools: what nurture groups achieve. *Emotional and Behavioural Difficulties,* **2** (3), 23–9.

Bowlby, J. (1971–80). *Attachment and Loss, Vols 1–3.* Harmondsworth: Penguin.

Castle, F. and Parsons, C. (1997). Disruptive behaviour and exclusions from school: redefining and responding to the problem. *Emotional and Behavioural Difficulties,* **2** (3), 4–11.

Department for Education and Employment (1997). *Excellence for All Children: Meeting Special Educational Needs.* London: HMSO.

Hayden, C. (1997). Exclusion from primary school: children 'in need' and children with 'special educational need'. *Emotional and Behavioural Difficulties,* **2** (3), 36–44.

Iszatt, J. and Wasilewska, T. (1997). Nurture groups: an early intervention model enabling vulnerable children with emotional and behavioural difficulties to integrate successfully into school. *Educational and Child Psychology,* **14** (3), 121–39.

Tyrer, P. and Steinberg, D. (1993) *Models for Mental Disorder* (2nd edn). Chichester: Wiley.

For us, this chapter is rich with the tensions and complexities inherent in debates about inclusive education. The intervention described is so much more inclusive in ethos than segregation in a special school – it is responding, one might argue, respectfully and with care; yet there is still an element of segregating and categorising. The age-norm dominated culture of schooling often means that pupils, like the ones described here, have to go outside ordinary classrooms to have developmentally appropriate education. Inclusive education surely requires us to open up our systems to find more positive alternatives in responding to diverse levels of maturity among pupils.

Part 2

Transitions

CHAPTER 7

Inclusion at Bangabandhu Primary School

Cathy Phillips and Helen Jenner

In this chapter, Cathy Phillips (headteacher, Bangabandhu Primary School) and Helen Jenner (Inclusion Officer with Tower Hamlets Local Education Authority) consider the central role that inclusive practice has played in developing the work of the school. They show how inclusive practice at Bangabandhu is based on a set of guiding principles. Those principles are characterised by respect for individual difference and openness to change. The article shows how definitions of good practice constantly change, led by responses to the diversity of the school's community. The authors do not claim to have every answer to the challenges the school has faced. However, they show how inclusive practice, supported by shared principles, can respond not only to individual circumstances but also to the concerns of whole communities.

History

Bangabandhu Primary School is situated in the east of Bethnal Green in the London Borough of Tower Hamlets. We are a community school and welcome children of all abilities, cultures, ethnic groups, political status and special needs. Sixty pupils a year join our two-form entry school and we have two nursery classes. The surrounding area is a mix of medium and high rise council flats with small areas of privately owned terraced houses. It is an area of considerable deprivation, with the majority of the school population being affected by substandard housing, overcrowding, unemployment or a lack of safe places to play.

Bangabandhu opened in January 1989 in temporary accommodation following an unprecedented rise in the size of the Bangladeshi community. Our name means 'Friend of Bengal' and is taken from the honorary title given to Sheik Mujibur Rahman, who helped found Bangladesh in 1971.

In 1991 we moved into our attractive, purpose-built building. It was described as barrier-free but this did not prove to be the case. Our first wheelchair users found that the level of the playground was 90 cm lower than the classroom floor and ramps had to be built to classroom doors. Fire doors did not open automatically and the toilets 'for the disabled' were too small. The vast majority of the initial school intake was Bangladeshi. Some children had been without a school place for several years. The

Bangladeshi parents, as new arrivals, had least access to the education system. The parents were also very concerned, in a climate of racism, for the safety of their children and wanted a school in their immediate neighbourhood. Our initial roll was almost exclusively bilingual, with children who had not attended school before or who had had extensive breaks in their education.

We worked very hard in the initial year to let the wider public know of our existence. The school is in an out-of-the-way location and was perceived by many as a private Asian school. We were able to increase our profile when we moved in to our new building. We leafleted the neighbourhood and invited everyone to open evenings to see the school. As the local community discovered the school and its reputation increased, the intake became more mixed in cultural and class terms and is now more representative of the wider community.

Many of the children enter the school with low levels of basic skills and there are still a number of children who join throughout the school from overseas or take extended leave with families abroad. Our school population is now approximately 65 per cent Bangladeshi, 15 per cent English, Scottish and Welsh, and the other 20 per cent come from a range of nationalities with Somali, Turkish and African Caribbean being the next most prominent groups.

Equal opportunities

As a new school we have made equal opportunities central to our practice. Antiracist teaching is an integral part of our provision and has a central place in the curriculum. From the start, we aimed to provide resources and a curriculum that reflected the nationalities and cultures within the school and a workforce that reflected the community. We have appointed support staff and, where possible, teachers who reflect the school population. Signs appear in both English and Bengali, and letters home are translated.

Teaching, assemblies and celebrations are planned with the diversity of our community in mind. We are predominantly a Muslim school and we ensure we are knowledgeable about what this means for our pupils, their families and many of our staff. We recognise, however, that for our pupils to have equal access to all that society has to offer, they need to know that Britain developed as a Christian society, many of its institutions shaped by Christianity.

Equal opportunities are at the heart of inclusion. We see equal opportunities as not about treating everyone the same but rather about meeting people's individual needs and celebrating individual strengths. Equality does not mean uniformity. It is about acknowledging and valuing the differences between individuals.

We recognise there is great tension between the government's standards agenda and their policy on inclusion. This tension has put great pressure on the school. We are concerned with social as well as academic progress. We want to foster young people who will be tolerant and able to make informed choices. We recognise that inclusion will weaken our performance in the league tables but are prepared to defend this position despite pressures to abandon an inclusive approach, narrow the curriculum and target resources at those children who will ensure that our position in the league tables improves.

Children with special educational needs

Once we moved to our new building, a teacher from a local special school approached us. She felt that many of her pupils were wrongly placed and would move to mainstream secondary schools. She wanted them to come to us on a part-time basis. Inclusion for pupils with significant special educational needs was, therefore, a gradual process for us. A few children became part-time pupils, several then moving to us full-time. We began to have pupils directed to us because of the suitability of the premises and the welcome and acceptance that pupils experienced. We also had a number of children from our own school population who were diagnosed with progressive conditions that would result in physical impairment. We also began to see a rise in the number of children on the autistic spectrum.

Our initial reaction was to look for experts 'out there' who would tell us how to meet these new needs. We actively sought any advice we could get from doctors, specialist teachers, physiotherapists, occupational and speech therapists. We also experienced at times feelings of frustration, disappointment and a lack of support. We came to realise that every child is an individual and that a label of cerebral palsy or autism did not necessarily tell you what that child needed next in the classroom with their learning or social skills. We are developing our own expertise with help wherever we can get it and will continue on this path. We have formed a productive partnership with Stephen Hawking School, a local special school.

We have had children on roll who are registered blind, with TAR syndrome (the child had no arms and poorly formed legs), 3 M syndrome, ataxia telangiectasia, cerebral palsy, spina bifida, brittle bone disease, autism, Down's syndrome and many other conditions. We knew nothing about some of these conditions until the children turned up and in some cases the diagnosis is so rare that little is known even in the medical world. We have learned that it is the individual child who is at the centre of our planning. For example, two children from a one-parent family were suddenly diagnosed with a serious degenerative condition. One child needed a teaching assistant as soon as possible as his movements were becoming more and more unstable. His mother was Turkish with limited English. We found a Turkish teaching assistant (TA) by advertising in the Turkish press in north London. Not all situations have been resolved so easily.

Adopting an inclusive approach requires us to recognise that we are always learning and that we may make mistakes. Ensuring that a school is thriving, making progress and raising achievement involves accepting challenges and taking risks at times. This risk taking is hard for everyone but particularly for new and inexperienced staff. It is important to listen to staff expressing their anxieties and concerns. We want people who constantly challenge themselves but we need to have the confidence to be able to say when we need help, be it training, more resources or whatever. In adopting an inclusive approach, staff learn that when something is not working then they have to change something, in the class, in their own approach or in the environment. They should not expect the child to change.

Induction of new children is a vital step in ensuring success. Photographs are introduced before the child arrives. A parent or teacher talks to the class about what the child can and cannot do, what they like and what they do not. We find that children who do not look the same physically do not then get stared at or asked inappropriate questions from curious children. If parents and staff have seen photographs displayed, they too do not react inappropriately. One of the most positive outcomes of inclusion is improved behaviour in the school generally and a high degree of disapproval if a term of abuse is used in the playground about physical characteristics or learning capabilities. Children who have had difficulties in schools with a less inclusive approach have transferred with success, though we have not eradicated name calling altogether.

Inclusion is a process. We will never get there completely but we can try! At first there was segregation in special schools, secondly, integration which said 'Yes, you can come to our school but you have got to fit in with us' and finally inclusion where we say 'Yes, please come and we as adults, pupils and our institution as a whole, will adapt as best we can in order to meet your needs.' This may mean adapting our attitudes and thinking, the curriculum, classroom organisation, furniture and equipment and the building.

The SEN Code of Practice allows inequality. Children with similar degrees of need do not necessarily all get a statement of special educational need: a statement can depend on the attitude and persistence of parents and the range of supporting evidence they can produce. The process of getting a statement can in itself lead to a focus on the need to change the child rather than the need to adapt and develop school provision. Inclusion should lead to greater equality, with resources shared more appropriately and children with more significant need being given an opportunity for greater independence, where possible.

Support staff

As we began to expand our special need provision, the number of support staff increased considerably. Some staff were general classroom assistants, others were special needs assistants, later to be called learning support assistants. There were different job descriptions and rates of pay for the two groups. In 1998 we made the decision to treat all assistants the same, to rename them as teaching assistants and ensure they had the same job description and the higher rate of pay. We were delighted when this happened nationally and welcomed the move from the DfES to increase the number and status of TAs. In recent years the school has been able to employ TAs directly and we have been able to create a management and career structure for them. While we want TAs to develop specialisms and interests, we also want all support staff to work with a range of children so that expectations are kept high, that there is variety of experience for staff, and all children feel that they have access to extra support at times. It is also important that teachers work with the full range of children in their class and do not become reliant on TAs taking responsibility for certain children. We also try and avoid children becoming dependent on one TA or vice versa, both errors we have made along the way. We also aim to employ the majority of TAs full-time. Training opportunities are offered such as the Open University STAC course and City and Guilds qualifications.

The Index for Inclusion

When our LEA asked us to pilot the Index for Inclusion in 1999, we found it a very useful tool for school development planning. Our initial focus was the role of the TA. Our main project focused on interviews with TAs and some teachers and pupils on the TA role. We discovered that our assistants had a high sense of job satisfaction and found the work rewarding. They needed improved opportunities for communication with teachers, more training and more time to prepare resources. Teachers recognised the vital work that TAs did and the contribution they made to children's progress. They also wanted more time to meet with their TA to plan and share information, and recognised the management issues involved with working with more than one adult in the class.

We changed assembly arrangements so that teachers and assistants could spend that time three times a week talking and planning together. Many TAs are also employed before the start and after the finish of the school day to allow more time to talk. Cover is provided for conferences with the SENCO and other professionals when needed. Ensuring there is enough time to talk, however, continues to be an area of concern.

Parental involvement

We had to work hard as a new school to gain parents' trust. We developed a number of social activities including our annual International Evening when parents and children contribute food from their country, wear traditional dress and listen to music from a range of places. Our last evening saw food from England, Scotland, Wales, Bangladesh, Israel, India, Japan, Morocco and Turkey. We hold a Mela in the summer term, similar to a summer fête, and have a range of stalls and events.

We have welcome meetings at the beginning of the school year when staff working in each year group are released at the beginning of the day to meet parents to talk about the year ahead and general expectations. Once a term we hold parent/teacher consultations where staff and parents can talk about children's progress and targets. We release class teachers for a day to allow those parents who would be reluctant or unable to come in the evening an opportunity to talk to the teacher. We also offer evening appointments for those parents who are working. A friendly reminder on the phone ensures that those who forget can still take advantage of this important meeting.

Parents and carers are also invited in to regular class assemblies when their child's class show and talk about some of the work they have done. Some classes have 'author's breakfasts', when family members are asked to join their children with refreshments to share their written work for the term.

A toddler group meets once a week with a toy library and is aimed at parents who will be sending their children to the nursery. It is very popular and mums, childminders, grandmothers and sometimes dads, have been regular visitors. A bilingual TA runs the group and ensures that newcomers feel welcome. The appointment of a bilingual receptionist has made it much easier for many parents to approach the school.

Parents have generally been very positive about our inclusion policies. The messages to parents are strong but happen through practice – seeing how children are included in class assemblies, outings and shows, for example.

The curriculum

We believe that a broad and balanced curriculum is essential for inclusion to be successful. An emphasis on sport and the performing and creative arts allows all children to participate more fully in the life of the school and opens up ways of communicating that do not always rely on the spoken or written word. Although we understand the importance of the core subjects in the curriculum, these subjects alone are not enough.

The proximity of central London offers a wealth of resources, and visits to museums, galleries and theatres are a regular part of the school curriculum. We welcome visitors to the school and have long-standing partnerships with the Guildhall School of Music and Drama and the Barbican Education Centre. We currently employ a dance company who are working with a range of children including those with physical and learning disabilities. Yoga is taught to two year-groups who are benefiting in terms of health and behaviour.

Artists in residence undertake a range of projects with the children. Children's confidence, speaking and listening skills and enthusiasm are all promoted and we see a growth in their literacy skills as a result.

Our behaviour policy

We believe that everyone at school is important and to be valued, is here for a purpose and has a positive contribution to make. We expect each individual to respect others, their families, cultures and beliefs. We aim to encourage self-discipline and keep rules to a minimum: rules are in place to support and maintain our ethos of care for each other, the community and the environment. We try and make our rules explicit, apply them equitably and ensure they are for the good of all.

We have a very strong policy on bullying and it is an item each term in school assemblies and in circle time. We try and ensure that everyone has a shared view on the definition of bullying in its widest sense in order to minimise its occurrence.

We see it as everyone's responsibility to ensure our policy is followed. Adults should at all times observe the same rules they expect of children. As members of staff we aim to be courteous and fair. This means keeping calm, listening carefully, being consistent in our dealings with others and using humour, praise and rewards wherever possible rather than sanctions, though these do, of course, have to be used at times. We have introduced a variety of strategies to support the inclusion of vulnerable or disaffected children including conflict resolution procedures, circle time, 'circle of friends' and playground management training for staff.

Children with emotional and behavioural difficulties usually present the most difficulties for staff. These children can cause the most stress, make us feel we have lost control, and can challenge our own emotional weaknesses. To better meet these needs, we are aiming at becoming a more emotionally literate school and put a strong emphasis on the emotional development of children and on raising their self-esteem. We still have work to do in this area.

A holistic approach

Additional teachers have been a feature of Tower Hamlets for several decades, with funding for pupils from minority ethnic backgrounds coming initially from the Home Office under Section 11 and then from the DfES. In the past, children might have received support under a range of different headings and may have worked with a SENCO, a Section 11 teacher and a TA within the space of a few days.

Now class teachers, together with their support teacher, meet termly to discuss the needs of each child and focus support appropriately. Decisions about support are based on the child's needs and on staff skills. We also employ two part-time workers, one who works with families with attendance problems and the other with those who have emotional or behavioural difficulties that prevent effective learning. We are also fortunate in being able to employ two part-time specialist teachers: one who works with children with speech and language delays and difficulties, the other with children with specific learning difficulties in literacy. We have also employed a speech therapist one day a week.

Teaching

Adaptability and flexibility lead to successful inclusion. We believe we need to look at the individual child and constantly evaluate what is in their best interests and those of the other children. An autistic child generally benefits from one-to-one tuition outside the classroom for part of the day because they find the normal classroom too busy to cope with all day. A child with Asperger's Syndrome is not made to join in an activity that he cannot understand and see as having no relevance to him such as competitive sport, but would be expected to join in physical activity to develop skills and keep himself fit. A child may spend all their time in the mainstream classroom but work for much of the day on an individual programme, fitting into general classroom activities whenever possible.

We discuss with individual children, and their parents, what they find difficult and devise with them strategies to help them cope or alternative activities. We also include them in the target-setting process for their individual education plans. This way, the teacher and TA gain much greater insight into the child's situation.

We believe all children at Bangabandhu have the same entitlement to the curriculum. If, however, a child is not benefiting from what is on offer to the class, withdrawal for some sessions or parallel individual or group sessions can be offered as long as there is greater educational value to the child than staying with the whole class. The aim will always be for the child or group to rejoin the class when ready – a timescale is set for this.

The LEA is committed to provide additional facilities at Bangabandhu following the closure of the special school, mentioned earlier. Our new resources will include two class bases, a practical area, a sensory room, a therapy room, a soft play room and an extended ICT suite. We currently have a number of children with complex needs who are in the mainstream classes. We hope future pupils will also spend most of their time there and that these new resources will expand our provision for all our children. The sensory room and soft play areas, for example, will be used by a range of children, not just those with complex needs.

Resources

Funding has been a difficult issue for us over the years, as it is for most schools. We have found it easier to manage the many issues around finance and inclusion now more of the school finance is delegated. We have a large budget and we need to look at it as a whole to ensure that our resources are distributed fairly. We have had to develop a relationship with the LEA that ensures access to the level of resources we feel we need and have had to learn to make realistic demands. It is important to review spending regularly and to be flexible. We are also able to be more pro-active now that we have more control and try to use resources for early intervention rather than wait until a child's difficulties become more severe.

We constantly look for appropriate resources that will support our teaching. These include specialist PE equipment that can be used by all children but is particularly accessible if you have restricted movement or poor sight. We are always looking for new ICT hardware and software that can support the curriculum and make it more accessible.

We carefully consider topics taught to make them relevant but also to open up the world to those whose circumstances leave them with very limited horizons. Working on an opera project based on *The Rake's Progress* was a great success with children and parents because we were sensitive to Muslim sensibilities in adapting the story.

Principles

Inclusion is about equal opportunities. We recognise that we have embarked on a process that may never be finished but aim to become more inclusive year by year. We believe in the need to build an inclusive society and that developing an inclusive approach to all aspects of school life can act as a pathway towards inclusion in the wider community.

We have established some basic principles. We consider all the children in our immediate neighbourhood have a right to attend our school. Every child has the same right of access and is entitled to appropriate support to meet their individual needs whatever their race, culture, faith, gender, sexuality, physical or learning impairment. We accept staff on the same basis.

Children with a language other than English, physical, learning or sensory disabilities, emotional or behavioural difficulties, have a right to the support they need in our classrooms. We recognise that all children have a right to learn and play together and that no one should be excluded because of their ethnicity or disability – this is discrimination. Our school community is open, positive and diverse and our school is accessible to staff, parents and carers with disabilities.

We understand that we have to challenge our thinking at all times – are we asking this child to fit into our routine or our preconceived ideas of what is best? Or are we really trying to adjust what we offer in order that every child feels secure, understands what is required of them and feels valued for what they are, not what we would like them to be? We believe that children do better, socially and academically, in inclusive settings and that any teaching or caring that happens in a segregated school can take place in an inclusive school. Inclusion supports school improvement and effectiveness.

Inclusion is a process that has the potential to develop friendship, respect and understanding. All children, with or without disabilities, benefit from inclusion. By aiming to meet the full range of needs in an ordinary setting, we can improve the learning environment for everyone – teachers and parents as well as children. The teaching and learning and social development that are right for inclusion are right for all children.

We recognise we have entered a process that involves changing and challenging systems and structures, adapting the curriculum, the buildings, language, images and role models. We also recognise that inclusion is not a single issue but involves a wide range of options and depends on a range of factors that include the individual, the setting and available resources.

What we have learned

We have come to some conclusions as we have worked towards being an inclusive school. We have learned that:

1 inclusion is a step on from integration;
2 a child does not benefit from having an individual at his/her side at all times – independence for that child is of prime importance;
3 a child who does need full-time support should work with more than one TA within a day;
4 a more flexible use of TAs is more productive than trying to ensure that each child with a statement of special educational need has his/her agreed level of support;
5 the needs of children at School Action (Code of Practice) and a full statement are often very similar, the only difference being the stage their paperwork is at;
6 outside agencies need to work with us in a planned way;
7 the class teacher has the central role in providing for the child;
8 all staff need training;
9 the specialist teacher has a key role.

Our aim has been to move gradually away from the position that we started with, where each child has a clearly defined entitlement to certain resources, to one where we in the school determine what resources are appropriate and how they are deployed.

Where next?

Our main priorities for the future are to:

● ensure that all our children are independent learners. We are concerned that as there are often several adults in the class, children can easily resort to their help rather than develop their own persistence and problem solving skills;
● ensure that staff expertise is known more fully and used effectively and that staff are encouraged to draw on and share their knowledge and skills to support learning;
● improve the welcome new staff receive when they start at the school. We want to ensure that new staff feel included and that their experience and observations are valued;
● improve the quality of communication between parents and the school. We have felt that parental involvement is a strength of the school but there is room for improvement and we want to develop further strategies to ensure all parents/carers feel valued, involved and confident in offering their concerns and contributions to the growth of the school.

Bangabandhu is, we feel, an exciting and challenging place where adults and children alike develop their skills, attitudes, learning and knowledge through a broad-based curriculum while developing strong links with the community. It requires everyone to work hard to maintain and develop this ethos. Ofsted recognised what had been achieved:

> Bangabandhu is a successful and effective school. Pupils with a wide range of attainment, including a high percentage of pupils for whom English is an additional language and a high percentage with special educational needs, achieve well and make good progress.
>
> Through excellent teamwork, excellent relationships and learning are maintained, reflecting the school's clearly stated aims.
>
> (Ofsted, June 2000)

We earned these comments because we embraced inclusion wholeheartedly when the school opened and before the word was in general usage. Inclusion is central to the life of the school.

> This chapter gives us the flavour of an inclusive school. As in some of our other chapters based in schools, we get a sense of work in progress. While no one claims to have right answers, the process of change is valued and encouraged and the goal is clear. The chapter shows us how important it is to establish clear principles, as a prelude to developing good and effective practice.

CHAPTER 8

Autism in special and inclusive schools: 'there has to be a point to their being there'

Priscilla Alderson and Christopher Goodey

Priscilla Alderson and Christopher Goodey researched the experiences of children with autism who attended either special schools or inclusive schools. Their observations and interviews with pupils and adults are discussed in this chapter in relation to the educational policy, practice and the nature of autism. Alderson and Goodey argue that evidence from this type of comparative study undermines the perceived reasons for the special schooling of children diagnosed as autistic.

Introduction

What kind of schools are most suitable for pupils affected by autism? [. . .] We observed 22 schools in two very different LEAs. East City has an inclusive policy and mixed-ability-range classes in mainstream coeducational, multi-racial, comprehensive schools, only two of the original eight special schools remain open and they are in a transitional stage. West County has 13 LEA special schools and units, further special schools run by voluntary organisations, and grammar or high (secondary modern) schools, almost entirely white, single sex schools and 23 private schools (Alderson & Goodey 1998). [. . .]

This paper considers pupils who were assessed as having autism or autistic spectrum disorder (ASD). They were in severe (SLD) and moderate (MLD) learning difficulties schools, an autism unit and in inclusive schools. We conducted small scale in-depth research, in order to achieve detailed qualitative observations of, and conversations with, disabled and disturbed pupils. Our findings are likely to be fairly typical of special schooling, judging from the literature and conference reports, and from lack of evidence that it is not typical. The qualitative research findings raise urgent questions about current theories, policies and practices in the education of these pupils. This article reviews meanings of autism, then one of us (PA) presents evidence from 'West County' LEA, and the other (CG) gives evidence from the inclusive LEA, 'East City'. We conclude by discussing theory and policy implications of the data.

Are definitions of autism coherent?

Scientists' theories are influenced by their time and place. Theories of autism concern an extreme narrowing that excludes everything except the person's own self. They were developed during the early 1940s, by Kanner in the United States, which felt isolated as a democracy between imperialist Japan and fascism in Europe, and also by Asperger in Vienna during the Nazi regime of racial hygiene and exclusion of all foreign elements (Proctor 1988). Decades later the theories were revived without reference to their political origins. Wing (1981) identifies three main characteristics of all autistic children: impaired social relationships, impaired communication, and impaired social imagination or imaginative play. Frith (1989: 10–11) notes that autism is often confused with other conditions. Following Kanner (1943) she proposes only two 'cardinal' features:

> **Autistic aloneness.** *Exactly* what this is *cannot be identified* with a specific behaviour. It can only be *inferred* from behaviour . . . This *intangible* difference of autistic children, pervading *all sorts* of behaviour, is highly conspicuous to the *experienced* clinician. [And] **obsessive insistence on sameness** . . . a *densely formulated* concept which *suggests* several factors at once: repetitiveness, rigidity, single-mindedness, pedantry, and inability to judge the significance of subtle differences.
>
> (Our emphases; Frith 1989)

Our emphases note the tensions between precision and uncertainty which characterise the literature on this complex condition. [. . .]

Experts differ on the range and severity of behaviours identified with autism. A National Autistic Society leaflet estimates that four or five people in every 10,000 have 'classic autism', but 15 to 20 people in every 10,000 have 'autistic-like conditions', and 'one in every 200 people is affected by [knowing someone with] autism.'

ASD includes Asperger's syndrome (1944) said to be characterised by: borderline or normal IQ; social isolation or naive, inappropriate social interaction; intensive interest in only one or two subjects; a narrow repetitive life style; limited or inappropriate intonation and body language; and poor motor coordination (Wing 1996). So many characteristics are linked to ASD, that a single person is unlikely to have all of them and few people are likely to have none of them at some time, leading to confusion and incoherence in definitions of autism and ASD. This leads to difficulty in selecting the most affected cases for special units and deciding precisely what special teaching techniques they require.

Advice to teachers

Our observations included a seminar for 200 teachers in West County about ASD, at which health professionals gave typical advice. A community paediatrician qualified most signs of ASD with 'may': 'Those at the milder end and those with SLD may not go through all the stages. Babies may not avoid eye contact. We don't now think that they all do not show affection.' Her cautious account perhaps encourages optimistic approaches and reasonably high expectations of affected children, yet it can also include many more children as having ASD. The doctor mentioned sets of contradictions: 'He [sic] may fail to notice other children or make friends, or he may be indiscriminately friendly and too loud and obtrusive. Language may be very much delayed or he may use very good grammatical structure. Dialogue is repeated rather than invented, though there can be original word creations.' The doctor concluded, 'Education and social environment can have marked effects on a child's happiness and overt behaviour, but the basic impairments remain.' This point questions how much teaching can affect mood and behaviour, how much it is mainly care and control, and how or whether special autism teaching differs from any other school teaching. Also, how far are learning difficulties attributable to autism or to other physiological or social factors?

A speech therapist then gave practical advice on encouraging social development, language, play skills, learning and self-esteem. She used a less equivocal style.

ASD is a communication disorder, in the way the child processes information . . . It is hard for them to extract any kind of meaning, oral or visual, so that they are confused. They need continuity, limited diet, to wear the same clothes, etc. The more stimulating the environment, the harder it is to cope with . . . Friends are the biggest issue in the clinic. They are desperately unhappy about lack of friends. We all have a duty to offer situations where they can be socially successful. Free times at school can be the hardest times when they can be very very vulnerable . . . Make sure you say the child's name **before** you give a general instruction to the whole class. Talk slowly in simple sentences and do not bombard the child with questions. When he/she asks a question make sure you are responding to his/her intentions rather than just the words he/she says otherwise you may be on the road to developing repetitive questioning. Always work from shared practical experience in all subjects.

These useful techniques apply to most young children. The advice raises questions about when adults should allow for a child's limitations, or try to compensate for, or resist or overcome them. Does a limited diet or wardrobe reinforce, or even establish, narrow rigidity?

An autism unit in West County (PA)

The unit observed is, in theory, part of the adjacent mainstream primary school, and shares the site also with a mainstream secondary and a large special school. There is almost no contact between the schools, they might as well be miles apart. The unit's 18 pupils are aged from 5 to 11. There are three teachers, four classroom assistants and two lunchtime supervisors. A notice on the front door says 'No child is allowed in before

9.15'. Children wait in their taxis, after a journey of up to an hour or more, then all enter the narrow hallway at once, while teachers and escorts exchange wry commiserations about their difficult charges. The school day of 9.30 to 3.00 includes breaks of up to 2.5 hours. The children mainly sit at a 'play table' with one box of equipment only per session, and shopping catalogues, waiting to work with teachers individually or in small groups at a 'work table'. Teachers spend long periods writing records, one spent half the day doing this. Each child has only very brief periods of tuition. The unit is very sparsely equipped, especially for the 6-year span some pupils spend there. Providing so few activities could reinforce autistic obsession. Alternatively boredom with repeated activity could be taken as attention deficit disorder.

The head of the unit said that some affected children are not diagnosed until they are aged 7 or 9. They 'drift along in school unnoticed . . . we can diagnose more of them, and there are more to cope with, some of them who were in main stream are with us now, they were a bit of a pain, a bit odd, they muddled through school, they were the cleverer and the milder cases.' She was unclear about parents' preferences, saying 'parents want them to go to local school and have local friends and community, so you can't steer the child to where the expertise is', but also that more boarding places are needed 'because of the stress on the family'. Partly to reduce pupils' travelling hours, 'three new units are being set up, and we're going to open a third class'. They are called 'integrated' because they share sites with mainstream schools, and will be for either MLD or SLD. West County staff emphasise the risks of attempting inclusive education: 'with integration there has to be some point to their being there', said the unit head, but the staff tend to assume that segregation is beneficial. The apparent increase in demand for ASD places is linked to many more cases being diagnosed and referred. The next sections describe how signs of ASD were demonstrated and treated in the unit.

Social relationships and communication

The characteristic peculiarity of gaze never fails to be present . . . They do not make eye contact . . . they seem to take in things with short peripheral glances . . . The use of language always appears abnormal, unnatural.

(Asperger, in Frith 1989: 9–10)

Profound aloneness dominates all behaviour . . . an innate inability to form the usual biologically provided affective contact with people.

(Kanner 1943)

Megan, one of the highest achievers, and Paul, the only black child present, clearly show an averted gaze, and make grimaces and abrupt gestures and sounds, the others are usually quiet and polite, work hard when given a task, talk coherently and look 'ordinary'. How do the staff give them special help with social skills? Unlike most teachers in our study who are friendly and helpful, the unit staff tend to avoid contact with me, and with the children. They teach different pupils each day 'so that they don't get attached to anyone'. This is a strange, marked contrast to mainstream primary schools which endorse children's attachment to their class teacher and expect younger ones to 'be upset' about a change of teacher.

Annie plays in the sand for over an hour at various times. She is deft, careful, imaginative and funny. She calls me (PA) 'baby' so I call her 'mummy' and she feeds me spoons of sand which in turn I feed to her, and we share cups of sand tea. The staff never remark on how well she plays, invents, and shares the small sand tray and small amount of sand with other children. Martin plays at digging for gold and mixing banana milk shakes. Then Nick arrives and Martin tries to ward him off by threatening to throw sand at him. The staff quickly chase Martin away, 'No we are *not* having you playing in the sand'. They ignore Nick disrupting Annie's play. At last Annie says, 'No we are *not* having you playing in the sand'. She is told off by the teachers, 'You must *learn to share the sand*'. Later Annie takes a dust pan and sweeps sand off the floor very competently, but no one comments on this.

Sandra, aged 11, frequently comes to sit next to me. She is said to shout at home, but never speaks at school and will board next term. She shows me her school books, and reads me a story with a mixture of tiny grunts and signs. During break time, she takes me to the small shaded area out of the blazing sunshine. Other children sustain eye contact and initiate friendly contact. From many examples, these details show levels of competence, good sense, imagination and sensitive interactions between the children which deny their autistic label. They play for long periods while the staff sit talking together, frequently discussing the children's limitations, as if they cannot hear, for example:

Teacher 1: She's psychotic.

Teacher 2: Yes. Not to say obsessive. Oh watch out for Paul. Look he's flicking his food, take his knife and fork away.

Lunchtime assistant. [Laughing and with irony] I wonder why? [She gives him a plate of shredded cabbage which he can only eat with his fingers.]

Classroom assistant: Oh look at him, I thought he was getting more civilised. I know you're going to be a naughty little monkey today, I can feel it in my water.

The children are hurried to finish their small portions and then all taken to the toilets at once. When they quickly reappear, several boys have wet trousers. The staff seem to assume that the children are too irrational to talk to. Neil weeps twice, for a long time with many tears and a teacher tells him to stop, but does not ask what the matter is.

Staff often admonish children, but seldom remark on their friendly co-operation, except occasionally to say it is 'amazing', 'too good to be true'.

Empathy and imaginative play

The most general description of social impairments in Autism is lack of empathy . . . indifference to other people's distress [and hypothetically] lack of the ability to recognize the existence of other people's minds . . . There is abnormal lack of imaginative activity, this refers to absence of pretend play.

(Frith 1989: 12, 154–5)

For about 30 minutes, Noel plays with plastic blocks and a plastic chicken. He builds a house for the chicken and calls some blocks eggs. He makes a fox, later called a wolf. The wolf tries to catch the chicken and break down the house and take the eggs. Interested to see Noel's capacity for empathy, I beg in a squeaky 'chicken' voice for help and mercy. Noel is sometimes the fierce wolf and as often the kind rescuer and house maker. He makes the chicken die and go to heaven, and is fluent and imaginative, funny, sometimes fierce, often kind. He builds a car for the chicken to ride in, and two bath rooms, and gives the chicken gentle baths. Later the wolf becomes a hamster who also dies and goes to heaven. Other children play imaginatively, as described earlier.

Links with other schools

This disturbance results in considerable and very typical difficulties of social integration. In many cases, the failure to be integrated in a social group is the most conspicuous feature . . .

(Asperger 1944)

The head of unit said: 'Yes, the LEA has an integration policy and there are a lot of units on mainstream sites, but how much they are integrated is quite individual. They don't make friendships anyway. If they can cope socially that is the hardest part, the lessons are the easy bit.' The pupils spend break times in a small yard and look through wire fencing at the other schools' playgrounds. This is discouraged. 'Don't put your hand through that fence! Either you'll be dragged through one way or you'll drag someone through to this side or there'll be biting.' If children have difficulty with communication, it is questionable logic to group them all together and away from articulate children at school, so also undermining their chances of making friends near their home, besides constantly seeing and treating them as subnormal. If lessons are 'the easy part' there seems even less purpose in segregation, for academic or social reasons. The special school system and attitudes impose isolation which is attributed to ASD.

Learning

> The children largely follow their own impulses, regardless of the demands of the environment . . . The children are simply not geared towards learning from adults or teachers . . .
>
> (Asperger, in Frith 1989: 9–10)

> They do want to do what they like doing, it's part of autism.
>
> (Teacher in unit)

Duncan waits patiently to play with the computer. Sitting opposite it, every time he looks up he cannot help noticing the brightly coloured games, with exploding coconuts and grunting monsters. He is told to learn to concentrate on his work. Other children have a turn each time he asks. At 11.50, he is allowed nearer the screen to watch. A teacher then slowly sorts out another game, working out how to click the mouse which one boy has done expertly, and typically doing easy tasks instead of showing children how to do them or checking if they already can. At last Duncan has a short go which he enjoys greatly, and then gracefully allows himself to be rushed off to lunch.

Many hours are spent playing computer games which involve touching the screen with a paintbrush to trigger a reaction. Everyone aged from 7 to 11 seems to do this easily, often much faster than the programmed timing. The computer is used to occupy rather than to educate. Annie completes a work sheet, colouring animals and correctly writing how many legs each one has. Then a teacher gives her another identical sheet without checking the first one. Annie fills in the second sheet incorrectly. A teacher walking by says, 'Oh that's silly, a snake can't have 27 legs'. Megan happily hums while busy writing and drawing. Then a teacher sits by her, and slowly looks through shopping catalogues, chooses a picture, cuts it out, glues it and sticks it on a page while Megan has to watch. Another teacher very slowly draws pictures and rules lines and eventually lets the watching child do some simple colouring. No work appears to be prepared before lessons.

Later, while two teachers write records for an hour, two assistants sort squared sheets with coloured patterns. One says, 'No, that's too hard for Noel, too complicated for him, give him this, no this.' Noel, aged 9 years, says, 'No, no, too young, that's too young. I'm too old for that.' He does the task quickly and easily, and is given another simple task and protests about having to use dull colours. After colouring a graph, Noel wants to cut it out but is not allowed to. A teacher very slowly cuts and pastes it into Noel's book, and writes what the exercise involved. The teachers exclaim in surprise that Noel has worked so well. Like the displays on the walls, most of the work is clearly done by the teachers and much is at nursery level. Special needs teachers are advised to teach in very small steps and review regularly, so that every small advance can be recorded to encourage the staff. The disadvantages of this approach have been widely discussed (Gardner 1993). The small tasks can easily seem pointless, boring, demeaning and frustrating to the children, and it is uncertain whether their skills improve through teaching, maturation or experience.

Therapy

Life is puzzling and unpredictable, so they need security, and protection from loud noises, pain, bright lights such as from wet surfaces. Don't shout because every loud noise will mean to them that you are angry. Provide a certain amount of predictability to reduce anxiety.

(Leaflet by West County LEA and Health Staff 1995)

The special unit is not a quiet, therapeutic haven for children who find ordinary school too stressful and distracting. The staff often shout angrily and there are noisy sessions, especially during the final half hour while everyone waits for taxis. There is no psychologist or counsellor, and psychologists seem to be unaware of the type of education they are recommending for the children they refer. Some sessions are called 'therapy', like 'music therapy', which appears to mean unstimulating repetition. Everyone sits on benches, listening to taped songs they know by heart. For example:

Now I need to get dressed (4 times)

Please pass me my clothes (4 times)

What shall I put on? (2 times)

Please pass me my pants (4 times)

Thank you for passing me my pants (lots of times)

Now I'll put on my pants (etc.)

The term 'therapy' can excuse frustratingly tedious lessons which are likely to increase disturbed behaviour (McNamara & Moreton 1995). By 2.20 pm, some children who have looked 'ordinary' so far begin to wriggle and wave. Yet any group of children aged 5–11 who spend years in this small unit, with the repeated activities, meagre resources, long journeys and negative staff might react similarly.

Discipline

The head of unit on discipline: How long is a piece of string? There are a million strategies. It has to be tailored to the child. If there's aggression you look at whether it is frequent or not, find out why, the cause, sit the child by you, separate him for a while, or present orders in a different way, or give them better ways of coping, get them to feel that they can have an influence if they express themselves in a better way. Communication is the major area they don't understand. The world is very confusing for them. You have to make the messages clearer, and see that they learn that they have to get on in the world. There are some rules that they have to keep.

What is the appropriate treatment for obsessive behaviour – to allow it, to try distraction, or firmly and explicitly to discourage it? Some teachers use threats, an unusually large teacher often says: 'I'll pick you up', he pokes and tickles children, and traps them into a large plastic barrel stood upright. Some teachers seem to want to ensure that children who want to do something (play with the computer or with lego or in the soft play area) cannot, and children who do not want to do it, have to, and they frequently emphasise confrontation. During break time, David, who reads and speaks very well, becomes increasingly agitated about being outside and keeps asking, 'How long, how long?' At last the door is opened, but a teacher pulls back the almost frantic David while another teacher calls out names from a list of the order in which pupils are allowed in with David last. A note on the wall says: 'David is obsessive about time. He needs to be spoken to and disciplined very firmly. Reward: a book of teacher's choice or toy of his choice but not clock'. Collective decisions about discipline can mean that teachers enforcing harsh rules need feel less personally responsible for increasing David's great distress.

The examples have been selected from many similar ones to illustrate general trends in this unit, and the special schools we observed for learning and communication difficulties. Staff in some other schools were more kind and gentle, but we saw similarly low teaching standards and expectations, and no informed, consistent ways of responding to behavioural difficulties.

Inclusive primary schooling in East City (CG)

Moreton is a resourced mainstream primary school with a special, all-age autistic class. Seymour School is resourced for children with severe or complex problems who are all fully included in wide-ability peer groups, and some pupils attend their local school with support. All the children we saw who were profoundly 'uncommunicative' (a problematic term as we shall show) have no speech or a few single words.

Seymour's head teacher said, 'We don't use the word "autism", we just see them as children.' She questions how much avoidance of eye contact and obsession with ritual affect people generally, including herself, and mentioned a psychologist who, when visiting the school, insisted on isolating a boy to test him and refused to respond to other children who talked to him. She is concerned that use of the label 'autistic' powerfully shapes perceptions and relationships, and considers that the school should adapt to the pupils and their differences, not the other way round. Questioning the idea of autism includes willingness to see any failures in communication as mutual and not simply as an effect of autism, with willingness to try other ways of communicating and breaking down boundaries in interactions between *all* the adults and pupils involved.

One former special school teacher said she finds that severely affected children improve notably when they join inclusive classes and she asks experts to visit Seymour, to challenge the theory that autistic behaviour is unalterable. She finds that the experts tend to assert that these children could never have been autistic, and she remarks they 'constantly alter the diagnosis, expanding it here and restricting it here . . . that's a vested interest.' It turns the diagnosis of ASD into a political rather than a clinical response, concerned with the power to allocate resources rather than with need.

Fifteen children were in class 8 at Moreton, with a teacher and five classroom assistants. It is a quiet area with some extra play and learning equipment, in the middle of the school to emphasise that it is not a separate unit. Each pupil has a different degree of integration into the peer classes, between 100 and 20 per cent of their time. During my visit, I am told that Aaron is brilliant at meccano, so try to show him some interesting things. He is not interested; perhaps he realises that I am not mechanically minded and that my behaviour is at odds with my real self. Eventually he decides to sit on my lap, although he doesn't look at me. The activity of the other boys in class 10 appears to be vague and aimless (in contrast to how they appear later in their peer classes). Their teacher comments on how angry the other children get during school outings, on behalf of the autistic children when they are stared or pointed at, and how much she feels class 10 can copy the 'normal' children, which they could not do at the special school where she once taught.

At playtime, I feel rather isolated in the playground until Alice, a big 11-year-old with no speech runs across the playground through a crowd and takes hold of my hands smiling. She plays with two other girls. A boy from class 10 walks and runs on his own, his arms slightly dangling, rather like other boys doing aeroplane impressions. Two infant-age boys play with another girl and help her when she wets herself. Later some children argue about who will have the privilege of fetching class 10 children to join their class.

In class 6, Alice and Satnam work with a classroom assistant, and a girl who had played with Alice pats her on the back occasionally. Alice has a story book with a word missing from each sentence, and she has to point to the correct word on a card. The playtime has illustrated the value to Alice of being able to communicate and the incentives for her to learn. She uses flash cards at school and home, as I did when I visited, and school friends talk to her on the telephone in the evenings. Satnam traces rows of capital letters neatly, making almost no eye contact, and swiping me lightly a couple of times, then he spits; Alice dribbles slightly. After they leave the table, a girl passing by sees that it is wet; she grabs a tissue and mops it up, unasked and apparently unplanned. It is not her table and she passes on.

In class 2, Anthony selects names words from flash cards helped by the teacher and a friend, while the others do a word search. Six-year-olds from the adjacent class come in to work with Anthony. Later, three 6-year-olds help him to do a coloured shape puzzle. Anthony says an occasional word or two, almost like echoes. Then we build a castle with large lego, then a boat and a bridge. I get Anthony to give me pieces and hand them to the friend to set up. Anthony loses interest quickly, but he is very interested in lego people, he keeps looking at a face with a hole in the back, and later peers under the bridge. He holds very little eye contact, but often looks towards me and chuckles to himself.

Gradual inclusion

During their interview, Alice's parents describe how class 10 have gradually been more included in the school. They began to sit in assembly and at registration with their peer class, they gain permission to have a packed lunch, and to play in the main playground and not a small 'quiet area'.

> *Alice's mother*: All the things we wanted for Alice, for her to take part in just like anyone else, used to have the same effect. First of all, they [teachers] thought of the problems it's gonna cause – not like, 'What can Alice get out of it?' It was, 'What sort of disruption it's gonna cause to the school?' . . .

> *Alice's father*: Alice makes it clear she does not want to be in class 10. She'll bring the board that says 'class 2' to one of the teachers, or she'll go for the door and try to get out of the room. She doesn't spend much time there . . . but surely she shouldn't be there at all if she doesn't want to be.

They kept Alice at home on Fridays, until the class 10 outings stopped. 'Every Friday morning used to be the outing day . . . to the supermarket. I said, "No, that's a special school thing, ten kids and seven teachers traipsing round Asda's to buy two bananas".' Alice's parents valued her 'willingness to *want* to be able to communicate'.

> *Father*: If Alice doesn't want to do something, she'll let you know in no uncertain terms – pulling away, making noises, but if she's doing something she really likes, then she'll show you all the joy. But with her friends, I think they've got their own communication system, which is all to do with facial expressions, the way they touch each other, that sort of thing . . . She'll spot someone, one of her best friends, she'll belt up towards them, grab their hands, smile at them, might make a noise. They'll say 'hello' back, and they'll start chatting to her.

> *Interviewer*: Is it an equal relationship?

> *Father*: I think it is, yeah. The group of kids that choose Alice to be their friend, they're fairly vulnerable theirselves. Kids that are very shy, kids that have problems in making relationships, kids that are very nervous, a lot of kids that don't want to be at school, that sort of child, yeah? Alice doesn't make the

demands that a lot of kids in the school make on them you know, 'You haven't got your Rebok trainers on' or 'Ooer, you look weird today, what you wearing?'

Interviewer: Is this just non-threatening, or does Alice offer something positive?

Father: Alice does give a lot back. She's really warm, she shows other kids that she's really happy to be in their company. At the end of the summer term there are all these kids in tears . . . A big strapping lad was crying because Alice is leaving. In particular for the boys, they've become such nice, caring kids, without mothering Alice. They're actually able to show a kid from the opposite sex that they care . . . The kids accept that, and there is this boy Peter who's cuddling Alice in the playground, and nobody's laughing at him.

Alice's head teacher described his efforts to change the school, though acknowledging the part played by families. He thinks autistic children give 'power' to the rest, which appears to mean confidence and maturity.

Friendships continued into the local secondary comprehensive, where former members of class 10 spend all their time with their peer class. A classroom assistant said he sometimes takes them, 'to our little room . . . we've got a mini library. Some of the other students say, "Please sir, can we come up with you?" And they come up and join in with them . . . although basically the idea of it is a haven or sanctuary for people who need it at a time of stress.' The assistant described his worst moment, 'when Satnam threw his first major wobbly. And it was bad. I took him out of the classroom initially and they actually had teachers coming out of their classroom from the second storey to find out what the screaming was about.' He added that this recurring event is no longer remarked upon. The pupils will 'come across and say, "Can we borrow your rubber?" and this is what they use as excuses just to make them feel at home. They really go out of their way to make them feel part of it.'

Education Policy and ASD

The autism unit illustrates the difficulties of attempting to diagnose such a condition. It is not clear which features are necessary and sufficient for a diagnosis, what precisely the unique educational difficulties associated with ASD are, the specific educational expertise pupils said to have ASD require, what unique needs they have in common to justify separate provision, 'the point to their being' in separate units, and how any benefits offered could justify the very high costs – financial, educational, emotional and social. Ironically, these costs are blamed on ASD and not on systematic discrimination. Autistic tendencies of isolation and self-absorption are more noticeable in the segregating education system itself, which appears to project and enforce these characteristics on to the pupils we observed. As we also illustrate in greater detail elsewhere (Alderson and Goodey 1998), comparative evidence of inclusive and special ASD schooling seriously challenges assumptions about the advantages of special schooling. The evidence also raises urgent questions for all LEAs and schools to reconsider their policies for pupils who are thought to have ASD.

References

Alderson, P. and Goodey, C. (1998) *Enabling Education: Experiences in Special and Ordinary Schools*. London: Tufnell Press.

Asperger, H. (1944) *Die autistischen Psychopathen in Kindesalter*, translation in U. Frith (ed.) (1991) *Autism and Asperger's Syndrome*. Cambridge: Cambridge University Press.

Frith, U. (1989) *Autism: Explaining the Enigma*. Oxford: Blackwell.

Gardner, H. (1993) *The Unschooled Mind: How Children Think and How Schools Should Teach*. London: Fontana.

Kanner, L. (1943) Autistic disturbance of affective contact. *Nervous Child*, **2**, 217–50.

McNamara, S. and Moreton, G. (1995) *Changing Behaviour: Teaching Children with Emotional and Behavioural Difficulties in Primary and Secondary Classrooms*. London: David Fulton.

Proctor, R. (1988) *Racial Hygiene: Medicine Under the Nazis*. New York: Harvard University Press.

Wing, L. (1981) Language, social and cognitive impairments in autism and severe mental retardation. *Journal of Autism and Development Disorders*, **11**, 31–44.

Wing, L. (1996) Autistic spectrum disorders: no evidence for or against increase in prevalence. *British Medical Journal*, **312**, 327–8.

This chapter has shown that the reasons for segregated education are not obvious to observers. There seems little that was exceptionally positive in, or distinctly related to, supporting the children's development in these settings. Alderson and Goodey argue that, in fact, the separation and grouping of these children acts negatively on how they are perceived and the educational and social opportunities they encounter.

CHAPTER 9

The Index for Inclusion: personal perspectives from early years educators

Peter Clough and Cathy Nutbrown

In this chapter Peter Clough and Cathy Nutbrown discuss the experiences of a small number of early years practitioners who have worked with the *Index for Inclusion* (Booth *et al*. 2000). They report on what the five practitioners said when interviewed about the concept of inclusion and the *Index* in particular. The interviews took place in March 2000 and again in July 2001 after practitioners had used the *Index*. This is not an evaluation as such, but an opportunity to engage with the perspectives of early years educators.

'Respectful educators will include all children; not just children who are easy to work with, obliging, endearing, clean, pretty, articulate, capable, but every child – respecting them for who they are, respecting their language, their culture, their history, their family, their abilities, their needs, their name, their ways and their very essence.'

(Nutbrown 1996: 54)

The *Index for Inclusion* was launched in March 2000 and a copy was issued to every state school in England. Developed by eminent leaders in the field of inclusion, the *Index* maps out a process designed to lead to radical change through the development of learning and participation of all involved in the life of a school (Booth *et al*. 2000). For some schools the *Index* has proved to be precisely the tool for development which they were seeking, whilst for others it has become just another ring-binder housed on a shelf full of such ring-binders: full of good ideas, viewed with good intentions, 'if only we had the time'.

Why are we talking about 'inclusion'?

Constructions of difference and difficulty

It has been argued that early childhood education at its best *is* inclusive education (Nutbrown 1998), because it is often the experience of those who work within the Foundation Stage that children with learning difficulties and/or disabilities are included *as a first option*. In such settings we would argue that inclusion is as much about *attitude* as it is about *response*. As Herbert demonstrates in the case of Steven:

This was the first time in her short career that Steven's reception class teacher had had a child with a Statement in her class. She was conscious that by choosing the inclusive option Steven's parents had accepted his need to interact with his peer group and not become, once more, dependent upon adults. She was reassured by the head that it was not a scenario of 'success or failure' and was given support to evaluate her own practice in a way which led her to believe that her established skills of providing a well structured and stimulating learning environment for all children were particularly relevant for Steven. She realised that it was her duty to attend not only to what was 'special' about Steven, but also to what was 'ordinary' and that there was no mystique to analysing tasks. She was already doing this and making them accessible to all children, including children with learning difficulties.

(Herbert 1998: 103)

The decisions made by parents and teachers in the case discussed above pointed to an outcome of inclusive practice. How an individual educator, an early years setting, a local authority or service constructs both a problem and its solution is determined by their characteristic habits of interpretation.

Roots of inclusion: routes to inclusion

It is worth taking a moment to consider how we have come to use the term 'inclusion' and to explore the roots of our present policy response to the education of young children with a variety of curricular, physical, emotional and social needs.

The psycho-medical legacy (1950s →)
This is understood as the system of broadly medicalised ideas which essentially saw the individual as being somehow 'in deficit' and in turn assumed a need for a 'special' education for those individuals.

The sociological response (1960s →)
This position broadly represents the critique of the 'psycho-medical legacy', and draws attention to a social construction of special educational needs.

Curricular approaches (1970s →)
Such approaches emphasise the role of the curriculum in both meeting – and, for some writers, effectively *creating* – learning difficulties.

School improvement strategies (1980s →)
This movement emphasises the importance of systematic organisation in pursuit of truly comprehensive schooling.

Disability studies critique (1990s →)
These perspectives, often from 'outside' education, elaborate an overtly political response to the exclusionary effects of the psycho-medical model.

Figure 9.1 Five key perspectives on educational inclusion (Clough 2000: 8)

Inclusive ideology and practices have emerged in only 50 years from within a situation of statutory, categorical exclusion. Special education itself has been transformed from the outside by civilising forces which have deconstructed and reconstructed its meanings and effects. The move – from segregated special education in special schools, to integration and the development of units within schools, to inclusion of pupils in mainstream settings – has been fuelled by the various ideologies and perspectives which marked their 'moments' in history (Clough 1998). It is possible to sketch out a rough history of the development of inclusive education which identifies five major perspectives (figure 9.1). Though never wholly exclusive of each other, they demonstrate historical influences which shape, in part, current views and practices.

By looking 'back' through these perspectives, it is possible to look 'forward' to the emergence of a more homogeneous response to inclusive education, where individual children's rights to inclusive education, as well as needs for individually appropriate education, are at centre stage from the start of their educational career. Looking back we can see how tests, labels and deficits dominated the identification of children's learning needs – a legacy from the psycho-medical model dominant in the 50s. As Sebba and Sachdev (1997) point out, educational 'labels' rather than categorisation 'labels' (for example: 'reading difficulties' rather than 'Down's syndrome') lead to more inclusive responses to children's learning needs. In the move towards inclusive education, recent developments have hinted at a convergence of thinking about inclusion and about how best this can be achieved. The *Index for Inclusion* is one example of such convergence, an outcome of a particularly fruitful collaboration which is designed to help schools understand what they mean by inclusion as well as to identify their inclusive practices and blocks to those practices.

Perspectives on inclusion

From the 'academy'. . .

> Some continue to want to make inclusion primarily about 'special needs education' . . . but that position seems absurd . . . If inclusion is about the development of comprehensive community education and about prioritising community over individualism beyond education, then the history of inclusion is the history of these struggles for an education system which serves the interests of communities and which does not exclude anyone within those communities.
>
> (Booth 2000: 64)

Tony Booth's position here, then, is that inclusive education is about education for all members of the community; all minority and oppressed groups. From this broad definition of inclusion it could be argued that Sure Start initiatives and Early Excellence Centres are, in effect, projects of inclusion in the early years.

From practitioners . . .

We asked five early childhood educators what they meant by the term 'inclusion'. Here they talk about their own understanding of inclusion and what their settings do to develop inclusive practice.

> It's about letting children with Special Educational Needs come to the school in their neighbourhood. I think that's right, but it doesn't always work out.
>
> Kay, nursery nurse, 2–5 years

> It's political. It's about social justice – giving every child the right to an education in their own community – which enables them to reach their full potential. For me, that means doing a lot of work to make sure that the staff here is aware, but also arguing for resources. Managing that is a challenge. The greatest need is for personal awareness – so I need money for staff development – installing ramps is easy – changing attitudes – challenging prejudice – that's the real issue of inclusion – it is a huge issue.
>
> Sue, headteacher, 3–10 years

> Well, I think inclusion is really about equality. About not shutting children out. If children are kept out of the system at this stage they'll always be different – seen as different. It's easy to say that though – not always so easy to include children – especially some who are very disruptive. Children with disabilities aren't a problem – I don't worry about them – they usually fit in well – it's children who can't behave – can't fit into the group – mess up the equipment, slop paint everywhere – throw things – bite – I tear my hair out over them. They're the ones that are in danger of exclusion and being separated off at five years old – that's terrible isn't it? But I can't help it – I have to survive, and I have to think about the rest of the children.
>
> Helen, reception class teacher, 3–7 years

> A lovely idea – inclusion – and when it's good, it's great! I have been able to have children in the nursery with Down's Syndrome and children with various emotional difficulties – abused children – but when they (the LEA) asked us to take in a child with autism, well, we had to say 'no'. Too risky – I was frightened that if we did – something terrible would happen and it would be my responsibility. So yes, lovely idea – but it really is an ideal that will never be achieved – total inclusion is impossible.
>
> Janie, nursery teacher, 3–10 years

I spend my life arguing for extra support for children with special educational needs who we're trying to keep in our school rather than send them to 'special'. Inclusion of all children in the community would be so much easier if it were the norm – the first resort – that's usually the case in the nursery, but as children go on into school that philosophy seems to fade and the first move seems to be 'how can I get rid of this one?'

Pauline, SENCO, 3–10 years

So, how typical are these voices on inclusion? To what extent can the political ideal of social justice be realised in practice in the early years of education? How far are these ideals of equity and fears of risk shared by early childhood educators generally? Wolfendale's 'snapshot of practice' includes many examples of work with children with special educational needs in the early years (Wolfendale 2000). This collection demonstrates the diversity of experience and attitude towards needs and to the concept of inclusion. Wolfendale presents many positive accounts of including young children with identified learning needs in nurseries or other early education settings; but there is another side to the coin, as our interviewees alert.

The failure of inclusion hurts; Nutbrown (1998) gives an account of a nursery teacher who, against her professional judgement, tried to include a child with autism in her nursery. Things went badly wrong because of endemic difficulties within the setting itself:

Martin was admitted to a nursery full of children with damage and dislocation in their lives – physical and sexual abuse, overwhelming poverty, disproportionate ill-health, numerous wet beds, and no end of broken hearts. Martin stayed for two weeks. Each day his teacher talked with his mother. Each day she told her what Martin had enjoyed, and of the struggle he had with his peers in the nursery. There were many troubled children in Martin's company, and though Martin was interested, bright and he was able, the nursery disabled him. In that setting he was not being included in a calm, ordered society. He was not a member of a predictable community, he was appended into a community of children and adults in chaos.

After two weeks Martin left. His teacher hoped he had not been harmed, but she knew the harm it had caused his mother. Martin went to a nursery a few miles away which had a special unit for children with special educational needs and which worked to include children from that unit into mainstream classes once they had become established in the school community.

(Nutbrown 1998: 170)

Martin's story is a warning that early years settings must be fit to include, and educators equipped with, appropriate professional development and management support. Berry's (2002) study of four children indicates that inclusion can work for some children and the factors for success depend upon the children's responses as well as those of educators and parents, and on the ability of the adults so involved to listen, really listen, to the children's voices.

The Index for Inclusion

The *Index for Inclusion* is a tool for school development. It is summarised as follows:

> The Index is a set of materials to guide schools through a process of inclusive school development. It is about building supportive communities which foster high achievement for all students. The process of using the *Index* is itself designed to contribute to the inclusive development of schools. It encourages staff to share and build on existing knowledge and assists them in a detailed examination of the possibilities for increasing learning and participation for all their students.
>
> The *Index* involves a process of school self-review on three dimensions concerned with inclusive school cultures, policies and practices. The process entails progression through a series of school development phases. These start with the establishing of a coordinating group. This group works with staff, governors, students and parents/carers to examine all aspects of the school, identifying barriers to learning and sustaining and reviewing progress. The investigation is supported by a detailed set of indicators and questions which require schools to engage in a deep and challenging exploration of their present position and the possibilities for moving towards greater inclusion.
>
> (Booth *et al*. 2000: 2)

So, the *Index* is intended to enable schools to 'sample' their cultures, policies and practices to see how they measure up to the view of inclusion articulated earlier by Tony Booth. This view embraces inclusion of *all* and addresses aspects of gender, class, race, religion, sexuality, social class as much as learning difficulty or disability.

Of course, we know from our research that some early childhood settings and providers have not encountered the *Index*. Because of the diversity of provision, some non-school settings missed the launch of the *Index* and have not yet been able to work with it, nor judge its usefulness to their setting. The *Index* is not 'just' about SEN and is distinct from statutory frameworks and structures such as the SEN Code of Practice 2001 (see Roffey 2001 for discussion of the legal context).

Using the Index for Inclusion

We were interested in how the *Index* made a difference to individual professional responses to inclusion; we wanted to know whether using the *Index* affected the personal 'routes to inclusion' of early childhood educators. After they had used the *Index* in their own schools and centres we returned to the five early years practitioners and asked them to reflect on their experience, and to talk about their own learning. We asked them five questions:

1. What were your first impressions of the *Index*?
2. Did the *Index* change your practice?
3. Did using the *Index* change your thinking?
4. What have you learned by working with the *Index*?
5. Would you recommend the *Index* to other early childhood education settings?

Here is a flavour of their responses:

Fantastic – a real eye opener. I never thought about some of the dimensions as being part of inclusive practice. I realise how inclusive we are! Of parents, of children from ethnic minority groups – It made me think – 'Am I being inclusive – as a professional?' Yes – I've really learned quite a bit – about me and my own attitudes – and about what other people who work here know too – and have shared.

Kay, nursery nurse, 2–5 years

It suggests setting up a co-ordinating group. That's important for large schools – but it works equally well in small settings where there are not large numbers of staff. We used it in a series of staff meetings. Got the children as well as staff to do questionnaires. It really raised awareness, amongst staff, children and also with parents. My Governors were interested too – even when it came to spending money! There's very good practice – and positive will – it is such an effective process – takes some sustaining though! We were encouraged to realise that we had many aspects of inclusive culture and our main task was to extend and develop what we did.

Sue, headteacher, 3–10 years

When they said we were going to do this I thought 'another initiative in another glossy folder'. I was sceptical – I admit – I wondered what the point was of doing another audit when we could have spent the time and money on a part-time support assistant for my class. But it was interesting – made me think – but whether it will make a difference in the end – well, we'll see.

Helen, reception class teacher, 3–7 years

I learned loads just by reading through the folder – thinking about the questions posed under the different dimensions – there's so much to think about – mind-blowing! It's a process that's never actually finished – but it feels very good. It is really about developing relationships – that's what it's about – valuing people enough to make relationships with them and then finding ways of working in that richness of diversity. He (the Head) said 'We should do this – take it home and see what you think.' As I worked through it, it all made sense – cultures, policies and practice – really obvious but it had to be laid out for us. So I took the folder back and said 'Yes – good idea – we should do this.' And the Head said 'Great! Will you set up the group?' It's been a lot of work but getting the children involved and the parents was really good – made a difference to the way we think about things now – I think. I would say that we're – most of us – at the point where we 'think' inclusion now – first.

Janie, nursery teacher, 3–10 years

Why do we need the Index for Inclusion?

The five people we spoke to have conveyed something of a personal response to the *Index* which suggests a change in themselves. We are left with the impression that there is a great deal of personal interrogation, personal learning, personal change which is an outcome of engaging with the *Index*. As Pauline says, 'we "think" inclusion now.'

Can such changes in thinking, in attitude, in realisation fail to result in changes in practice? As Kay told us, 'That whole idea that "inclusion" isn't just the latest PC term for SEN – that was really refreshing.'

A key point in the interviews was the development of a shared language for discussion. Sue commented 'We've got a language now to discuss things within the school' and this change in language resulted in Pauline negotiating a change in her title as Special Educational Needs Co-ordinator. 'I've asked to be called the Learning Support Co-ordinator now. It doesn't really fit, being a SENCO, in an inclusive school!'

Their work with the *Index* in their settings, they told us, made a difference to them as individuals. It was not always easy, as Helen admitted, 'It was painful at times. I had to confront and admit some personal prejudices.' But it seems that these early childhood professionals would want to recommend the *Index for Inclusion* to others, in other settings, so that they can find out for themselves.

'It's not something you can get second hand – you have to be part of the thinking, part of the change'.

Acknowledgements

We would like to thank Kay, Sue, Helen, Janie and Pauline for sharing their experiences and perspectives with us. Thanks also to Sue Webster for her comments on an earlier draft of this article.

References

Berry, T. (2002) *Does inclusion work? Simon's Story*. In C. Nutbrown (ed) *Research studies in Early Childhood Education*. Stoke-on-Trent: Trentham.

Booth, T. (2000) *Reflection*. In P. Clough and J. Corbett (2000) *Theories of Inclusive Education: a students' guide*. London: PCP/SAGE.

Booth, T., Ainscow, M., Black-Hawkins, K., Vaughan, M. and Shaw, L. (2000) *Index for Inclusion: developing learning and participation in schools*. Bristol: Centre for Studies in Inclusive Education. The *Index* is available from: CSIE, 1 Redland Close, Elm Lane, Redland, Bristol BS6 6UE.

Clough, P. (ed.) (1998) *Managing Inclusive Education: From Policy to Experience*. London: PCP/Sage.

Clough, P. (2000) *Routes to Inclusion*. In P. Clough and J. Corbett (2000) *Theories of Inclusive Education*. London: PCP/Sage.

Herbert, E. (1998) *Managing Inclusion in the Early Years*. In P. Clough (ed.) *Managing Inclusive Education: From Policy to Experience*. London: PCP/Sage.

Nutbrown, C. (ed.) (1996) *Respectful Educators: Capable Learners – children's rights and early education*. London: PCP/Sage.

Nutbrown, C. (1998) *Managing to Include? Rights, responsibilities and respect*. In P. Clough (ed.) *Managing Inclusive Education: From Policy to Experience*. London: PCP/Sage.

Roffey, S. (2001) *Special Needs in the Early Years: collaboration, communication and coordination* (2nd edn). London: David Fulton.

Sebba, J. and Sachdev, D. (1997) *What works in Inclusive Education?* Ilford: Barnardo's.

Wolfendale, S. (ed.) (2000) *Special Needs in the Early Years: Snapshots of Practice*. London: Routledge Falmer.

Early years education has a vital role to play in the development of inclusive education. It is here that best inclusive practices are often developed and modelled. With the help of tools like the *Index for Inclusion* and, equally importantly, a culture of openness and dialogue, transition towards greater inclusivity can be a rich learning process for all involved. A version of this article first appeared in *Early Education* 2002. Since that time a second edition of the *Index for Inclusion* has been published (in 2002) and is available from the Centre for Studies in Inclusive Education. Our research into early years educators' perspectives on special educational needs and inclusive practices continues.

Peter Clough is Professor of Education in the graduate School of Education at Queen's University Belfast.

Cathy Nutbrown is Senior Lecturer in Education at the School of Education, University of Sheffield.

Chapter 10

Changing from a special school to an inclusion service

Carol Bannister, Vivienne Sharland, Gary Thomas, Vivian Upton and David Walker

The development of inclusive education is often described as a journey. This chapter outlines the particular journey of one special school and how it transformed, over time, into an inclusion service. The authors describe the key elements and stages of this transformation and they suggest ways in which other schools can be supported in becoming more inclusive.

The special school

Princess Margaret School (PMS) was a Barnardo's special school for children and young people with physical disabilities. Opened in 1966, it educated more than 50 day pupils and 40 boarders; 30 years later, in 1996, it became an inclusion service, providing a range of support for children attending local mainstream schools. When managers at PMS began to consider inclusion as an option for future development, they did so within a context of considerable achievement and success as a special school. But although the quality of service offered was seen as a strength, it also could operate as a barrier to change. On many occasions, variations on the theme of 'If it ain't broke, don't fix it', were to be heard from staff, parents and professional groups.

Looking around: developing ideas and making plans

Before making any decisions about the future of the school it was agreed with Barnado's managers that the school's management team would look at examples of best practice elsewhere. Consequently, it was necessary to visit a range of schools and projects and to attend the first international workshop on inclusion. At this early stage, inclusion was only one among a range of options being considered; others explored included the development of the school as a resource centre to include a pre-school intensive therapy centre.

First steps

After intensive discussions, the senior management team produced a vision for the school, which they called the school's 'purpose' (or mission statement), of which Table 10.1 is a shortened version. This committed the managers to action in three areas: empowering pupils; developing services; and influencing the wider environment. The second and third areas represented a major shift of direction for the school.

Table 10.1 The school's 'purpose' or mission statement

1) We should empower individuals by:
  ● maximising each young person's potential;
  ● enabling young people to be their own advocates;
  ● fully involving families, the children and the young people in their education.

2) We should help to develop inclusive schools and services by:
  ● providing a high quality set of services and resources to children and young people with disabilities, their families, their carers, and the community;
  ● evaluating and adapting services as circumstances, or needs, change;
  ● creating opportunities for staff development.

3) We should influence the wider environment by:
  ● being advocates for young people's right to be included;
  ● being actively involved In the debate regarding inclusion in the wider community;
  ● influencing and encouraging change in other organisations' attitudes and services.

The practical ramifications of this change in outlook were two-fold. Firstly, an advisory teacher (physical disability) was appointed, funded jointly by Barnardo's and the LEA (Local Education Authority). Secondly, LEA and PMS managers involved other members of staff and other groups within Barnado's in developing inclusion.

Beginning integration: the appointment of an advisory teacher

The post was developed jointly between Somerset LEA and Barnardo's during 1991–2. The teacher's time was divided equally between supporting those mainstream schools in Somerset which already offered places to pupils with disabilities, and working at PMS to support staff and to develop an integration process, whereby pupils could transfer from PMS to mainstream schools. The process was deliberately called an 'integration' procedure, the aim of which was to make it possible for pupils 'to fit' into the chosen school. There was, originally, no plan to work with the schools over an extended period in order to assist them to become more inclusive.

The futures group

During this period the school's managers established the 'futures group', which included staff representing each department in the school and which met regularly over two terms.

Its aims were to develop thinking about inclusion in the school, and to produce a strategic plan in consultation with stakeholders including parents, mainstream schools and the LEA.

Making inclusion happen

In 1993/94 a major area of development was in the further education department as it already had strong links with mainstream colleges. Staff were experienced in inclusion and numbers in the department were falling owing to more and more pupils being integrated into local colleges.

The teacher in charge of the Year 4/5 group in the primary department put forward a proposal that her class should be transferred to a local mainstream primary school. Over the previous term the children had had a weekly afternoon session based at this school, and the experiment had been judged to have been successful. It was therefore decided to transfer (in September 1994) the class, the class teacher, the classroom assistants and the services of the Princess Margaret School's physio and speech and language therapists to the primary school.

Parents were split on whether to accept the proposed changes or to retain the existing service. Two parents were enthusiastic and positive about the proposals; one set decided to pursue a different option for their children. After full consultations between parents, staff at the primary school and PMS staff, all of whom would be closely involved, the decision was taken to pursue the link for four main reasons:

- without the link the curriculum opportunities for this particular group would be limited as a result of small class size, different ages and abilities, and a variety of communication difficulties (only one child in the class used verbal speech and there was a gender imbalance towards boys);
- PMS managers felt that the primary school staff and governors shared a commitment to inclusion and would be determined to make it work;
- children who had already attended the primary school part-time were enthusiastic;
- PMS staff were convinced that the children's educational and social opportunities would be significantly enhanced in the primary school.

A joint policy statement was drafted which established the aims of the partnership as:

- giving pupils from PMS as full an experience of mainstream education as possible;
- ensuring that PMS pupils are fully included in all aspects of life at the primary school;
- enhancing the primary school children's understanding of equal opportunities and the needs of those with disabilities;
- evaluating this kind of inclusion for all pupils and staff.

In the event, only two of the five children were transferred to this particular school: one remained at PMS; the other two were placed by their parents in their local mainstream schools, supported by Somerset LEA. Therefore, of the original five, four children transferred to mainstream schools but only two were transferred to the particular school concerned.

PMS managers pursued a deliberate policy of generous staffing support for these two children. In addition to normal primary school staffing, PMS provided a full-time teacher and two 'full-time equivalent' classroom assistants, plus speech and language therapy and physiotherapy input. This high staff/pupil ratio was justified on the grounds that the partnership with the primary school was unknown territory, and that there were likely to be heavy demands on staff.

Following these early successes in integration, the special school was left with a roll that was unbalanced in its age distribution. The Senior Management Team (SMT) was clear in its view that this situation was untenable in the long term. After lengthy discussions it was therefore decided that the next inclusion phase would be in two stages:

- 1995 No referrals accepted to Year 7. Transfer of Year 10 and Year 11 to mainstream schools. Preparation of KSI and Year 8 children to mainstream schools, for completion in the following year;
- 1996 Final transfer of KS l and Year 8 to mainstream schools. Acceptance of *new* referrals into mainstream support provision.

The decision to transfer the *older* pupils (in Years 10 and 12) into mainstream earlier than the *younger* children was based on the fact that:

- Year 10 pupils would be able to embark on a full GCSE programme, rather than the limited one that PMS could offer;
- there were only three Year 11 pupils and consequently a limited peer group;
- some of the younger children (in Year 8) had multiple impairments (including two with no speech). The systems and resources in the mainstream schools were not sufficiently prepared for these pupils and a more lengthy process of preparation was required.

The Inclusion Project personnel

The 'primary school project' was the seed from which the inclusion service grew, as ideals were turned into practice. Major organisational changes were necessary, not only in the style of work required, but also in the structure of the establishment as some staff would inevitably lose their jobs. The consequent discussions with staff about these changes were less traumatic than had been envisaged, and the following transcript of an interview with David Walker, the headteacher, in which he talks about the process, indicates its nature:

I went round every member of staff, in small groups, to the kitchen staff, everyone – because this was about redundancies . . . And that was an interesting experience because I got all kinds of reactions, almost none of them the ones I expected! The kitchen staff for example – there'd been lots of anxiety and worry in the senior management team about, you know, they'd been here a long time: what were they going to do, and so forth. So when I met with them, I'd geared myself up, you know: 'This is going to be a group who are really upset'. And they said, 'well actually we thought that was about it – we'd worked it out anyway ourselves . . .' I mean it wasn't what I'd expected: suddenly people were into their plans . . . So again, one of my assumptions had to be rethought: this wasn't a disaster for everyone. For some people it was, clearly, but nothing like the numbers I think that I'd assumed. And some of that team were up for early retirement or whatever . . . so there's all those kind of different things coming out. I think that was a real learning point for me. I don't know quite how to put it. It's a sense of 'We've finally got ourselves clear. This is what we're going to do'. And the value of that was that then other people could begin to plan and react to it. So the staff suddenly – all this stuff had been talked about and talked about – when was it going to happen? Suddenly then, there was a very clear time-scale. And they could then begin to make plans – what was going to be best for *them* . . .

(Thomas *et al.* 1998: 94)

Table 10.2 indicates the way in which the special school staff became an *inclusion* service, and shows the significant organisational and personnel changes which have taken place.

Table 10.2 From a special school to an inclusion service

Princess Margaret School (73 children; 40 boarding)	Somerset Inclusion Project (18 children; none boarding)
1 principal	1 project leader
1 deputy principal (education)	
1 deputy principal (care/social work)	
1 administrator	1 project administrator
14.5 teachers	5 teacher coordinators (inclusion coordinators – see next section)
12 classroom assistants (LSAs) (full-time equivalent, in fact, 25 part-timers)	20 classroom assistants (LSAs) (full-time equivalent)
25 residential social workers	
2 nurses	
4 physiotherapists	2 physiotherapists
1.5 speech and language therapists	1.5 speech and language therapists
1 volunteer co-ordinator (40+ volunteers)	1 volunteer coordinator (20 volunteers)
1.5 family social workers	1 family social worker
5 kitchen staff	
7 ancillary staff (cleaners, drivers, etc.)	
2 technicians	
4 administrative staff	1 project secretary

(from Thomas *et al.* 1998: 105)

Maintaining momentum

No major organisational change of this kind is smooth, and this was no exception. The question needs to be asked: What kept the inclusion process on track in the face of organisational obstacles? Answered quite simply: The rewards were great and the benefits were evident. In particular:

- young people were talking about their experiences. For the Year 11 pupil transferring at the end of his school career it was 'the best year of my life';
- parents were witnessing increasing motivation in their children, who were achieving academically and were enjoying increased social inclusion both in and out of school;
- school staff in partner mainstream schools were commenting on the positive impact on the school culture of having children with disabilities in the school.

The project in practice

During the process of inclusion, a number of factors were identified as critical to the success of the project. One was the development of the role of the *teacher coordinator* as the special school teachers, with their own classes of children, took on the role and managed the effective inclusive education of the children who were formerly in their classes.

The role of the teacher coordinator

The role of the teacher coordinator is constantly evolving in response to the changing needs of the children and the mainstream staff, and has three broad responsibilities:

- *curriculum* . . . The curriculum is differentiated by the teacher coordinator through regular liaison with class teachers and support assistants. This work was particularly important at the beginning of the project, before the 'host' teachers gained ownership. At that stage curriculum delivery and balance was the total responsibility of the teacher coordinator who managed the support assistants and had a hands-on role in the classroom. Good practice was developed and children were actively encouraged to model appropriate language and behaviour;
- *liaison* . . . The teacher coordinator also liaises with physiotherapists, speech and language therapists and parents at regular planning meetings and arranges all the annual review processes. He or she also provides a focus for external agencies (educational psychologists, school transport, occupational therapists and LEA staff) and arranges informal meetings, when necessary, which take two forms:
  i)   informal liaison at hand-over times, at break-times, at lunch-times and at the beginning and end of the school day;
  ii)   a formal weekly meeting to discuss, to review and to set targets;

- *management* . . . The teacher co ordinator manages the 'development and improvement' of the inclusive process in schools. In one mainstream primary school (a pioneer partner in the project) the teacher coordinator was invited to join the management planning team and, consequently, it was possible to reach clear agreements about staff development and training in key areas.

These three broad areas provide a firm framework for the role, and now, in the second and third years of working in the mainstream, the role of the teacher coordinator and support assistants has evolved considerably. For example, the increased confidence and skills of all staff, and the 'ownership' of the new pupils by the host schools, means that the teacher coordinator is able to work with more schools and children, as the project develops. The role of the teacher coordinator can now be likened to that of a peripatetic SENCO (special educational needs coordinator) for the project pupils, and some aspects of coordination have been passed to the support assistants. Class teachers assumed more responsibility for planning, for the delivery of the curriculum and for direct liaison with support assistants in their classrooms. The input of assistants was valued by class teachers, and decision-making and differentiation on a daily basis was increasingly becoming part of their role alongside regular liaison with speech and language therapists, physiotherapists and parents.

One teacher coordinator (in a secondary school) was asked to list her responsibilities, and they included:

Work with students' schools and the LEA

- trouble shooting, problem solving, challenging discrimination;
- training mainstream staff in differentiating the curriculum;
- ensuring physical access to classrooms;
- advising staff on inclusion;
- (with the senior management team) to increase opportunities for inclusion and to adapt policies;
- (with the LEA) to implement plans for the adaptation of a range of facilities;
- supporting pupils in all aspects of their school life;
- developing Individual Education Plans;
- monitoring and evaluating inclusion.

Work with LSAs (learning support assistants)

- informal training;
- day-to-day support;
- staff development and appraisal;
- team building.

Work with parents

- regular contacts;
- distributing information about programme, events and pupil progress;
- ensuring consistency of approaches between home and school;
- transition, and formal and informal reviews.

Administration and management

- record keeping;
- the co-ordination of reviews, meetings, therapy, transport and respite care;
- the budget;
- examination arrangements;
- secondary to FE transfers;
- timetables.

Conclusion

If special schools are to work in different ways in helping mainstream schools to become more inclusive as suggested in the Government's Green Paper (DfEE 1997), there are possible alternatives (Thomas *et al*. 1998). We have shown in this article how it is possible for a special school to become an inclusion service. If we were asked to give advice to other such schools on the processes involved, we would suggest the following:

- discuss, as a school, your ideals. Not everyone might agree with them, but try to reach a consensus. If the aims are to promote inclusion, ways towards inclusive practice should be devised;
- write a statement on your purpose and educational philosophy, and make it widely available;
- discuss your ideas with other stakeholders: parents, students, the LEA and those local mainstream schools which are likely to take your children. Build on any existing integration schemes;
- establish a 'futures' group to determine ways of bringing about change. Draw a time-line and set objectives;
- discuss your plans and their financial implications with your LEA;
- be prepared to slim down as an establishment if you decide on a complete transformation, from a special school to an inclusion service. Bear in mind that some children and their parents may wish to remain in special education and to transfer to other special schools, and that some staff may wish to take early retirement or redundancy;
- indicate in the plans, ways in which teachers will become teacher coordinators and give details of the enhanced role of LSAs.

References

DfEE (1997) *Excellence for all Children: Meeting Special Educational Needs*. London: DfEE.

Thomas, G., Walker, D. and Webb, J. (1998) *The Making of the Inclusive School*. London: Routledge.

This chapter illustrates how a vision of what inclusive education might be was used to underpin the development of an entirely new service. The transformation began by sharing this vision widely and led to developments that endeavoured to put the pupil, rather than existing educational structures, first. Consequently, the new service involved significant changes in organisation, personnel and practices.

CHAPTER 11

Voices from segregated schooling: towards an inclusive education system

Tina Cook, John Swain and Sally French

This chapter looks at 'inclusion' from the viewpoint of disabled people who have experienced segregated education. The authors review the literature in this area and then explore the views of pupils who are in the process of transferring from a special to a mainstream school. These perspectives are often absent from discussions of inclusion. However, the authors argue that voices from experiences of segregation should be central in constructing an inclusive education system.

Introduction

A local education authority (LEA) we shall call Romantown has begun reorganising its special educational needs provision under a policy flag of 'inclusion'. The changing policy and associated changes in provision and practice are, at least in general terms, being undertaken in numerous local authorities around Britain. One aspect of Romantown's reorganisation involved the closure of an all-age school we shall call Adamston, for pupils with physical disabilities, a school which first opened in the 1920s. The pupils from this school have been placed (in September 1999) in a range of provision, particularly in mainstream schools with 'additionally resourced centres' and newly-opened special schools for pupils with learning difficulties. (The reorganised system did not include a school for pupils with physical disabilities.) We explored the pupils' views about their education, and the changes they were experiencing, in a project in which a photograph album of pupils' memories of Adamston was created.

In this chapter we have three related aims:

(1) to present an analysis of the judgements disabled people bring to bear on their education, from experiences of segregated schooling, through a review of the literature;

(2) to explore the views and experiences of Adamston pupils prior to the closure of their school under the policy of inclusion;

(3) to examine the contribution of disabled adults' and pupils' views in moves towards inclusion. In attempting to realise our aims, our overall argument became that moves towards inclusion must be founded on the participative involvement of disabled people (adults and pupils) in changing education.

Whilst the judgements, views and experiences of both the adults and pupils were different and diverse, gathered from stories about residential and non-residential schooling situated in socially, historically and geographically disparate communities, it became clear that there were common themes that linked their stories. They were predominantly about being what James and Prout (1990: 6) term 'passive subjects of structural determinations' and not being actively involved in the construction of their own lives. The themes that linked them together are around perspectives of both feeling and being excluded from decision-making processes that fundamentally affected their lives, and the imperative for disabled people to participate in debates about their experiences and processes of change which shape and transform their experiences.

In attempting to realise our aims, our overall argument is that moves towards inclusion must be founded on the participative involvement of disabled people (adults and pupils) in changing education.

Inside stories: histories of segregated schooling

In general terms, much of the research on disability, including disabled children, has ignored the views and experiences of disabled people themselves. Non-disabled people have researched disability and given their perspectives. Histories of segregated schooling are, for the most part, the official histories of non-disabled people and professionals, documenting such things as changing numbers, and types of schools and official rationales for changing policies. Furthermore, research into disability has focused primarily on medical and psychological issues, rather than on the disabling environment. These critiques have led to a growing literature on the problematic nature of disability research (Barnes and Mercer 1997). In relation to research with disabled children, Robinson and Stalker state:

> While there is a well established body of knowledge about the way parents experience life with a disabled child, children's own accounts of their lives are largely missing, their voices have not been heard.
>
> (1998: 7)

Shakespeare and Watson (1998) make the point that children can have profound experiences of life, including disability, and yet they have not been consulted or taken seriously by academic or professional 'experts'. A recent exception is the 'Life of a Disabled Child' project, which has focused on disabled children's perspectives and experiences as social actors within a disabling environment (Priestley 1999).

The literature on disabled people's experiences of segregated education is not extensive and comes mainly from disabled adults reflecting on their childhood experiences. In reviewing what disabled adults and children say about their education it becomes apparent that their experiences are varied and their views are diverse.

Themes do emerge, however, in terms of what is seen to be important about their education. These themes, of educational standards, personal and social liberation and education as an experience in itself, will be explored first.

Educational standards

Educational standards have consistently been important for disabled people. Segregated schools are judged by insiders in terms of what is taught, how it is taught and the effectiveness of the teaching they experience. The educational standards experienced by disabled people in segregated schools have generally been low (Barnes, 1991). […] Many special schools placed a huge emphasis on practical tasks like cleaning and gardening. Henry, a man with learning difficulties, recalled:

> We used to play games, learning to read and write, spelling and how to clean places up – how to wash windows, how to clean anything you can mention.
> (Potts and Fido 1991: 68)

In addition to low educational standards, physically impaired people frequently complain about the amount of time spent in various forms of therapy. Phil Friend, who features in Davies's book, states:

> . . . looking back from the age of nine to sixteen, the primary concern of that school was to 'therup' me. It was nothing to do with education really.
> (Davies 1992: 37)

Similarly, deaf people complain that their education was eroded by an obsessive emphasis on the ability to lip read and to talk (Craddock 1991). These views are supported by Alderson and Goodey who state:

> Too many therapists in a school can divert the school's main remit away from education so that learning is fitted around therapy and students risk being further disabled academically.
> (1998: 154)

Poor educational standards in special schools, though common, were, however, never universal. Selective schools for visually impaired, hearing impaired and physically impaired children, who were judged to be academically able, have existed for many years, preparing their pupils for university or entry to some professions. Disabled people who have attended such schools sometimes express satisfaction with the education they have received.

Personal and social liberation

The experience of education also has meaning in the broader terms of how it impacts on the lifestyles and quality of life of disabled people. Disabled people may judge the education they receive in terms of empowerment–disempowerment and oppression–liberation. Some disabled people find that they receive a superior education and have a more favourable lifestyle than their non-disabled siblings and peers by virtue of being excluded. Martha, a Malaysian woman with a visual impairment we interviewed, was separated from a poor and neglectful family at the age of 5 and sent to a special residential school. She said:

> I got a better education than any of them (brothers and sisters) and much better health care too. We had regular inoculations and regular medical checks and dental cheeks.
>
> (Swain and French 2000)

Martha subsequently went to university and qualified as a teacher, which none of her siblings achieved. [. . .]

A recurrent theme in the accounts given by disabled adults is the confidence they gained by attending segregated schools. John O'Shaughnessy, a man interviewed by Willmot and Saul, said:

> I remember my very first day at Uffculme as a very shy 14-year-old lad who had spent half of his life at home, ill with asthma and wrapped in cotton wool . . . I left Uffculme two years later an $11\frac{1}{2}$ stone, self-confident young man ready to face the working world.
>
> (1998: 168–9)

The positive social effects of being with similarly disabled people can even emerge within highly abusive institutions:

> Attending special school at the age of nine was, in many ways, a great relief. Despite the crocodile walks, the bells, the long separations from home and the physical punishment, it was an enormous joy to be with other partially sighted children and to be in an environment where limited sight was simply not an issue. I discovered that many other children shared my world and, despite the harshness of institutional life, I felt relaxed, made lots of friends, became more confident and thrived socially. For the first time in my life I was a standard product and it felt very good.
>
> (French 1993: 71)

[. . .] Although some disabled people have found that the experience of special education gave them self-confidence, others have found the opposite to be the case (Leicester 1999). Eve, a visually impaired woman, said:

There was too much discipline. They were ever so strict. They used to run people down all the time and make you feel that you were useless. They used to make you feel that you were there as a punishment rather than to learn anything. They didn't understand children at all, never mind their sight. They used to expect you to do what they wanted and they used to get really cross if you couldn't see something, or you couldn't clean your shoes properly, or do anything they wanted you to do; what confidence I had they took it all away.

(French 1996: 33)

Education as an experience in itself

A major theme throughout the literature documenting disabled people's experiences of segregated education is the quality of the experience in its own right. As for non-disabled people, one way of judging experiences is in terms, for instance, of enjoyment and happiness or boredom and unhappiness. John O'Shaughnessy, who went to an 'open air' school, said of his experiences, 'In later years my thoughts drift back to the happiest two years of my childhood' (Willmot and Saul 1998: 169). However, regardless of impairment, accounts of physical, sexual, psychological and emotional abuse are commonly disclosed by disabled adults, especially those who went to residential schools. Harriet, who attended a school for visually impaired girls in the 1950s and 1960s, recalled the physical abuse:

We went to bed at five o'clock in the evening and we didn't get up until seven o'clock in the morning but we weren't allowed to get out of bed to go to the toilet. I was very unsettled because I'd gone to foster parents at the age of three and then to school at the age of five, and one night I wet the bed. The prefect on duty realised what had happened and she tried to cover up for me, she got me out of bed and put me in the bath, but one of the matrons came along. She picked me up out of the bath, just as I was soaking wet, and gave me the hiding of my life . . . I yelled and screamed, it terrified me.

(French 1996: 31)

[. . .] It should not be assumed, however, that all insider experiences of segregated schools are negative in terms of the quality of the experiences themselves. Some of the people interviewed by Willmot and Saul (1998), speaking about their experiences in 'open air' schools, suggested that even though the regimes of these schools were institutional and harsh, they regarded their time there as a highly positive experience, including in terms of the basic necessities of life such as food. [...] A strong and recurrent theme in the accounts of disabled people who have attended residential schools is the distress at being separated from their families, particularly when very young. Chris, a young man we interviewed (French and Swain 1997), recalled being very unhappy and crying every Monday morning as he waited for the bus to take him back to school where he was a weekly boarder. He was much happier when transferred to a 'special' unit in a mainstream school. [. . .]

Many disabled adults have found that the experience of segregated education interfered with, or even ruined, their family relationships. Richard Wood, who is physically impaired, said:

> I think it destroyed my family life, absolutely, I don't know my family . . . I never looked forward to going home in the school holidays . . . I never felt I belonged there . . . within two or three days I couldn't wait to get back to school because I really wanted to see my mates.
>
> (Rae 1996: 25–6)

Detachment from the entire home community is also a common experience of disabled people both during school holidays and when they leave school. Lorraine Gradwell, a physically impaired woman, recalled her isolation during school holidays:

> I didn't have any contact. There was one little girl who sometimes came to play. I think that was because her mum knew mine and it was a bit of a duty for her. We played together, but I couldn't really understand why she was coming.
>
> (Rae 1996: 7)

Even children who live at home and attend a special unit in a mainstream school can find themselves isolated from their peers in their immediate home environment. Peter, a young visually impaired man we interviewed (see French and Swain 1997), said, 'It's hard because my friends are up there . . . I find it hard to mix with them round here because I don't go to their school and I don't know them.'

We turn next to the voices of pupils in a day special school for pupils with physical disabilities. They are also voices from segregation, but speak from and of some very different experiences. Their experiences are particularly pertinent to our analysis as their school has been closed under a policy of 'inclusion'.

The pupil project

This analysis is based on a project conducted with pupils at Adamston School during July in the half-term before it closed. The project involved the planning for and production of a book of photographs by the pupils of things they wanted to remember about their school. We hoped to involve pupils in discussions about Adamston, their experiences there, and their thoughts and feelings about the closure of the school and their future.

We worked with two groups: three primary-aged pupils and four secondary pupils, who participated on a voluntary basis and whose parents were aware of their participation.

[...] At the time of the interviews, the secondary pupils who were placed in new schools had all made visits to those schools, but all three primary aged pupils maintained that they had not seen their future school. The research project was carried out at the school over three sessions.

Session one involved pupils in the planning of the project. They decided what they were going to photograph and why the picture was important to them. A demonstration was provided in two ways:

- one of the researchers showed pictures of herself at work and explained why she had taken the photos;
- an instamatic camera was used with each group to allow the pupils to take trial photos.

The project was planned by each pupil drawing and noting (with the assistance of the researchers) possible pictures for the book. The session was tape-recorded and the tapes were transcribed.

Session two was the photo taking session. Each pupil was given a disposable camera to take photographs for inclusion in the book. The photos were taken in pairs: one for possible inclusion in the school memories book and the other for each pupil to have his or her own personal record of the school.

Session three involved pupils in selecting photos for and making both their own personal records and the school memories book. Each photo chosen for the school book was accompanied by a caption, which was discussed and agreed by each group. The school book, then, had two sections: one put together by the primary group; the other by the secondary group. This session was also tape-recorded and the tapes were transcribed.

We chose to use this method to try and elicit pupils' views about their school and its closure for the following reasons:

- taking photographs was something the pupils would enjoy and that would engage their interest;
- some of the pupils were young and some had learning difficulties, which could have made it difficult for them to develop abstract conversations and concepts using direct interview techniques (Lewis and Lindsay 2000). The concrete nature of the task could help focus their attention and discussion;
- the pupils would work on this in a group, and through talking about their experiences together we hoped the pupils would be more comfortable and more expansive;
- it would allow us to return to the topic at a future date with an obvious starting/reference point.

It was clear that all the pupils were engaged in and enthusiastic about the project. [...] Whilst this approach had a number of strengths in terms of the collection of data, there were a number of difficulties.

All the children in this small sample were able to communicate verbally. Children using augmentative communication aides or with whom participation in standard communication would be difficult, were not included. We were acutely aware of not being able to listen to these children at this point, and hope to work with them in the future. [. . .]

There were ethical problems, including questions of informed consent. Though the pupils did seem enthusiastic, it was not clear whether the enthusiasm was directed at the project or was motivated by the opportunity to be absent from regular classes.

Though the views of a small number of pupils could be explored in depth we had no control over the explanations provided by teachers. We did find that we had to devote some time to explanations at the start of session one. There were limitations, too, in sampling. By asking the staff to recommend pupils we were unsure as to whether there was any selection of pupils other than on a voluntary basis. We were aware that there were other children who could have different views about Adamston and its closure, who were not put forward by the staff.

Given the hierarchy of adult/child interactions and the focus we gave our work compared with the immediate interests of the pupils, our awareness of directing their thoughts and contributions was necessarily heightened. We tried not to use direct questions, but allowed the pupils to develop conversations around the photographs.

Deciding what was pertinent within the data was complex and we tried to avoid 'lazy interpretation', as described by Alderson and Goodey (1996), that concentrates on inconsequential responses furnished by the children. It was not always easy, however, to spot the 'consequential' responses and there were times within our first trawl of the data when children's responses were ignored as irrelevant, but later thought to be extremely pertinent. The basis for choosing relevance tended to be when the children insisted on having discussions, sometimes along *with* the researchers, but sometimes *despite* them.

We found too that pupils' thoughts and feelings about their future placements and the reorganisation were not easily addressed. The immediate focus for the project was the immediate context for the pupils, that is the closure of their school, their memories of the school and what they valued. The more abstract questions about their future had to be raised by the researchers.

Views from Adamston

Perhaps inevitably the pupils' discussions covered a wide range of topics. However, three broad themes did recur:

- education as an experience in itself;
- inclusion as belonging;
- feelings of exclusion.

Education as an experience in itself

Their experiences were predominantly positive and related almost wholly to the quality of the experiences themselves, rather than to any educational standards or aims. The teachers who featured in the books, for instance, were said to be 'cool' or a 'good laugh', rather than because they were skilled at teaching. The school was valued as 'the best' because it was 'different'.

Pupil: This school's much better. I wish it had never closed.

Pupil: There's something different about this school.

Researcher: So what's different about this school?

Pupils: Lots of things. Horses. Sports Hall. The teachers are different. They're funny.

When asked what they would miss, 'friends' was the first answer and most pupils had predominantly taken photographs of their friends. They appeared to have very strong friendship bonds with each other across both gender and age range.

Amongst the secondary pupils there was the general camaraderie of leg pulling and teasing, often around 'snogging', 'skipping lessons together behind the sports hall', the 'disgusting nature of school dinners' ('I'd rather eat horse muck'), people being 'boring farts', and their mutual purported dislike of anything that suggested work, e.g. 'Maths. French. IT.'

The primary pupils demonstrated their strong friendships in a much more straightforward manner. 'I like knocking about with my friends. I like C. I really like knocking about with him because he's a real sort of friend.' They showed confidence in their friendships. When one child stated that 'my favourite things I like doing is playing with my friends', another's immediate response was 'he must mean me'.

There was evidence within both the secondary and primary pupils' talk of mutual understanding and recognition of the needs of others for greater amounts of help at certain times. For example, all the secondary children were keen to place a photograph of S, a wheelchair user, in their album. When deciding on the caption one suggestion was:

Pupil: Every week S's class goes out [said with a trace of envy in his voice].

Pupil: Yes, but that's not really their problem because at the weekend they can't get out so they have to go out with the teacher. They can't get out with their parents because their wheelchairs are too heavy.

The relationships with the staff in all areas of the school were consistently highly valued by all seven pupils. It was cited as the aspect of the school they would praise most highly. They described them as 'funny', 'mental', 'dead crazy', 'excellent', but also as 'kind' and 'helpful', not only towards them but towards their friends.

> *Researcher*: Why do you want a picture of J [staff member] in this book?

> *Pupil*: Because she's nice and she helps, she helped M anyway.

> *Pupil*: She helped me and all.

The pupils had a lot to say about their shared history. Some children had taken photographs of the nursery because they said that was where they had originally met their friends; it was their history. A number of the pupils appeared to be fascinated by the fact that the Teachers' Centre had once been the school, and so wanted to include a photograph of that in their book. Another source of evidence of shared history came from discussions around performances and outings they had made. The primary school pupils described a band they had formed. They had played to the school and remembered how it had made them feel.

> *Pupil*: We get together as a group and we practise and then we put on a show for everyone.

> *Pupil*: Even the physios.

> *Pupil*: And it's great because we're all excited.

> *Pupil*: Do you feel all good inside when you've done something?

This led to a number of 'feeling good' and 'do you remember' conversations among the pupils that were about doing things together and being part of something within school.

Inclusion as belonging

Some judgements of Adamston were embedded in the pupils' expression of loss at the closure of the school. Some expressions of the loss of the community were poignant. One pupil told us, 'The thing is the school is closing. And the thing is when you leave a school you can come back to see it, but we can't come back and see it.' Another, talking about the book of photographs, stated, 'So like you know when I go to my new school I'll be able to take this and show them who my old teacher was. And I won't know how I'll be able to see my old teacher, and I wanted to be able to see this.' The central theme seemed to be pupils' feelings of inclusion in the Adamston community in the sense of belonging.

The school had a small residential unit (referred to as 'resi'), which provided the secondary pupils the opportunity for overnight stays. This, it seemed, was consistently highly valued and would be missed.

Pupil: Resi is going to be a really big one for me. It's absolutely excellent. It's probably one of the best things about the school.

Researcher: What do you like about resi?

Pupil: You don't have to be at home being bored. All your friends are there . . . your own room.

The school had riding stables and many of the children found it hard to imagine leaving the horses.

Pupil: Well I do really want to see them again and I will see them again but I know I'll not see them at school, but I can sometimes come and visit them can't I? Or even there might be some at my other school . . . cos this is one of the things I want to do . . . I've got loads of photos of Sparky [horse] here.

The pupils struggled to understand loss. A primary pupil who had been known to one researcher when she was young, but whom she had not seen for four years, appeared to use this experience as a springboard to try and develop her understanding about loss and connections. Despite the researcher inexpertly trying to return the conversation to the topic of Adamston, the pupil repeatedly asked questions and made statements about having known the researcher. This can be seen as an exploration of her own previous experience of history, loss and change.

Pupil: It's really sad that I'm going.

Researcher: Do you think you'll enjoy your new school though?

Pupil: Well, here I will come back and see them.

Researcher: But they are not going to be here are they?

Pupil: Yes they are [said in a questioning voice but also assertive].

Researcher: Who is?

Pupil: You know Mrs T? She'll still be here . . . I've got [lists children] in already. Have you known me for ages?

Researcher: I knew you when you were little, yes. But I haven't seen you for a long time. Your mum used to bring you to the hydrotherapy pool at the Centre.

Pupil: Did you used to work there?

Researcher: Yes. And then you went to AW Nursery.

Pupil: Did you come and see me there?

Researcher: Yes, I saw you there as well.

Pupil: So did you used to come to my house?

Researcher: No, I don't know where you live.

Pupil: It's in [region of the city].

Researcher: I would go past it but I didn't come to your house.

Pupil: Do you know [gives her address]? Its got a red door. Do you know the one? You go past the fence, my next door neighbour's fence, and my house is in the middle. [. . .]

Pupil: You know when you were at the Centre, what did we used to call you?

Researcher: T, you've always called me that.

Pupil: Didn't we call you 'Mrs' something?

Researcher: No, we've always called ourselves by name at the Centre.

This pupil had clearly set an agenda here and was determined to direct the conversation. Her insistence demonstrated the importance for her of teasing out history, renewed contacts and change.

The primary pupils repeatedly talked about using the photographs they had taken as a link between the past and the future

Researcher: Why do you want to keep these [particular photographs]?

Pupil A: They have all my memories in . . . and I want to take some of my friends in secondary . . . because they have been my friends for quite a long time.

Pupil B: Physios. I want to take a picture of them in this school and then in my new school.

The older pupils offered their thoughts on leaving the school less readily than the primary children, but when they did, their conversations included both anger and sadness. In a conversation about why the school might be closing, one pupil suggested the governors were to blame.

Researcher: So you think the governors have closed the school?

Pupil: Yes.

Researcher: Why do you think they wanted to do that?

Pupil A: Because they opened their big mouths.

Pupil B: It's not fair. It's not fair on anyone. It's not fair on us.

Researcher: In what way?

Pupil: Because there's a lot of people here that need help, physios . . . and it's not fair on them.

Feelings of exclusion

In separate interviews, their parents had reported what they considered evidence of anxious behaviour, one parent reporting that her child had restarted having fits during this unsettled time. Teachers too reported incidents of unsettled behaviour within the school such as a certain amount of disinterest and disaffection within the classroom that was uncommon in that environment. The central theme embedded in pupils' anxieties seemed to be feelings of exclusion from Adamston, their school.

There was evidence within the interviews that pupils were feeling anxious. Most had worries about their new placement. When asked if they were feeling they were going to be all right in their new school, they offered a mixed response ranging from definite 'no' and 'yes', to 'probably' and 'don't know' replies. With secondary school pupils replies were often tinged with teenage bravado and it was not always possible to engage in conversations with them about their thoughts on their new schools.

All the pupils, both primary and secondary, said how they would miss their friends, especially as they did not live in the same neighbourhoods and Adamston was the main point of contact. One primary pupil, whilst acknowledging he was going to miss his friends, was pragmatic about this and was making arrangements to go and stay with them. He also said:

Pupil: It's quite a big move and I'm a little bit frightened and it's going to be funny at first but I think I'll get into it.

Secondary pupils reported:

Researcher: You went to (mainstream) again on Tuesday?

Pupil A: Got more homework.

Pupil B: It was rubbish.

Researcher: Why was it? Why do you say that?

Pupil B: Because it's not like Adams, it's not a special school. Plus it's boring. All the teachers are boring.

Researcher: Why do you want to go to a special school?

Pupil B: Because I've got (medical conditions) and I'm incontinent.

Researcher: And you don't think they can cope with that in a mainstream school?

Pupil B: No [An emphatic 'no' which ended this discussion].

Others worried about practical details that had not yet been resolved, such as transport. Many pupils took photographs of the Adamston bus drivers and the buses. They associated them with 'great trips out' and 'getting out of lessons'. The bus photographs prompted a discussion with a primary pupil who, whilst looking at all his photographs of the bus, stated that his new school was not near his home and he did not know how he would get to his new school.

One primary pupil, who had not been placed in the local school attended by his sibling, despite it having an additionally resourced centre for children with physical disabilities, worried both about the travel across the city and the size of the classes. He reported that he had seen his younger sibling in a large class and didn't know how he himself would manage, but he was pragmatic about it: 'they decide what's best for us and I'm willing to take a chance . . . I'm willing to do it.' He could not tell us why such choices had been made and he himself had not been involved in the decision making. A secondary child referred to this non involvement in decision making.

Pupil: Well most of the kids here have to go to mainstream. I'm going to Daleview (special school). That's the only school I can go to.

Researcher: Why are you going to Daleview? Did you decide you wanted to go to Daleview?

Pupil: No I got a letter. From the Civic Centre.

Researcher: So they decided?

Pupil: Well, yes. And my mam. The first time my mam went to visit the school they wouldn't let us go.

Some of the secondary pupils felt the closure had not been fair, on either themselves or others and felt quite angry about it. Others could engage with their new school, to a certain extent, and were beginning to make visits, but demonstrated mixed emotions and loyalties.

Researcher: And what do you think of the [new] school generally? Do you like going there?

Pupil A: Yes, but this school's better . . .

Pupil B: This school's much better . . . in Harpers Lee you get shouted at all the time.

Researcher: Did you get shouted at when you went?

Pupil A: No.

Pupil B: We were late so we got shouted at.

Including insider voices from segregated settings

One way of interpreting the views of disabled people presented here is in terms of the pros and cons, or arguments for and arguments against, segregated schooling. This has been the dominant discourse since the 1944 Education Act, if not since the inception of mass schooling. Given that there has been no significant decrease in the number of disabled pupils placed in segregated schooling over the past 30 years, this debate is at best sterile and, at worst, maintains the status quo.

There is another way of understanding these views and experiences, however, which looks towards inclusive education. Listening to the insider voices from the wide variety of experiences in segregated settings, from historical contexts and Adamston, we are struck first and foremost by the variety itself. They speak of abuse, but also of belonging. If there is a dominant common story, it is of subjugation in a context of unequal power relations between disabled and non-disabled people. Historically, it is a story of disabled children being subjected to various forms of abuse. At Adamston, it is a story of disabled children being subjected to the loss of their community, originally created by non-disabled people through a policy of segregation and then terminated by non-disabled people in the name of inclusion.

Adamston was a small community which provided social, emotional and psychological security for these young people. It is not at all surprising that young people want to hold on to the community they are part of. The re-organisation–closure of their school and placement in the new system–has been done to these young people. They (even more than their parents) have been powerless. The idea that pupils could or should be involved in policy-making or even decisions about their placement in the re-organised education system did not arise for the pupils themselves or anyone else involved. They were completely excluded from the consultation process and did not attend their annual reviews at which decisions about their placement in the re-organised system were discussed. Only once did a pupil appear at her own annual review. She burst into the room asking, 'What are you saying about me?' The meeting immediately stopped and she was gently ejected. The decision at the meeting was that this 14-year-old should attend a mainstream school. No account has been taken of these disabled pupil's views in the planning of inclusive settings. No account has been taken of what these young people valued about their education, how their views might affect processes of change, or what they would look for, and need, to feel included, in a so-called inclusive setting. Similarly, no account has been taken of disabled adults' views, their experiences, their culture.

From the evidence in this paper, insider voices from segregated schooling have much to say about inclusion and the process of changing towards an inclusive system, whether they are the voices of disabled adults who speak from experiences of abuse or they are the voices of disabled young people who speak from experiences of belonging in a long-established community. We shall pin-point just four specific messages.

1. There are positive personal and social effects for disabled people from being with similarly disabled people. Inclusion cannot be realised through the denial of disability.
2. Inclusion has a powerful psychological dimension of belonging. Whilst being included, in educational policy terms, is about having access to ostensible universal standards of education, the confidence that comes from social inclusion is the context for such access.
3. Moving pupils around the system of schooling, especially outside their own neighbourhoods, has dramatic and traumatic consequences for the lives of individuals.
4. Young disabled people can tell us what inclusion means for them.

Most important, however, is the general message that moves towards a more inclusive education system must begin with the inclusion of the voices of disabled children and adults. Insider voices from segregated schooling should inform the processes of change from a segregated to an inclusive education system, if 'inclusion' is not to perpetuate the subjugation of disabled people in other settings.

References

Alderson, P. and Goodey, C. (1996) Research with disabled children: how useful is child-centred ethics? *Children & Society*, **10**, 106–16.

Alderson, P. and Goodey, C. (1998) *Enabling Education: experiences in ordinary and special schools*. London: Tufnell Press.

Barnes, C. (1991) *Disabled People in Britain and Discrimination: a case for anti-discrimination legislation*. London: C. Hurst and Co.

Barnes, C. and Mercer, G. (eds) (1997) *Doing Disability Research*. Leeds: the Disability Press.

Craddock, E. (1991) Life at secondary school. In G. Taylor and J. Bishop (eds) *Being Deaf: the experience of deafness*. London: Pinter Publishers.

Davies, C. (1993) *Lifetimes: a mutual biography of disabled people*. Farnham, Surrey: Understanding Disabilities Educational Trust.

French, S. (1993) Can you see the rainbow?: the roots of denial. In J. Swain, V. Finkelstein, S. French and M. Oliver (eds) *Disabling Barriers – Enabling Environments*, pp. 69–77. London: Sage.

French, S. (1996) Out of sight, out of mind: the experience of and effects of a 'special' residential school. In J. Morris (ed.) *Encounters with Strangers: feminism and disability*, pp. 17–47. London: the Women's Press.

James, A. and Prout, A. (1990) Contemporary issues in the sociological study of childhood. In A. James and A. Prout (eds) *Constructing and Reconstructing Childhood*. London: Falmer Press.

Leicester, M. (1999) *Disability Voice: towards an enabling education*. London: Jessica Kingsley.

Lewis, A. and Lindsay, G. (eds) (2000) *Researching Children's Perspectives*. Buckingham: Open University Press.

Potts, M. and Fido, R. (1991) *A Fit Person to be Removed: personal accounts of life in a mental deficiency institution*. Plymouth: Northcote House.

Priestley, M. (1999) Discourse and identity: disabled children in mainstream high schools. In M. Corker and S. French (eds) *Disability Discourse*, pp. 92–102. Buckingham: Open University Press.

Rae, A. (1996) *Survivors from the Special School System*. Bolton Data for Inclusion, Data No. 2. Bolton: Bolton Institute.

Robinson, C. and Stalker, K. (1998) Introduction. In C. Robinson and K. Stalker (eds) *Growing Up with Disability*, pp. 7–12. London: Jessica Kingsley Publications.

Shakespeare, T. and Watson, N. (1998) Theoretical perspectives on research with disabled children. In C. Robinson and K. Stalker (eds) *Growing Up with Disability*, pp. 13–28. London: Jessica Kingsley.

Swain, J. and French, S. *(2000)* Towards an affirmative model of disability. *Disability and Society*, **15**, 569–82.

Willmot, F. and Saul, P. (1998) *A Breath of Fresh Air: Birmingham's open-air schools 1911–1970*. Chichester: Phillimore.

Cook, Swain and French's work reveals the importance of inclusion for pupils, both socially and also in the decision-making processes within the school. As with other chapters in this book the importance of listening to pupils is highlighted. This is essential if exclusionary and subjugating practices are not to be transferred into new settings.

Part 3

On the margins

Interviews with young people about behavioural support: equality, fairness and rights

Paul Hamill and Brian Boyd

This chapter presents findings from a yearlong research project undertaken by researchers from the University of Strathclyde. Eleven comprehensive schools in Scotland were involved and the aim of the study was to evaluate the effectiveness of in-school support systems for young people who display challenging behaviour. Pupil support bases had been set up in most of the schools aimed at reducing exclusion rates and these were examined from the perspective of all stakeholders – teachers, parents, young people and key inter-agency personnel. The chapter focuses on the views of the young people who, although often perceived as disruptive, disaffected, and troubled, articulated clear messages for all professionals.

Children's rights in the Scottish context

Article 12 of the *United Nations Convention on the Rights of the Child* (UN 1990) asserts that the child has the right to express his or her opinion in all matters affecting him/her. This theme has, in recent years, gained prominence in Scotland. The *Children (Scotland) Act* (Scottish Office 1995) emphasised that children have participation rights in relation to the decision-making process which affect them as individuals. These participation rights have now been extended by the *Standards in Schools (Scotland) Act* (SEED 2000a) to cover rights in relation to school development and education authority plans which impact upon the young person's quality of life. This focus upon taking into account children's views is now high on the social and educational agenda. Promoting the participation of young people in decision making has been an evolving process in Scotland and this can best be illustrated by considering briefly the Scottish context and in particular some practice which has impacted upon the process.

In 1978, an organisation entitled 'Who Cares? Scotland' was established to give a voice to young people who were being looked after by local authorities. This development highlighted the importance of giving this group of vulnerable young people a voice in relation to issues that are relevant in their lives and it was widely recognised as a major step forward.

In 1995, a national initiative entitled 'Connect Youth' was launched, aimed at creating a network whereby young people could exchange ideas and good practice which would promote their right to be heard. This initiative played a part in the development of the Scottish Youth Parliament established in 1999, which aims to promote equality for all young people and to encourage them to play their role in influencing change. The Scottish Alliance for Children's Rights took this a step forward in 2000 when they produced 'A Proposal for a Commissioner for Children in Scotland'. The commissioner would be an independent voice in relation to children's issues.

There is clear evidence therefore to suggest that positive developments are emerging within the Scottish context. However, we still have a long way to go and many young people remain silent and are not in a position to influence the policies and practice that shape their lives. This is particularly true in relation to young people who are disadvantaged and disaffected. This was summed up by the Scottish Office in 1998 as follows:

> In families in danger of being socially excluded the scope for children's needs to be overlooked is even greater.
>
> (para. 2)

One group of young people who are often excluded from Scottish schools are those whose behaviour can be challenging or disruptive. According to Hamill and Boyd (2000), these young people have:

> difficulty in developing social competence, adjusting to social contexts and in learning to follow normal and accepted behaviour patterns.
>
> (p.24)

In short they have special educational needs and, like all young people, they also have the right to participate actively in decisions about their education and welfare. These rights are clearly articulated in *A Manual of Good Practice in Special Educational Needs* (SOEID 1999) which is currently one of the benchmarks of good practice in Scotland.

Inclusive education

Young people whose special needs arise because they have social, emotional and behavioural difficulties are often excluded from the mainstream school, or from classes within the mainstream school, because their behaviour is deemed to be challenging and disruptive. The body of research literature in relation to inclusive education has grown considerably in the past few years, yet, although voices promoting inclusion are now heard increasingly and the arguments for inclusion appear to be overwhelming, inclusion for these young people is still not a reality (Thomas *et al.* 1998; Allan 1999; Mittler 2000).

Advocates of inclusion argue that it is vitally important therefore to establish first and foremost the young person's right to be included. It is only when this has been achieved that effective channels of communication can be set up to enable him/her to exercise the right to express a view in relation to the decision-making process. At present, few of these young people see themselves as having any real say, particularly in relation to one of the biggest decisions impacting upon their lives, namely, the decision to exclude them from school.

In Scotland, as elsewhere in the United Kingdom, the issue of social inclusion is a dominant theme particularly in the educational context. The most recent legislation in Scotland, the *Standards in Schools (Scotland) Act* (SEED 2000a), confirms the intention to create within Scottish education a presumption of inclusion and this principle has been clearly set within the legislation. In accordance with this belief, there has evolved in Scotland a strong focus on ensuring that young people who are disaffected are not excluded from our mainstream schools. This is of course easier said than done, as it often involves changing deep-rooted negative attitudes and expectations. Some professionals still see exclusion as a natural response to what they perceive as disruptive behaviour. Cullingford (1999) sums this up when he says:

> the number of exclusions from school increases each year and one explanation is that exclusions are seen as an inevitable response to difficult and disruptive pupils who come to school already disaffected.
>
> (p.94)

Cooper (1993) reminds us that it is not easy to define problem behaviour as it results from a:

> complex interaction between contextual factors and aspects which the individual brings to the situation.
>
> (p.9)

This complexity poses real challenges for those who want to create supportive, inclusive environments where the voices of these young people can be heard. They often appear as defiant rebels but all too often this persona masks a vulnerable, unhappy individual who finds it difficult to communicate his/her feelings, let alone exercise the right to participate in the decision-making process (Campion 1992; Chazan *et al.* 1998; Pomeroy 2000).

In 1999, the Scottish Executive Education Department (SEED) published the *New Community Schools Prospectus* which focused upon the intractable problems many excluded young people face. These relate mainly to poverty, underachievement and indiscipline. One of the recurring themes in the prospectus is the need to reduce pupil disaffections, tackle social exclusion and raise attainment. Emphasis is placed upon inter-professional collaboration and working in partnership with young people where they are no longer perceived as silent partners. These themes were echoed in the Beattie Report (SEED 2000b), which explored issues relating to implementing inclusiveness and realising potential. Once again the need to maximise the participation of all young people in mainstream schools was highlighted and the need to remove attitudinal barriers was given prominence.

If we are serious about ensuring young people exercise their right to express themselves in relation to matters that have a significant impact on their lives we must ensure this applies to all young people; including those who are disruptive. It is not enough to give a young person a voice; we must also be prepared to listen and act upon what they say. However, we must also take time to ensure we understand what it means to experience social, emotional and behavioural difficulties.

Young people with social, emotional and behavioural difficulties

In Scotland, the label 'social, emotional and behavioural difficulties' is applied to a wide range of young people whose needs lie on a broad spectrum, from those who are occasionally disruptive and whose difficulties are short-term to those whose behaviour is extremely challenging or who have serious psychological problems. Defining this group of young people is a difficult task as the complexity and diversity of need make a simple definition impossible. It is clear, however, that one common factor is that these young people become disaffected and are at great risk of underachieving both educationally and in relation to their own personal development.

This adversely affects not only their own education but also that of their peers. Social, emotional and behavioural difficulties manifest themselves in different ways. Some young people are aggressive and sometimes violent, while others are isolated, withdrawn and introverted. While it is important to recognise that every individual is unique it should also be recognised that there are characteristics that are present to varying degrees in all young people who display 'challenging behaviours'. These characteristics, which are outlined in Part 3, Section 6 of the Scottish Consultative Committee on the Curriculum report entitled *Special Educational Needs Within the 5–14 Curriculum – Support for Learning* (SCCC 1994: 2) include low self-esteem, difficulties with learning and poor interpersonal skills. [. . .]

The research

Throughout 1999–2000, a research study undertaken by researchers in the University of Strathclyde evaluated provision for young people with social, emotional and behavioural difficulties (SEBD) in mainstream comprehensive schools. The main focus of the research was to throw some light upon the effectiveness of the in-school pupil support bases in reducing rates of exclusion. [. . .]

The researchers included all the significant individuals, specifically young people, parents, teachers and other professionals, and a range of research techniques were employed including semi-structured interviews, observation schedules, questionnaires, support analysis grids and documentary evidence. An ethnographic case study approach was used to explore how the strategy had evolved and the focus was upon how individual pupils, their families and schools interact. The overall study was set within an action research context which provided an opportunity for collaboration between the researchers and those professionals who work with and support young people within a realistic and sometimes challenging context. Emphasis was placed at all times upon the cycle of feedback linking the researchers, the school communities, parents, other professionals and the young people. The overall aim was to transform environments through the process of critical enquiry. We hoped that the transformative power of such an approach would empower those who work with young people and shape the eventual research outcomes. The bulk of the data was qualitative and, in relation to its analysis, the researchers adopted the descriptive narrative approach outlined by Strauss and Corbin (1990). Consequently the material was analysed in a way that accurately described and reconstructed it into a recognisable reality. This allowed all of the significant players a voice but blended their ideas into a series of themes expressed and shared by a number of individuals. This involved interpreting the data in a way that ensured that the voices of all participants were heard but which, at the same time, brought together related issues within the evidence. The research team were particularly keen to ensure that the voices of the young people were heard. This report therefore focuses on the perceptions of the young people involved in the study.

The sample

In partnership with the behaviour support staff in the 11 comprehensive schools, a group of young people with SEBD was identified for interview. Each individual had been excluded from school on more than one occasion and frequently accessed the pupil support base due to disruptive behaviour. The purpose of the interview was explained to the young people and both their permission and that of their parents was obtained prior to interview. The young people formed focus groups composed of four or five individuals and a total of 45 young people were involved. All of the young people were in the age range 14–16 years and were currently in the final year(s) of compulsory schooling. There were 34 boys and 11 girls in the sample.

A semi-structured interview schedule was used, focusing upon the young person's perceptions of learning and teaching, the curriculum, behavioural issues, the pupil support base and exclusion.

The interview methodology was underpinned by the work of Rogers (1980, quoted in McIntyre and Cooper 1996). He suggests a range of approaches in order to facilitate the interview process, particularly in relation to young people. These include empathy, unconditional positive regard, congruence and repeat probing. McIntyre and Cooper also set out a series of steps to be followed when interviewing young people, including defining relationships, negotiating access, selecting techniques and enacting appropriate relationships. The Strathclyde research team adhered closely to this model.

Emerging issues

At the heart of this research study was a concern for human rights, equal opportunities and social justice. The qualitative nature of the research enabled the researchers to understand more fully how the use of pupil support bases as an inclusive strategy impacted upon the in-school experience of these young people. [. . .] Methods of data collection reflected the qualitative nature of the research and, within this context, the semi-structured interview schedule was used to elicit extremely rich data from the young people. It was surprising how consistent all of the young people were in relation to the views expressed, and the issues selected for discussion reveal a very high level of conformity.

Curriculum

The research literature in relation to young people whose behaviour can be challenging consistently points to how an inappropriate curriculum can exacerbate behavioural difficulties (Fogell and Long 1997; Cole *et al.* 1998; Montgomery 1998; Porter 2000). This theme was echoed repeatedly by all of the young people in the sample:

> The teacher told me to get on with the work. I couldn't do it but he just said I should be able to. He asked me questions and I didn't know the answer. I ended up swearing at him and he then threw me out and told me to go to the Pupil Support Base.

> Mrs X treats me like a person. She knows I am a bit slower and she makes the worksheets interesting and fun. Other teachers find the most boring page and tell you to copy it then I get fed up and start messing about.

There was a widespread view expressed by the young people that the curriculum on offer was often inaccessible to them as it did not meet their needs. When they were unable to respond to the curriculum, they felt that they were perceived as being to blame whereas, in reality, the inappropriate curriculum was a potential source of behavioural difficulties. Thus the perceptions of these young people confirm the research findings as summarised by Porter (2000):

> a relevant curriculum is both a preventative and interventive measure in relation to disruptive behaviour.

(p. 118)

Exclusion – equality, fairness and rights

All of the young people interviewed agreed that, in certain circumstances, exclusion was an effective strategy. They readily discussed occasions when they had been excluded and the extent to which they felt it had been an appropriate strategy:

> I got excluded for shouting and arguing with the teacher and for fighting with x. I know I did wrong and I can accept that I should have been excluded.

However, the young people did not always perceive the process to be fair and they consistently used words like 'equal', 'fair', 'respect' and 'rights' to elaborate upon this theme:

> I only argue with teachers who don't treat me fairly. I like teachers who respect you and don't just automatically blame you. Mr X treats everyone equally but Mrs Y doesn't.

Being treated disrespectfully by teachers was clearly seen as a provocation to disruptive behaviour (Tattum 1982; Olsen and Cooper 2001). Conversely, when these young people felt they were treated with genuine positive regard they were less likely to be challenging (Charles 1996; Cooper *et al.* 2000).

The young people saw themselves as victims who were picked upon and made scapegoats:

> If everyone in the class is carrying on the teacher always picks on me and puts me out. It's not fair. I always get the blame and it's not right.

This view was often linked to the young person's perception that, in the eyes of some teachers, they had a reputation. Once this had been established it seemed almost impossible for the young person to shed this image which, in their opinion, negatively influenced some teachers' attitudes and expectations:

> I'm in fourth year now and I definitely have a reputation. Some teachers just automatically think of me when something bad happens.

One crucial factor which often emerges in the research literature as a measure of how inclusive a school community is, is the extent to which everyone is valued and treated equally (Thomas *et al.* 1998). Again this was a recurring theme which the young people raised. They often expressed views that revealed that the theory of equality did not always translate into practice:

A lot of teachers do try and treat everyone equally but it's not true that all pupils in this school are equally valued. Some teachers convey a sense that they don't like pupils and treat you as if you are not worth bothering about.

Thus the young people conveyed to the researchers a very clear view that the decision to exclude is a very complex issue. The work of Cullingford (1999) reinforces the view expressed by these young people and confirms the validity of their personal experience of being excluded. They are the individuals who experience exclusion at first hand and although on occasions they accept the decision, more often than not they feel that their view is disregarded as invalid.

Learning difficulties

Thirty out of the 45 young people interviewed emphasised the connection between learning difficulties and misbehaviour in class. This relationship has been well documented in the literature (Cooper 1993; Hewett 1998; Garner 1999; Pomeroy 2000). However, this group of young people felt that some teachers had not yet grasped the importance of making the link between learning and behavioural difficulties. There was a feeling that teachers varied in relation to the efforts they made to support young people who experienced learning difficulties and this could lead to disruptive behaviour:

I was in English and I couldn't read the worksheet. I asked the teacher for help and she just ignored me so I just asked my pal for help and the teacher gave me a row. I shouted out and she said she was not having me in her class.

These young people consistently made the point that, in most classes, all pupils are expected to tackle the same work. They did not see a lot of evidence of differentiation in action and this posed a problem for them:

I hate it when I am in a group and I can't do the work. It's really embarrassing and I feel terrible. If people laugh at me I lose my temper and then I am sent to the Support Base because of my behaviour.

However, the young people were keen to emphasise that many teachers are extremely helpful and supportive:

Mr X knows I am dyslexic. He doesn't shout at me – he explains things and helps me get it right. He makes me feel that I can do it. I don't get put out of his class.

The crucial factor was that the teacher and the young people were very clear that it was the teacher who made the difference and that not all teachers were, in their opinion, effective or inclusive.

Teachers

As one might expect these young people had a lot to say about their teachers and the role they played in creating inclusive or exclusive classroom cultures. They understood how complex and stressful the teacher's job could be and they spoke highly of the many teachers who, in their opinion, do a first class job:

> The teacher's job can be really hard. They have to try and help everyone and everyone wants this or that at the same time. It's hard for the teacher to cope.

> Teachers have a difficult job to do. Most of them do their best to help us to learn but some pupils are prepared to work and some are not. Some people like me can be a bit rowdy and sometimes distract others and the teacher gets mad and stressed. So would I.

The young people tended to refer to what they perceived as effective teachers as 'good' teachers. The researchers tried to tease out what this meant and concluded from the evidence that the young people were expressing, in their own language, the view that the most effective teachers made an effort to include everyone:

> Mrs X is a good teacher. She listens to you and treats everyone fairly. She is strict but she is fun as well.

> Good teachers have a relaxed kind of class. They respect you and are like a sort of friend. They see you as a person and listen to you. A lot are like that but a lot aren't.

However, there was also a considerable amount of evidence to suggest that not all teachers were equally effective in promoting positive behaviour. As far as these young people are concerned, the teacher is the key. They accepted that some young people can be so disruptive that they are unwilling to respond positively to any teacher but they were also well aware that teachers varied considerably in their ability to relate to young people. One very articulate boy summed it up eloquently as follows:

> Good teachers help you and spend time with you. They understand how you feel, they respect you and give you a chance. Bad teachers don't listen, treat you like dirt, pick on you, think they are always right and boss you around all the time.

The young people were not prepared simply to accept the treatment they received from 'bad teachers' which they perceived to be unfair. They consistently expressed their determination to resist what they perceived as injustice. Even though they understood that ultimately they would be the losers in that they might be excluded, they were not prepared to be passive victims of unfair treatment. They often made a conscious decision to challenge these teachers who in their opinion abused their authority.

I always challenge Mr X because he never treats me right. As far as he is concerned everything is always my fault. If he shouts at me I am going to shout at him.

I'm not letting her (teacher) get away with treating me as if I'm dirt. She is not getting away with that so I stand up for myself because it is just not right to treat someone as if they are worthless.

Pupil support bases

In Scotland there is an increasing trend to open in mainstream schools Pupil Support Bases. All of the young people interviewed had spent time in these Bases and wanted to share their experiences with the researchers. There was unanimous agreement among them that the Pupil Support Base was helpful and sometimes prevented them from being excluded:

I don't see eye to eye with some teachers so I come here (Pupil Support Base). I know if I stay in class I'll just get thrown out of the school.

The young people often made a clear distinction between some of their class teachers and the teachers who managed the Base provision:

The teachers in the Base understand my problems. They know about my life outside school. I can talk to them.

These young people wanted their class teachers to be more like the teachers who supported them in the Base. They recognised qualities in the Base teachers that were not, in their opinion, evident across the school as a whole. The young people also expressed a strong feeling that the Pupil Support Base was often used inappropriately by those whom they perceived to be ineffective teachers:

I didn't get a chance to misbehave in Mr X's class. I just walked in and he shouted at me to go to the Base.

Mrs X said she was not here to teach people like me. I'd only stepped over the door and she said – 'Base!'

A quarter of the young people in the sample did admit that they sometimes misbehaved in order to be sent to the Base. They preferred the supportive ethos in the Base where they felt more secure:

Sometimes I don't like the teacher or the subject is boring. I cause trouble so that I get sent to the Base.

All schools had in place whole-school policies in relation to indiscipline and the promotion of positive behaviour. The majority of the young people were well aware of these policies and how they should operate in practice. These policies emphasised the importance of praise and rewards and teachers were expected to create learning environments that were motivating and stimulating. The young people were, in general, supportive of these policies:

> We've got a behaviour policy in this school. You can get badges for good behaviour and you can get stickers in your card and get vouchers for McDonald's.

However, there was a widespread view expressed by all of the young people that all teachers were not consistent in applying school policy. Some teachers took a very rigid approach whereas others used the system more flexibly and interpreted policy in relation to individual need.

Conclusion

One of the most effective ways of securing young people's rights is through improving and extending educational opportunities available to them. Currently in Scotland one of the features of good practice which is highlighted within the context of education is the need to ensure all young people:

> have the right where appropriate to participate actively in decisions about their education and welfare. Their feelings and views should be valued and respected.
>
> (SOEID 1999: 22)

In the wider arena of school effectiveness research, the absence of the student voice has been an issue for a decade or more. Nieto (1994) argues that:

> One way of beginning the process of changing school policies is to listen to students' views about them; however, research that focuses on student voices is relatively recent and scarce.
>
> (p.396)

Rudduck, Chaplain and Wallace (1996) acknowledged that there are obvious problems in legitimising the contribution of the pupil voice in schools' own improvement practices. The University of Strathclyde study, by giving a voice to some of the most disaffected students within secondary schools, has confirmed Rudduck et al.'s conclusion that:

> . . . young people are observant, are often capable of analytic and constructive comment and usually respond well to the responsibility . . . of helping to identify aspects of schooling that get in the way of their learning.
>
> (p.8)

Young people designated as having SEBD are often characterised as getting in the way of the learning of their peers. However, the incidence of learning difficulties among these young people with social, emotional and behavioural difficulties suggests that they too need to have a voice to express their experience of learning failure. Rudduck *et al.*'s view that we should take seriously young people's accounts and evaluations of their learning, teaching and schooling is borne out by the insights the young people displayed in this study.

The researchers tried to ensure that young people whose behaviour could be challenging and who were often excluded had an opportunity to exercise their right to share their feelings and views. The aim was to raise confidence and self-esteem and ensure the young people felt their opinions were valued.

The Strathclyde study allowed the young person's view to emerge and gave them a voice. It is clear that, when this happens, these young people are keen to have their voice heard. They want to have their say and it is important to remember that what they have to say may or may not correspond to the teacher's viewpoint and experiences. Nonetheless one must acknowledge these perceptions and accept them as valid because they are an expression of what the young person believes.

As professionals we must accept that all young people have the right to have their voice heard. This can be particularly difficult if the messages they convey cause us to reflect upon and critically analyse our own practice. In relation to the present research study the young people had much to say to us as professionals and hopefully we are listening to, valuing and responding to their views. We may be surprised just how knowledgeable and articulate young people can be and so we give the last word to one wise young man.

> An inclusive teacher never makes you feel like a second class citizen. They listen to you and don't just ignore what you think.

References

Allan, J. (1999) *Actively Seeking Inclusion*. London: Falmer Press.

Campion, J. (1992) *Working with Vulnerable Young Children*. London: Cassell.

Charles, C. M. (1996) *Building Classroom Discipline: from models to practice*. New York: Longmans.

Chazan, M., Laing, A. F., Davies, D. and Philips, R. (1998) *Helping Socially Withdrawn and Isolated Children and Adolescents*. London: Cassell.

Cole, T., Visser, J. and Upton, G. (1998) *Effective Schools for Pupils with Emotional and Behavioural Difficulties*. London: David Fulton.

Cooper, P. (1993) *Effective Schools for Disaffected Students: integration and segregation*. London: Routledge.

Cooper, P., Drummond, M., Hart, S., Lovey, J. and McLaughlin, C. (2000) *Positive Alternatives to Exclusion*. London: Routledge.

Cullingford, C. (1999) *The Causes of Exclusion*. London: Kogan Page.

Fogell, J. and Long, R. (1997) *Spotlight on Special Educational Needs – emotional and behavioural difficulties*. Tamworth: NASEN.

Gamer, P. (1999) Schools by scoundrels: the views of disruptive pupils in mainstream schools in England and the United States. In M. Lloyd-Smith and J. D. Davies (eds) *On the Margins: the educational experience of problem pupils*. Stoke on Trent: Trentham Books.

Hamill, P. and Boyd, B. (2000) *Striving for Inclusion – the development of integrated support systems for pupils with social, emotional and behavioural difficulties in secondary schools*. Glasgow: University of Strathclyde.

Hewett, D. (ed.) (1998) *Challenging Behaviour – principles and practice*. London: David Fulton.

McIntyre, D. and Cooper, P. (1996) *Effective Teaching and Learning: teachers' and pupils' perspectives*. Buckingham: Open University Press.

Mittler, P. (2000) *Working Towards Inclusive Education – social contexts*. London: David Fulton.

Montgomery, D. (1998) *Reversing Lower Attainment – developmental curriculum strategies for overcoming disaffection and underachievement*. London: David Fulton.

Nieto, S. (1994) Lessons from students on creating a chance to dream. *Harvard Educational Review*, **64**(4), 392–426.

Olsen, J. and Cooper, P. (2001) *Dealing with Disruptive Students*. London: Kogan Page.

Pomeroy, E. (2000) *Experiencing Exclusion*. Stoke-on-Trent: Trentham.

Porter, L. (2000) *Behaviour in Schools – theory and practice for teachers*. Buckingham: Open University Press.

Rudduck, J., Chaplain, R. and Wallace, G. (eds) (1996) *School Improvement: what can pupils tell us?* London: David Fulton.

SCCC (Scottish Consultative Committee on the Curriculum) (1994) *Special Needs Within the 5–14 Curriculum – Support for Learning*. Dundee: SCCC.

Scottish Office (1995) *Children (Scotland) Act*. Edinburgh: HMSO.

Scottish Office (1998) *Report of the Consultative Steering Group on the Scottish Parliament*. http://www. scotland.gov.uk/library/documents-w5/rcsg-18.htm.

SEED (Scottish Executive Education Department) (1999) *New Community Schools – The Prospectus*. Edinburgh: HMSO.

SEED (Scottish Executive Education Department) (2000a) *Standards in Schools (Scotland) Act*. Edinburgh: HMSO.

SEED (Scottish Executive Education Department) (2000b) *Implementing Inclusiveness – Realising Potential*. The Beattie Committee Report. Edinburgh: HMSO.

SOEID (Scottish Office Education and Industry Department) (1994) *Effective Provision for Special Educational Needs*. Edinburgh: HMSO.

SOEID (Scottish Office Education and Industry Department) (1999) *A Manual of Good Practice in Special Educational Needs*. Edinburgh: HMSO.

Strauss, A. and Corbin, J. (1990) *Qualitative Analysis for Social Scientists*. Cambridge: Cambridge University Press.

Tattum, D. (1982) *Disruptive Pupils in Schools and Units*. Chichester: Wiley & Sons.

Thomas, G., Walker, D. and Webb, J. (1998) *The Making of the Inclusive School*. London: Routledge.

UN (United Nations) (1990) *Convention on the Rights of the Child*, Articles 12 and 23. New York: UN.

The need to listen if we are to learn from each other is a recurrent theme in this volume and Hamill and Boyd are powerful in illustrating this. This chapter leaves us in no doubt that all pupils have something worthwhile to contribute to the debate about how best to support learners.

CHAPTER 13

Disadvantage and discrimination compounded: the experience of Pakistani and Bangladeshi parents of disabled children in the UK

Qulsom Fazil, Paul Bywaters, Zoebia Ali, Louise Wallace and Gurnam Singh

This chapter discusses a study of the circumstances of 20 Pakistani and Bangladeshi families with one or more severely disabled children living in Birmingham, England. Parents and other adult carers were interviewed about their material circumstances, use of services and wellbeing. Importantly, the study found that these parents did not have as high levels of informal extended family support as can be assumed. Nor did they access formal support without difficulty. Thus, often disadvantage and discrimination compounded to make for difficult lives.

Introduction

While definitions of childhood disability remain complex and contested (Beresford *et al.* 1996; Ahmad 2000a), it is estimated that around 400,000 disabled children are currently being brought up in the UK with over 100,000 being described as severely disabled (Department of Health 2000). Of these, around 17,000 families are thought to include more than one disabled child, with some 7,500 families having two or more severely disabled children (Tozer 1999). The vast majority of such children live at home with their families for most of the time. [...] The growing research evidence about the experience of such families, particularly two recent national surveys (Beresford 1995; Chamba *et al.* 1999), demonstrates that they face widespread disadvantage and discrimination, particularly if they are members of minority ethnic groups. This article reports further evidence of the interaction of disability, ethnicity and disadvantage from a qualitative and quantitative action research study of families of Pakistani and Bangladeshi origin with a severely disabled child living in a Midlands city.

Families with disabled children in the UK experience many interlocking facets of disadvantage and discrimination (Ahmad 2000a). This has contributed to the development of the concept that it is the family as a whole that is disabled by the unjust society in which it finds itself. Parents and siblings, like disabled children, are also subject to stigma, marginalisation and discrimination. Within this experience, two key dimensions are central. First, disabled families in general face greater chances of (long-term) material deprivation than families without a disabled child. Second, against that problematic background, they commonly experience a variety of obstacles in accessing the range of information and services which it is known would have a positive impact on their lives (Beresford *et al.* 1996). In combination, as Ahmad (2000b) rightly argues, such disabling conditions constitute barriers to disabled people exercising their rights and responsibilities as citizens.

As Chamba *et al.* (1999) have demonstrated, families from minority ethnic groups with a disabled child face additional barriers to full citizenship, compared to majority families, as the consequences of the further impact of individual and institutional racism on their material circumstances and access to services. Chamba *et al.* undertook a large national survey of ethnic minority families with a disabled child recruited through the Family Fund Trust and only included if they had been eligible for a grant. This was taken as a measure of the severity of the children's impairment. [. . .] They underlined the differences which lie between and within minority ethnic groups, as well as those between the minority and majority populations. Within the minority populations studied, those from Pakistan and Bangladesh are worst placed in both the key dimensions identified.

Evidence of comparative material disadvantage can be seen in, for example, the income, housing circumstances and access to private transport of families with a disabled child. In 1997, 65% of ethnic minority couples with a disabled child surveyed by Chamba *et al.* (1999) had incomes of less than £200 a week, although the 'modest but adequate' budget for a family with two children and a car calculated by the Family Budget Unit was around £450 (McClusky and Abrahams 1998). Yet it is widely recognised – not least by the families themselves – that having a disabled child brings increased costs. As Modood *et al.* (1997) found that over 80% of all Pakistani and Bangladeshi households had less than half average incomes (compared with 28% of white households), it is not surprising that Chamba *et al.* found that disabled families from these groups were the most likely to have low incomes, despite the fact that only 2% were lone-parent families.

Low income in families with disabled children, often linked to comparatively low levels of employment, is compounded by differential knowledge of and receipt of benefits. Roberts and Lawton (1998) found that disadvantaged families make relatively fewer applications for Disability Living Allowance (DLA) and their applications are less likely to be successful. Minority group parents were less likely to be receiving DLA care, with mobility components and Invalid Care Allowance, and less likely to be awarded higher rates of DLA than majority group parents (Chamba *et al.* 1999). Parents from minority groups who said they understood English well were more likely to be in receipt of benefits than those who did not. This factor also affects different minority groups differentially. Only 29% of Bangladeshi and 53% of Pakistani respondents to the national survey (predominantly mothers) identified themselves as having a complete understanding of spoken English, compared with 64% of Indian respondents (Chamba and Ahmad 2000), with similar degrees of difference for reading and writing. Interpreting services were not being provided to between a quarter and a third of those who were said to need them.

In the two national surveys, housing conditions were widely reported by families with a disabled child to be unsuitable for their needs, across a variety of forms of housing tenure (Beresford 1995; Chamba et al. 1999). Overall, six out of 10 ethnic minority families reported that their home was unsuitable for the care of their child compared with four in 10 in Beresford's survey. Here, too, Pakistani and Bangladeshi families were particularly likely to face multiple problems, with an average of 4.2 problems per family reported compared with around 3.5 for African Caribbean and Indian families (re-analysis of data in Chamba et al. 1999). Six out of 10 Bangladeshi families also had no access to a private car compared with one in four of Indian families.

Parents of all ethnic identities describe problems in the coordination of services as well as in availability, quality and timeliness (Beresford 1995). The difference in familiarity with English coupled with the failure of service providers to work equally effectively in languages other than English, are major mediating factors in the reduced levels of access to services of minority ethnic families with a disabled child. As Ahmad (2000b) points out, language counts for much more than just a means of communication, but is a significant primary barrier to families securing the information – about their child's impairment and information about services – which is a precursor to service access.

Parents from minority groups face the additional problems of the stereotype of extended family availability and willingness to provide care. Even though there is evidence of increased levels of extended family involvement by Pakistani and Bangladeshi families, only a quarter of such families reported receiving 'a lot of help' from family members (Chamba et al. 1999). It is not clear whether these somewhat raised rates of informal help are the *cause* or rather the *result* of the absence of formal services. Other assumptions, for example, that minority families do not like to send their children to respite care facilities, also seem, on the evidence, to be a reflection of the perceived lack of trust that the service provided will be appropriate to the needs of their children (and will not expose them to overt racism), rather than a cultural preference.

In summary, while all ethnic minority parents of disabled children face significant additional disadvantage compared with the white majority, which is itself discriminated against, there are deep differences between different ethnic minority groups. A parallel form of the inverse care law operates (Tudor Hart 1971) in which those families most likely to be facing material deprivation and disadvantage (Pakistani and Bangladeshi families) are least likely to be receiving services, least likely to be able to understand professionals' information or processes, and least able to express their own requirements effectively in a language service providers will understand.

One paradoxical finding of the national surveys was that, despite this evidence, Bangladeshi and Pakistani families reported fewer problems with service providers than the other ethnic minority groups. This reflects the wider finding that 'disadvantage is associated with both poor quality service provision *and* low expectations' (Chamba *et al*. 1999: 22). The issue of low expectations and of a relatively low expression of dissatisfaction with a variety of services exemplifies one of two significant, if inevitable, limitations of the method adopted by Beresford *et al*. (1996) and Chamba *et al*. (1999): a written, postal survey. First, while Chamba *et al*. made considerable efforts to help participants complete the questionnaire, the process clearly did not allow for any questioning of respondents, to seek more detailed exploration of the key issues which lay behind the statistical data. The approach also meant that the data relied on self-report, and was untested against the observations of a third party, the perceptions of professionals or confirmed data about actual service provision, income, benefits and so on. This inevitably left certain questions about the meaning and significance of the data unanswered.

The remainder of this chapter reports on some findings of a study designed to test the impact of providing an advocacy service to Pakistani and Bangladeshi families with a disabled child aged between 5 and 19 years. The first stage of the study involved establishing baseline data about the social circumstances and service needs of the families concerned and it is this data which is reported here. The findings are presented in three main sections:

- evidence of material disadvantage
- access to services and support
- family support and social well-being.

As this was a study of just 20 families, the objective is to add depth to the evidence outlined above that disadvantage and discrimination are compounded for minority ethnic families with a disabled child, not to provide comparison with the national postal surveys. It aims to add to understanding of the lives of such families, the barriers they face in accessing services and the consequences for their well-being. The disadvantaged circumstances the families described and the absence of well coordinated services are further evidence of the presence of institutional discrimination in health, education and social care services.

Methodology

Pakistani and Bangladeshi families were identified to take part in an action research project. A new advocacy service was established by East Birmingham Family Service Unit (EBFSU), a local project of a national voluntary sector organisation providing preventive and support services for children and families. For the research project, 20 families to whom the advocacy service was to be provided were identified from new cases referred to EBFSU between October 1999 and March 2000. All contained one or more severely impaired children aged between 5 and 19 years old. Families were interviewed initially to identify their existing needs prior to receiving the help of an advocate.

Interviews were conducted with adult family members in their own homes at a time convenient to them. Each interview involved a semi-structured questionnaire devised by the research team which explored the family's social situation and contact with service providers. Each participant was also screened for psychological well-being using the General Health Questionnaire (GHQ28; Goldberg 1981), for social support using the Social Support Questionnaire (SSQSR; Saranson *et al*. 1987) and for self-esteem using the the Self-Esteem Scale (SES; Rosenburg 1965).

Results

The families

Fifteen families were of Pakistani origin and five were of Bangladeshi origin. The families were referred via local schools, community nurses, health visitors and social workers. In each family, all those adults who were involved in the caring of the disabled child were interviewed. In total, 39 people were interviewed: 20 mothers, 16 fathers and three family members who played a role in caring. We had anticipated that carers might also include older siblings and other extended family members. However, of the 20 families interviewed, only three carers were not parents. These carers included one sister and two grandmothers. Mothers were the main carer in 19 families and a father was the main carer in one family.

Four families did not have a father living in the household; all these families were of Pakistani origin. This was more than a quarter of the Pakistani families. It is unclear whether this is unusual, as the incidence of single-parent Pakistani families is unknown and, in any case, the numbers involved in this study are very small.

The average age of mothers and fathers was 35 years and 41 years respectively. The majority of families had more than four children, two families had seven children and five families had six children. Families had an average of 4.5 children. The majority of parents were first-generation Pakistanis or Bangladeshis. Only four parents were second-generation Pakistanis. All four of these were married to first-generation Pakistanis.

Findings: evidence of material disadvantage

Housing

Eight families out of 20 (40%) owned their own homes, six (30%) families lived in local authority housing and six (30%) lived in houses provided by private landlords.

Thirteen out of the 20 families (65%) said that their house was unsuitable. Of these, seven families (35%) felt that their house was not appropriate for adaptation and wished to move to a more suitable house. The other five (25%) had a range of reasons for the unsuitability of their house, from small items such as a raised stand to reach the toilet to needing a suitable area for their child to play in.

The seven (35%) families who said that their current accommodation was not suitable for adaptations and wished to move lived in some very adverse conditions. These families had severely disabled children, did not have lifting equipment and had to carry their children up and down the stairs. Four of these families (20%) slept downstairs in fairly small back living rooms. In this room they had the child's bed, and one or two settees. In the daytime, they used it as a sitting room and in the evening they slept on the settees so that they could keep an eye on their disabled child. These parents had been sleeping like this for many years and all four of them have been trying to move to suitable local authority accommodation for a number of years.

One father reported that discriminatory attitudes of landlords led to difficulties in finding private rented accommodation. He lived in a three bedroom house with five children and wanted to move. He explained his difficulty in finding accommodation in the private sector:

> Private accommodation is difficult as people see T's disability and will not rent a house to us as they are afraid that he will damage their property.

Employment

Nine families had a father working outside the home. Of those working fathers, five worked in shops or factories and four were self-employed. The self-employed consisted of three taxi drivers and one shop owner. None of the mothers worked at the time of the first interview. During the period of the advocacy project, one mother started work as a dinner lady at the local school. Two mothers who were students were both single parents.

Costs of living and barriers to claiming income

Five (25%) out of the 20 families reported difficulty in managing with their income and eight families stated that there were items that they needed, but were unable to afford. These families reported a need for essential items, including beds, cooker, clothes, washing machine and fridge. A particularly striking finding was that 17 families (85%) were unaware of the Family Fund scheme from which such essential items could have been claimed.

Mothers with partners were, in general, not sure about the benefits that the family was receiving. They told the researchers to ask their husbands about benefits and finances. Benefits were perceived as being stigmatising. For example, one mother believed that they were entitled to family credit. When the father was interviewed he said that he was managing and did not wish to claim benefits as this would not reflect well on him. The mother reported that the family struggled on wages of £150 a week. They had six children. Another mother explained that her husband had not wished to claim benefits for the disabled child as he did not want people to think that he could not look after his child and that they were living off her money. He had been persuaded to claim by a community nurse.

The complexity of the issues surrounding making a benefit claim is exemplified by a third mother, who had been advised to claim benefits in respect of a daughter aged 9 months who needed a lot of care with feeding (she also had a 9-year-old disabled daughter). She was afraid to make the claim for her daughter as she felt that by claiming benefits she would be labeling her baby daughter as disabled and 'tempting fate', as she was afraid that she would also become disabled like her older child. At the time she believed that her baby only needed care with feeding, not that she was disabled.

Findings: accessing services and support

Evidence of problems in accessing services

We asked families about the service providers that each family had contact with in the 6 months prior to interview. Families reported relatively little contact with professional service providers; few families were closely linked with service providers other than the school and the general practitioner. However, in general, families had difficulty in understanding the role of the service providers, identifying who they were and where they came from. In some cases, families knew nothing more than the first name of a worker who came to the house. [. . .]

The families most likely to be in contact with service providers other than the general practitioner (GP) and the school were those families with children who needed frequent medical care. These families had contact with community nurses and one family had contact with a health visitor. The person who had the most contact with the service providers depended on which of the two parents spoke English. [. . .]

Service providers who were particularly difficult to identify were housing and social services. Only one family had a social worker whom they could name. Housing staff were difficult to identify as the Housing Department did not allocate a named individual worker to a family.

Since families found it difficult to recall who visited and which organisations these visitors came from, there may be more service providers involved than we were able to identify. However, from the families' perspective, if a user cannot describe who a service provider is, where they come from, what services they can provide or how to contact them, their value is substantially reduced.

TABLE 13.1 Services families wanted contact with

Would like contact with	Number of families
Respite care	6
Practical help	5
Housing	5
Social worker	4
Somewhere to get a wheelchair	2
Someone to help with child's behaviour	2
Mobility allowance section	1
Somewhere to get household items, such as bed, fridge	1
Physiotherapist	1
To know more about the illness	1
Someone to sort out footpath	1

Outstanding service need

Fourteen parents stated they wanted contact with service providers. They had either previously been in contact with these services but had lost contact or had never been in contact before. Number of service needs for families ranged from seven families who had at least three service needs they wanted help for to seven families who had fewer than three service needs they wanted help for. A number of parents did not know which service to contact but stated they wanted to contact a service that would satisfy their stated need (Table 13.1).

Families' experience of and contact with professionals and services

Schools. Parents said that they visited their child's school when they needed to. In general, the majority reported being satisfied with the school and felt that the schools were very good at looking after their children. One mother said that her child was doing things at school she did not do at home. She had learnt to use the toilet and was using Makaton language skills at school, even though she would not use it at home. She recalls finding out whilst visiting one day at school that her daughter was able to feed herself.

> I found out that she eats by herself at school one day, I saw her eating there and I was gob smacked, so now I cut her food and she eats it.

However, three families stated that they were afraid of visiting the school, as seeing the disabled children scared them. These families did not attend school reviews, as they stated that they found it distressing. We discovered from the schools concerned that very few of our parents visited the school for annual reviews.

Four parents had areas of dissatisfaction with the school. Three families were concerned that their children came home with bruises. One mother whose child came home with self-inflicted bruises felt that the school was not doing enough to keep him happy. She commented that:

if H is happy he won't bang his head on the floor, I think that they should take extra care, the school is a special school, that's what special should mean, that they should give him special attention. Two weeks ago he came home with a big cut on his head, last week he had a black eye. I didn't have the time to go to the school because I am under so much exam pressure, trying to study, but I spoke to the school guide (*a school guide accompanies the children on the bus to and from school*) and she said she didn't know what happened. Nobody had told her.

One family was concerned about the standard of their children's education (they had two children who went to a special school). The mother said:

I feel that the school system is hopeless and that the children have got worse. They can't write, they were not this bad before they went to school, but since they went to this school they have got worse. They have picked up bad behaviour which they bring home and then carry out at home. S bites her hand and sucks her thumb, she never used to do this before she started at this school. I think she has picked up this habit from other children.

The extent to which a disabled child will be able to meet the parents' expectations for literacy and writing may be limited. In this case, after interviewing the teachers it was apparent that the parents had expectations for their child that exceeded the school's assessment. The family reported having little contact with the school. Such a gap in expectations and accompanying dissatisfaction with services is the kind of outcome that is likely if communication between service providers and families is weak.

Social services. Two families received help from social services in the form of extra care hours provided by a care worker. However, they reported problems in getting these hours sorted out. Both mothers said that social services often took weeks to deal with a request for care hours and then often allocated hours when they were no longer needed.

Four families stated that when they needed to contact social services they had to speak to the duty social worker. These families said that they got extremely frustrated with having to tell their story again and again every time they spoke to social services, and to a different social worker each time. The social services department had recently introduced a new system where families have to leave a message and then someone rings them back, which caused much frustration.

Respite care. Of the 20 main carers, only one mother said that she had recently had a break from caring. She had one disabled daughter, who she had left with her husband and mother-in-law while she went to Pakistan. However, the belief that Pakistani and Bangladeshi parents with a disabled child are not interested in respite care was not confirmed. Nine of the families said they did not want respite care, but three families (15%) had taken up respite care in the past year and wanted to do so again, and a further six families (30%) who had not had respite care wanted it. Two mothers (10%) were not sure about respite care, but said that they would consider it if they needed to. [. . .]

Access to appropriate housing. Seven families were waiting to be moved to a new property. These families have been waiting for many years with little recent contact. [. . .]

Housing services were reported by a number of families to be unsympathetic. One family reported an attitude that can be seen as lacking in cultural awareness. The parents had six children and wanted to be moved to a larger house with more bedrooms. They had a daughter in her early twenties living with them. The housing officer had advised them that their daughter should move out and get a place of her own. This annoyed them as they said that if the officer had been Pakistani then they would have understood that Pakistani families do not let their daughters live on their own.

GPs. Families did not report any problems with the doctor and said that they were happy with the service received from the family doctor. This service is the one with which families had the most contact. However, contact with the GP had clearly not provided a gateway to the range of health, social care and other services which families would have valued.

Hospital specialists. In seven families, the disabled children were currently under the care of a hospital specialist. Two fathers and one mother were able to name who they saw at the hospital. Six out of seven mothers knew neither the name of the specialist nor the hospital. Two families reported missing hospital appointments for their child. One mother said that they found it difficult to take their son by car and taxis cost a lot of money, so they missed many appointments. Another family reported that they missed their last appointment to see the specialist as they had forgotten.

Community nurses and health visitors. Four families reported contact with a community nurse and one with a health visitor. These families were very happy with the health visitor and community nurse involvement, and the support that they received from them. They said that the nurses, as well as helping them with the child's welfare, also helped them fill in forms for housing, social service care hours and occupational therapy services.

Physiotherapists. None of the parents had had contact with a physiotherapist in the past 6 months. The reason for this may be that the physiotherapists have all their contact with the child at the school. It is of concern that parents have little contact with physiotherapists and also that parents may not even be fully aware of the role of the physiotherapist. One family were not sure what the equipment they had been given was for – they sent it to school, but were not sure if the school were using it.

> He goes to hospital and he has these clothes to straighten his legs. Mom sends the clothes to the school and the school are supposed to put the clothes on him. They said that they would do it. They think that by having these clothes we might be able to straighten his legs but they're not sure. I'm not really sure what the clothes are supposed to do. [. . .]

An important barrier to access

Families were asked if they thought that the ethnicity of the service provider was important in service provision. Eight parents said that the ethnicity of the service provider was important. The majority of these were mothers and the main reason given for ethnicity being important was language barriers.

> If they had an Asian assistant at the school then we would have somebody who could speak my wife's language and she would be willing to go to school.

> It would help if somebody spoke Urdu but I managed to communicate with her (school nurse). My main problem is language.

> It would be better if someone spoke my language then I could ask the questions without an interpreter.

One parent's response suggested that more than just language was at issue:

> It would be a great peace for me if I could directly understand and speak to a Bengali doctor. It would really be peace of mind for me.

However, another mother talking about her experience with Asian staff within the Housing Department stated that *'ethnicity can make things worse, when there are Asians who do not listen.'*

Findings: family support, mental health and social well-being

The belief that extended families are a rich source of help in Asian families was not evident in this sample. Only two mothers had help from a member of the extended family, the help mainly consisting of babysitting. This is a much lower level of support than that found in the national study of mainly white families in which one in five parents stated that they were helped a lot by their family (Beresford 1995).

Parents from minority ethnic groups and those with low incomes have previously been reported as less likely to belong to a support group (Beresford 1995). None of the parents in our study belonged to a support group and only two parents had contact with another parent of a disabled child. Three mothers expressed the view that they would like to meet other mothers with disabled children.

One in five mothers also reported no help from their partner. This is similar to Beresford's (1995) findings, in which one in five respondents stated that they received little or no help from a partner. Not receiving any help or break from caring inevitably leads to tiredness. Physical energy is an important coping resource and, as a result of increased workload, parents with a disabled child have an increased vulnerability to stress.

Not surprisingly, given the previous evidence, we found that not only were Pakistani and Bangladeshi families in the study socially and economically deprived, they also suffered from high levels of anxiety and depression. Mothers were found to report substantially more somatic symptoms, anxiety and insomnia, and symptoms of severe depression than fathers. Altogether, 11 out of 39 parents (28%) were found to be above the severe-depression threshold score of 10. This included eight mothers (40%) and three fathers (19%). [. . .]

In addition to being amongst the most social and economically deprived in the population, doing most of the caring and receiving little or no social support outside the family, some women also reported experiencing domestic violence and/or being blamed for bearing a disabled child. Four women reported incidents of continual domestic violence. Those women also reported that they did all the caring duties concerning the disabled child and that their husbands gave little or no help. [. . .]

Five of the women said that their partners blamed them for having a disabled child. One mother said her husband would not accept that his daughter was disabled, so she had left him after years of physical abuse. Six mothers reported that their marital relationship was directly affected as a result of having a disabled child. Two of these women's husbands had left them. They explained why.

> My husband blamed me for this (having a disabled child), he said that it is my fault . . . he never comes to see him . . . he says if I marry again he will take H.

> My husband couldn't take the responsibility for A, she needed a lot of care and attention so he left.

One mother had left her husband temporarily as he blamed her for producing a disabled child.

> Because of the disabled child we had lots of family problems, when I was expecting the second baby, (her first child is disabled) I left my husband. Some

people mediated and helped us get back together. He used to tell me that I was an unlucky person and that is why this has happened to me. Now that we have this house provided by the council for A he doesn't say such nasty things about the child as he can see the benefits.

Discussion and conclusion

The evidence of this small-scale study complements and supplements the data available from the national surveys about the experience of families with one or more disabled children. It reinforces the understanding of disability as a product of impairment coupled with socially created discrimination rather than individual tragedy. It demonstrates again that families of disabled children are caught up in the disadvantage which results. It extends knowledge of the ways in which different dimensions of structural and individual discrimination, based in disability, 'race' and gender, interact to create inequality and unjust suffering. A number of significant points emerge, of relevance to policy makers, practitioners and researchers, as well as to disabled people and the disability movement.

This study suggests that there may be a significant number of families with severely disabled children in the UK who are not known to and do not know of the Family Fund, which has been set up to provide basic equipment, labour saving devices and other necessary everyday household goods. The Family Fund is designed to support families facing the combination of reduced income, reduced prospects and additional costs that characterises the lives of the majority of disabled families. It is likely that families who are not aware of the Fund, or who do not understand the process involved in applying to it, will contain an excess of those for whom English is not a first language, of which the Pakistani and Bangladeshi communities contain substantial numbers. The absence of these families from the Fund's books raises questions about the representativeness of the national studies (Beresford 1995; Chamba *et al*. 1999), which may have under-estimated the level of disadvantage and inadequate access to service provision.

This specific point about contact with the Family Fund can be extended into a second general point: that having contact with one service patently did not ensure that other services were accessed. All the disabled children in these families were attending school and most had been in contact with their GP in the last 6 months. However, contact with other services, desired by the families, had not followed. Neither the health nor education systems offered a clear gateway to information about and access to the range of services that may be available to disabled families.

It is not surprising, therefore, that, in this locality at least, there was also no single point of coordination of services for families, no first point of contact, no one to look at the families' circumstances holistically. Far from service provision being integrated across the different agencies and professionals so that families experienced a seamless, needs-led service, it was the absence of systematic services which came through most strikingly. Undoubtedly, limited skills in the use of English by the families was a major barrier – though not the only barrier – here. Over three decades after the main contemporary period of immigration from the South Asian sub-continent, service providers still had not got effective means of offering services to non-English speakers or to those who are not familiar with the basic structures of the British welfare system. [. . .]

The evidence of this study does not support either the view that 'Asian' families are necessarily part of a care-giving extended family or that Pakistani and Bangladeshi families do not welcome the offer of certain kinds of services, such as respite care. The interviews found a variety of circumstances being faced by families which were diverse in nature; some single parent, some two parent families; some with adults in employment, many without; some with grandmothers providing support, many without. Equally, the families had a variety of expressed needs and attitudes to service provision. As in the case of the majority community, only some families want a break from care provided by the disabled child's overnight stay with paid carers (Beresford 1995). For all parents, the quality of the care being offered – its appropriateness to the needs of the child – is a key dimension of the decision to accept help. Two things are clear: service providers should not make assumptions about the services which a particular family might want or value, and the level of service provision is substantially below that which families currently desire. That applies to Bangladeshi and Pakistani families just as much as, if not more than, other groups.

Finally, the study gives evidence of families who are remarkably resilient. Under profoundly difficult material, practical and emotional circumstances, the parents, particularly the mothers, were continuing to provide care to their children. However, the costs to those families are substantial as evidenced in the high level of psychological ill-health which the parents demonstrated. Neither the disabled children nor their siblings were interviewed for this study, but they undoubtedly also bear the costs of the combination of disadvantaged circumstances and inadequate service provision that has been demonstrated.

This study set out to examine the circumstances of what were likely to be members of the most disadvantaged groups of families with disabled children in the UK, so it is not surprising that disadvantage and institutional discrimination were found. It was set in a particular inner city location and might not reflect the circumstances of similar families across the country more generally. However, the findings parallel and give additional depth of evidence to those national studies to which we have referred throughout and we have little doubt that they could be replicated in many other parts of the country. The fact that the results are expected, should not dull our response. The distance between the experiences of these families, and the model of a security net of welfare services providing care and protection to all the country's children is immense. The widespread disadvantage and discrimination experienced routinely by families with a disabled child in the UK in the twenty-first century is compounded for the families who talked to us by everyday institutional and individual racism that is the backdrop to their lives.

References

Ahmad, W. I. U. (ed.) (2000a) *Ethnicity, Disability and Chronic Illness*. Buckingham: Open University Press.

Ahmad, W. I. U. (2000b) Introduction. In W. I. U. Ahmad (ed.) *Ethnicity, Disability and Chronic Illness*, pp. 1-11. Buckingham: Open University Press.

Beresford, B. (1995) *Expert Opinions: a national survey of parents caring for a severely disabled child*. Bristol: Policy Press.

Beresford, B., Sloper, P., Baldwin, S. and Newman, T. (1996) *What Works in Services for Families with a Disabled Child?* Ilford: Barnado's.

Chamba, R. and Ahmad, W. I. U. (2000) Language, communication and information: the needs of parents caring for a severely disabled child. In W. I. U. Ahmad (ed.) *Ethnicity, Disability and Chronic Illness*. Buckingham: Open University Press.

Chamba, R., Ahmad, W., Hirst, M., Lawton, D. and Beresford, B. (1999) *On the Edge: minority ethnic families caring for a severely disabled child*. Bristol: Policy Press.

Department of Health (2000) *Quality Protects: disabled children, numbers and categories*. London: Department of Health.

Goldberg, D. P. (1981) *The General Health Questionnaire 28*. Windsor: NFER–Nelson.

McClusky, J. and Abrahams, C. (1998) *FactFile '99*. London: NCH Action for Children.

Modood, T., Berthoud, R., Lakey, J., Nazroo, J., Virdee, S. and Beishon, S. (1997) *Ethnic Minorities in Britain: diversity and disadvantage*. London: Policy Studies Institute.

Roberts, K. and Lawton, D. (1998) *Reaching its Target? Disability Living Allowance for Children*. Social Policy Reports No. 9. York: Social Policy Research Unit, University of York.

Rosenburg, M. (1965) *Society and Adolescent Self-image*. Princeton, NJ: Princeton University.

Sarason, I. G., Sarason, B. R., Shearin, E. N. and Pearce, G. N. (1987) A brief measure of social support; practical and theoretical implications. *Journal of Social and Personal Relationships*, **4**, 497–510.

Tozer, R. (1999) *At the Double: supporting families with two or more severely disabled children*. York: Joseph Rowntree Foundation.

Tudor Hart, J. (1971) The Inverse Care Law. *Lancet*, 27 February, 405–12.

It is easy to become caught up in a euphoria about inclusive education and social inclusion. This chapter brings us down to earth with a bump. The account of this research is a powerful reminder of the very significant barriers to inclusion and social justice. It is also, however, a powerful reminder of how important it is that we begin to address these barriers through approaches that involve the school and wider community.

CHAPTER 14

Teachers and Gypsy Travellers

Gwynedd Lloyd, Joan Stead, Elizabeth Jordan and Claire Norris

This chapter discusses some of the findings from a project looking at how teachers in Scotland perceive, and respond to, the culture and behaviour of Traveller children. The authors discuss in particular the extent to which schools respond to cultural diversity when this challenges notions of 'normal' school attendance and behaviour. Important links are made between disciplinary exclusion from school and broader social exclusion.

Introduction

This chapter raises issues about how teachers define discipline and good order in schools. As Munn, Johnstone and Sharp (1998) point out, the level of indiscipline in schools is an emotive topic. Thus any aspect of a pupil's actions which might be seen to be threatening to good order may be viewed negatively by teachers. The study reported here looked at how certain behaviour by children from Gypsy Traveller families can become construed as disruptive to 'good' discipline. There are a number of ways in which this construction of Gypsy Traveller children's behaviour as problematic can be understood. Sometimes this can be seen as lack of cultural knowledge by teachers of Gypsy Travellers' lives, equally sometimes a lack of knowledge, or indeed a rejection, by the pupils of the norms and values of schools. Teachers themselves may often not reflect critically on the culture of schools; rather they may individualise problems, focussing on the single pupil. The position of Gypsy Travellers in Scotland as a marginalised group, many of whom feel under threat from the settled world, can be reflected in their experience of school. There is a parallel here with the experiences of some disabled groups who have argued that the response of the educational system to difference involves a privatising of controversial public issues (Troyna and Vincent 1996).

Gypsy Traveller children in Scotland

The Council of Europe identifies two main groups of Travellers, Gypsy Travellers and Occupational Travellers, the latter group including, for example, Show and barge people. (Others sometimes include a third group, 'new age' travellers.) Our project focused on Gypsy Travellers and Show Travellers; however, the findings discussed below show a more complex situation for Gypsy Travellers, upon whom this paper concentrates.

It is difficult to know the number of Gypsy Travellers in Scotland. Estimates vary from three- to five-thousand nomadic Gypsy Travellers and possibly another twelve-thousand housed (Gentleman 1992; Liegeois 1987). Traditional and understandable fear of authority probably means that any official figures underestimate the numbers who think of themselves as Gypsy Travellers and who share common cultural beliefs (Braid 1997; Reid 1997). There is disagreement among both Traveller communities and academics over the legal recognition of Gypsy Travellers as an ethnic minority in terms of the race relations legislation. Although this is formally recognised through a Court of Appeal judgment in England, this is not always considered to be legally applicable in Scotland (Jordan 1996). [...]

While there is some diversity of opinion over the correct descriptive terminology the term Gypsy Traveller seems to be the most often currently used by organisations representing the community itself, such as the Scottish Gypsy Traveller Association. By Gypsy Traveller we mean those who consider themselves to be part of this community, whether still nomadic or housed, and who share the common knowledge, speech, customs and manners historically associated with that culture. Our definition is, therefore, principally one of self-ascription.

Research previously undertaken by the Scottish Traveller Education Project (STEP) and by Save the Children Fund (SCF) suggests a low level of school attendance by Gypsy Traveller children, especially at the secondary stage (Jordan 1996; SCF 1996). There is an official dispensation which allows for a reduction in the number of school attendances required from Traveller pupils, to allow for seasonal work travelling. Economic and legal changes in recent years do however make it increasingly difficult for Gypsy Travellers to maintain their nomadic life-style.

The research – methods

The impetus for the project was provided by evidence, both anecdotal and from other research in England and Scotland, that some Traveller children were being excluded from school (OFSTED 1996). The research questions sought to explore whether our initial understanding, that Traveller pupils' behaviour was an issue in some schools, was substantiated by closer investigation. If some Traveller pupils' behaviour was an issue, how was it described and made sense of by teachers, pupils and parents? What responses were made to the behaviour and what strategies were used by schools?

Interviews were conducted with a range of staff (31), mainly learning support, guidance and school managers, in twelve schools, urban and rural, where Travellers were known to have attended, and with Show Traveller parents (10) and young people (6) and Gypsy Traveller parents (7) and young people (18) in different parts of Scotland. Traveller support workers, mainly teachers, were also interviewed (15).

Interviewers used a semi-structured interview schedule as a topic guide but our aim was primarily to create an interview climate where teachers, parents, children and young people felt able to talk freely without too much control from the researcher. This approach is described by some researchers as a non-directive interview (Cohen and Manion 1994). This was particularly important for Traveller parents and young people, understandably suspicious, who needed to be reassured that we really were going to listen to what they had to say. Much of the content and direction of the interviews was determined principally by the respondent, the interviewer using the schedule to ask questions or raise issues if these had not come up. (The interview guides are given in the Appendix.) [. . .] Care was taken, however, to avoid making suggestions or leading respondents. The majority of interviews were taped and transcribed; a small number of respondents preferred not to be recorded and in these cases detailed notes were taken.

Some deliberate validation was also built into the project through the process of interviewing of Traveller support staff. Their views were important – as a group they have a mixed 'outsider/insider' status working both on Traveller sites and with numbers of teachers and schools. They were thus able to offer a valuable comparative perspective. In the early stages of the project six Traveller support workers were interviewed together, using focus group techniques and recorded with tape and video. Three were subsequently reinterviewed towards the end of the project with the purpose of obtaining their views of the developing analysis.

We interviewed both housed and mobile Show and Gypsy Travellers, identified and contacted for us by 'gatekeepers', individuals with an existing relationship of trust with Traveller groups. The Travellers interviewed were not chosen as in any way representative of their communities; they had something to say and were willing to talk to us. We recognised that these groups are heterogeneous and so aimed to gather personal experiences from which we could form impressions and develop themes, rather than generalisations.

We make no claim for scientific neutrality, indeed we are explicit that our interest stems from a concern for social justice. [. . .]

The research – findings

The research looked at the school experiences of both Occupational (Show) Travellers and Gypsy Travellers and the whole findings are described in a project report (Lloyd *et al*. 1999). A key finding of the study was the difference in the views of school staff on the two groups of Travellers. Teachers in schools where Show Travellers had attended were almost all highly positive about having Show Traveller pupils in school and did not see their presence as disruptive, other than in relation to the disruption to the routines of the class because of irregular attendance. Although teachers saw irregular attendance and absence from school as perhaps the major issue for both groups, the pupils themselves, Show and Gypsy Travellers, identified name-calling by other pupils as the strongest negative feature of their school experience.

This chapter concentrates on Gypsy Traveller pupils, whose behaviour was perceived by staff to be problematic and who were sometimes formally excluded.

Was the behaviour of Gypsy Traveller children an issue for schools?

There were a wide variety of views and perceptions expressed by the staff interviewed. In some respects they reflect those likely to be argued about all children in school in that some children's behaviour is considered to be a problem by some teachers, in some schools and at some times. The notion of behavioural difficulties is inevitably subjective and contextually varied (Cullen *et al*. 1996; Munn *et al*. 1998).

> You get children with behavioural problems who are Travellers and you get children with behavioural problems who aren't.
>
> (B: Traveller Support)

Most of the school and Traveller support staff did describe some incidents and circumstances where schools had defined the behaviour of some Gypsy Traveller children as problematic. A small number said that there had never been any particular issue with the behaviour of the Traveller children. Sometimes this was then contradicted by reference to circumstances where there had been problems. In some secondary schools not all staff were aware that the school had identified and responded to perceived problems. For example, the behaviour support teacher in a secondary school described the exclusion and referral to the Children's Hearing System of two Gypsy Traveller girls, but two of her colleagues appeared not to be aware of this. In secondary schools there were sometimes quite different views expressed by staff in the same school, for example the four teaching colleagues quoted below.

> We've never had any situation where the Travelling people have been different from anybody else.
>
> (A: Deputy HT, Secondary)

> There are conflicts, I hate to say there is a 'them and us', they have a way of life where they do certainly appear to care for each other but equally well, they see the rest of the community as being the great unwashed where the problems are.
>
> (B: PT Guidance, Secondary)

They voice their opinion in not too pleasant a manner sometimes . . . I could take it because I knew him, but certainly in front of a mainstream class it wasn't acceptable . . . He didn't see a lot of point to the curriculum . . . it was difficult for us too because if he was withdrawn from these classes it meant he was sitting down there and it was time that was special for others too. If he was there, he demanded attention. With the staffing level it was difficult to make sure the others were getting the attention as well. That was a problem.

(C: Special Education Teacher, Secondary)

He had real run ins with authority which was major, quite a major disruption, fighting and swearing and such things. On the other hand he was quite pleasant to adults. He did have a problem with integration . . . there was little parental backup, the parents didn't see the value of school or higher education . . . If we're talking difficulties, the biggest difficulty is attendance, they just don't attend . . . no matter how nice they are, how well they integrate, the attendance thing is always the thing that hits most, even more so than just discipline.

(D: Guidance Teacher, Secondary)

There were no teachers who argued that the behaviour of all Gypsy Traveller pupils was a problem for the school. Several made a point of beginning with a positive statement, even when they subsequently mentioned difficulties with individual children.

For the most part their behaviour is good, if not better than many of their peer group . . . Within the school there is no doubt that we have come up against behavioural problems with the kids . . . we have also had difficulties with those Travellers who have been settled, even though they have been settled for quite some time. One of the major issues is truancy.

(F: PT Learning Support, Secondary)

How did teachers make sense of Traveller behaviour?

Again, there was a considerable range of views and understandings of Gypsy Travellers' actions in school. The interviews often contained quite contradictory observations, for example several teachers stated that they felt that the difficulties presented by a particular pupil were not related to cultural background but then went on to give examples that suggested that the teacher was indeed viewing the behaviour as significantly influenced by their background. Sometimes teachers were emphatic in their view that the cultural background of the pupil was not a factor in the teacher's perceptions, implying that perhaps to recognise difference was in itself inappropriate.

I've never, never thought of him as any of the Travelling people, he was difficult because he could flare up very easily. My impression was that was part of his background and he had a sort of defence mechanism . . . maybe the language is the one thing we've noticed more . . . he's not scared to say what he wanted. I wouldn't say that was typical of Travelling people but he maybe, that might have been that they accepted it more on the site. We've never had any situation where the Travelling people have been different from anybody else

(A: Deputy HT, Secondary)

In some instances the teacher's own implicit prejudice or stereotyping was apparent. For example, a teacher in charge of a secondary special class, where several Gypsy Traveller young people had been placed, talked 'positively' about two pupils, contrasting this with looking like a 'tinker'.

They were very acceptable, they were nicely dressed, they turned up nice, they didn't make themselves different in any way . . . they were actually very clean and tidy . . . they didn't make themselves out to be Tinker girls – their hair was nice and what not . . .

(C: Special Education Teacher, Secondary)

Perhaps paradoxically, the teachers who acknowledged that schools could face problems with the behaviour of Traveller pupils were those with the most knowledge of and empathy with cultural difference, as in the case of Traveller support teachers. They were the most likely to say there is an issue which they see in the schools they visit. They were clearer in their positive acknowledgement of difference and their perception of how this difference might become constructed as difficulty by schools.

Several support teachers and other staff made the point that all children can choose to be difficult in school and also that sometimes Traveller children face difficulties in their lives which are not peculiar to Traveller communities. Thus, though some Traveller children were seen to have required extra support in school because of family bereavement, alcohol or other drug use or physical or sexual abuse, in this respect they would be no different from children from the settled community.

Perceived lack of cooperation in class, e.g. not following instructions

Some difficulties may be the consequence of lack of knowledge. Schools' ability to operate is contingent on pupils knowing how to behave and knowing when they break the rules. Often the Traveller pupils might have missed the beginning of the first class in primary school, may not have been to nursery school and, therefore, have missed the everyday learning about how you act in class.

The boys had no real knowledge of how to behave in a large group . . . sorry, how we expected them to behave, which is maybe a different thing . . . they would sit and talk, shout out, refuse to do any work, walk around the place – which in a class of thirty is something that is very difficult to accommodate . . . I feel that in the case of the Traveller boys they were just behaving normally to them. They weren't setting out to disrupt.

(G: PT Guidance)

The structure of classroom norms may be implicit and difficult for the Traveller child to access. It may represent a difficult transition to insideness for children used to spending much of their time outside.

I think the thing at the P (primary) 1 level with the behaviour is that it is such a culture shock for the child, you know . . .

(E: Traveller Support)

Just a whole new ball game to be even within a building with corridors and so many rooms.

(C: Traveller Support)

And rules – 'you sit down' (in teacher instruction voice).

(F: Traveller Support)

Research into teachers' views of discipline in schools generally suggests that the biggest issue is low level disruptiveness, talking, hindering other children and not cooperating (Munn *et al*. 1998). It was suggested that Gypsy Traveller children may get into trouble for the same kinds of reasons as other children, for example, not having a pencil or not doing their homework, but that for some Traveller children these may happen more often because of the circumstances of travelling and life on site.

Difficulties related to late coming and to absence

Erratic patterns of attendance created difficulties. Problems of attendance were sometimes, but not always, associated with actually travelling. Several teachers mentioned problems of attendance by housed Travellers.

One of the difficulties when they did come back was that if they had been off for a great deal of time, like other kids, they had fallen behind and therefore the disaffection if you like, started at that period when they came back and it was in all subjects.

(F: PT Learning Support Secondary)

Unpredictable patterns of attendance were recognised by all the Traveller support teachers as disruptive to class and subject teachers. Sometimes it may be that this exacerbates a problem a teacher was already having with a class.

> It's a case where fourteen Travellers arrived at a school within a week, most of them settled very well but there's five gone into the P1 class and one boy, by anybody's standards anywhere, has behavioural problems. You get children with behavioural problems that are Travellers and you get children with behavioural problems that aren't. But it has had a catalytic effect on the class who were difficult anyway. There is one child who has come in who the other children perceive as being beyond control. And it's not just that he is a problem in that class, but he has awakened, or reawakened, the possibility for that type of behaviour, the other children had settled quite well. So in terms of that class, yes the child is being perceived as a huge problem. They're trying to deal with it positively but there is a huge problem.
>
> (D: Traveller Support)

> Well you can appreciate you've got bad days and you've got a class like P's class which is disruptive and then you've got them settled to work and then the door opens and P comes in
>
> (J: Learning Support T Secondary).

Problems to do with missed curriculum and specific learning dificulties

Frustration was expressed by several teachers recognising the difficulties presented by irregular attendance and their wish to see children making identifiable progress.

> If they move between areas, move between schools, they might find that in one school they have done a section of work, when they get to another school they are only starting it so they repeat it all but they've missed the bit that they did before.
>
> (B: PT Guidance Secondary)

Several teachers suggested that sometimes difficulties in schools might be related to a high level of dyslexia amongst Gypsy Traveller boys. This is a problematic assertion as it is difficult to separate the notion of a specific learning difficulty from the overall issues associated with a historically non-literate culture, inconsistent school attendance and missed learning.

Problems with friendships/peer group relationships

Varying patterns of attendance were also seen to lead to difficulties with friendship and peer group relationships.

The poor attendance means that they never establish real friendships because it happens so often. They're always on the outskirts in the class if they're not attending regularly. They're always on the fringe because they haven't built up relationships over the years and if they find they can't build relationships with children it's very difficult for them to mix in.

(H: Traveller Support)

Some teachers felt that it was difficult for Gypsy Traveller pupils to establish friendships outwith their own community. Sometimes children would spend break times checking on the wellbeing of siblings or of other Traveller children.

Difficulties related to name-calling / bullying of Traveller pupils and fighting

Some teachers felt that there would always be name-calling.

I would say that you are bound to get a bit of name-calling and that sort of thing, I think that's inevitable . . . I'm sure there's a bit of name-calling but they never complain about it . . . they tend to tough it out.

(D: Guidance T, Secondary)

Others thought that it was not an issue in their school although the evidence from the interviews with children, families and Traveller support teachers suggests that it is virtually universal and that many pupils do not feel supported by schools in facing it.

(Q. What about relationships with other children?) Poor. Two reasons: firstly they kept themselves to themselves, they don't naturally mix, this is girls and boys: secondly because of the background they come from, they do at times come up smelling or dirty, they get called 'tinkie' or 'blacko', in this part of the country it's 'tinkie' and 'blacko'. To this they would rarely react violently, they would come and complain and would use this as an excuse for not coming to school for the next three weeks.

(G: PT Guidance, secondary)

I think he gets on well, but he is a wee bit smelly at times, a wee bit scruffy, he has an English accent, so he is different and he will be picked upon from time to time. Not because he's a Traveller but because he's different.

(A: Deputy HT Secondary)

There's a lot of prejudice in the area about Traveller children. They use a horrible word, I can hardly bring myself to say the word, but they say 'scoot' as a derogatory word for a travelling pupil. They would use it for any one they saw who was dirty or scruffy. That is one of the problems, I have to say, that many

travelling children are not very clean which other children don't like at all . . . it
really is a form of racial prejudice and it has to be tackled as seriously as that.

(N: Traveller Support)

[. . .] For most teachers in schools the bullying and name-calling was not seen as part
of an overall racism, although one or two did see this broader view which also tended
to be expressed more often by Traveller support teachers.

Certainly the anti bullying policy and strategies (are) in place within the school.
It's not seen as a racial problem just as a general bullying thing.

(N: Traveller Support)

A number of teachers suggested that bullying and name-calling were sometimes used
as an 'excuse' not to attend school.
Most schools mentioned fighting in the playground as an issue, often as a response
to name-calling but also sometimes between Gypsy Traveller children.

. . . it's playground and it usually focuses on the boys because there is a tendency
for them to be fiercely competitive. They're fiercely competitive among
themselves and it leads to rough play. If they have a fall out, a quick aggressive
battering is a very quick quite satisfactory solution to them.

(HT Primary)

It (i.e. exclusion) was for fighting. One boy was swearing at the teacher but
mainly it's been fighting outside school.

(N: Traveller Support)

The issue of racist name-calling and bullying is addressed in more detail elsewhere
(Lloyd *et al.* forthcoming). It may be that teachers in some schools have not reflected
on their duties under the law to provide education free from discrimination and
harassment or that they do not perceive this to be an issue with respect to Gypsy
Traveller pupils. Traveller support staff were more likely to perceive the bullying and
harassment as racist than teachers in schools.

Style of addressing adults and sense of justice

These were commonly identified as an issue for schools. Children often addressed
school staff as if they were equal adults, sometimes making personal comments which
the teachers found difficult. One Traveller support teacher argued that Gypsy Traveller
children have not learned the 'social dishonesty' expected in the settled world.

. . . if you are talking to a Traveller child, he or she will speak to you as an adult. Now in school that can appear to be cheeky because children tend on the whole not to speak to teachers like that.

(A: Traveller Support)

[. . .] I think one of the difficulties is the difference in Travellers' perceptions of fairness. It's difficult because by the time a Traveller boy is twelve he is thinking of himself as a man and speaking on equal terms with adults and this is not acceptable (to teachers). It's just so difficult to match the registers.

(L: Traveller Support)

Several teachers like the one above commented on the sense of fairness expressed by Gypsy Traveller children and suggested that this sometimes got them into trouble at school.

The boy that was with us lasted till about the end of 3rd year then he just couldn't cope any more. It was very frustrating for us because he was quite a bright boy and what we could offer him in his support class did not give him the breadth and balance, it did not give him what he needed. Now for him to conform in a mainstream situation was very difficult for him, he was bright, he was cheeky, he had to be disciplined. He had a real sense of justice if he thought something was wrong. He had his own values if he thought somebody was being unfairly treated. His language, if he did get annoyed he found that very difficult to control and of course in certain situations it doesn't always work.

(C: Special Education Teacher)

Difficulties associated with transition to secondary school

Lack of knowledge of school and classroom routines is also mentioned in relation to the transition from primary to secondary school when Gypsy Traveller pupils may arrive late and miss the introduction and induction phase. Attendance becomes much more sporadic and tails off completely for many Gypsy Traveller pupils (SCF 1996). Peer group relationships and bullying may also become more problematic.

It's like going from P7 to secondary, October is too late to try and fit into S1

(F: Traveller Support)

Once the boys reached the age of 12, 13 they didn't want to come to school, they were disruptive, they couldn't be put in a class with other children, they just completely disrupted the place and we found that a tremendous problem.

(G: PT Guidance secondary)

Another issue identified at the secondary school level was refusal to participate in particular subjects, for example PE. Several teachers argued that some secondary subjects were seen as irrelevant for Gypsy Traveller pupils. As for other pupils it may also be the case that sometimes a particular subject may be liked because of the teacher who teaches it:

> He liked science because he got on well with the science teacher and the science teacher really talked to him and they really got on well.
>
> (C: Special Education Teacher)

Discipline at secondary level becomes more complex as subject teachers vary in their approach:

> Some secondary teachers are very free and easy about things like chewing gum and what the noise level is . . . and that's accepted that within a secondary school there are variations.
>
> (J: Traveller Support)

Difficulties deriving from travelling life and being on a site

Traveller support staff felt that school colleagues had little understanding of the impact of life on a site, rather than in a house or of the culture and customs of travellers living in a trailer.

> One of the things I feel about issues around behaviour is, for example, within a school, teachers don't understand the perspective of Traveller life and how the child's behaviour can change totally when they start getting ready to leave. There are other examples like a funeral or something major going on at the site, just like children in houses where they have something going on with their family but Travellers have more incidents like that and it comes through more in their behaviour.
>
> (A: Traveller Support)

Difficulties associated with local neighbourhood poverty, and delinquent subcultures

Several teachers mentioned that both housed and nomadic Gypsy Traveller families often live or stay temporarily in areas of multiple deprivation. Changing patterns of employment may make it difficult for Gypsy Travellers to obtain work and some were seen by schools to be living in circumstances of great economic disadvantage. A few teachers, especially where there were locally housed Gypsy Traveller families, talked about the problems for the school and for the families where Gypsy Traveller young people had become involved in the local delinquent subculture, for example, in one case with drug dealing. Some Gypsy Traveller parents also referred to this and, for some, their fears of their children getting into this kind of trouble were an argument against participation in secondary education.

Gender issues

Most of the teachers' views differentiated between boys and girls. As has been found elsewhere, boys were more likely to be in trouble in school, to be seen as aggressive and more confrontational (Crozier and Anstiss 1995; Lloyd 1992). Girls were more likely to be seen as accommodating to the school norms.

> It's hard to say but our experience would be the girls integrated better. I can think of several girls, P's sister for example, who came into school and had friends and went through school and she was – you'd never know she was a Travelling person, you never associated her with P. She fitted in perfectly well, had friends, came to school.
>
> (D: Guidance T Sec male)

When girls were difficult they were regarded as particularly problematic, especially when they were involved in violence.

Exclusion

Although formal disciplinary exclusion did happen to Gypsy Traveller pupils, it seemed often more likely that conflict with teachers led to non-attendance. Where pupils were excluded there were issues around the formal procedures, for example, where the procedure was to write formally to parents inviting them to attend a meeting before their child would be readmitted it was often the case that this meeting never happened. Some Gypsy Traveller parents may not be able to read such communications. Often, however, the pupil may be removed from the roll by their parents after a problem before reaching the stage of exclusion.

Some teachers suggested that Traveller pupils may have consciously or unconsciously behaved in a disruptive way leading to exclusion from school as a strategy to avoid attending school.

> . . . he was finally excluded for urinating in a bowl up at home economics and making it very obvious that he done this and so on and so forth. Whether he was deliberately trying to get himself excluded, or he was making a statement, I'm not a hundred per cent certain, but he was not a pleasant lad to have within the building.
>
> (N: AHT Secondary)

One support teacher saw the continual exclusion of a boy from school in the context of what was being done by neighbours to his family.

> One of the wee boys I'm working with just now is in a situation where the family have been forced from the housing scheme they were in because of discrimination. His behaviour has always been a problem and he's been excluded.
>
> (P: Traveller Support)

Another saw the exclusion having a negative impact on a pupil.

> In one particular case, I think this boy changed remarkably after he was excluded. I think he saw it as unjust. He's in secondary school and he became very withdrawn and quite hostile. He's been in a lot of confrontations with teachers since then although he hasn't actually been excluded . . . He's now stopped attending and we feel it stemmed from the exclusion and his perception of a strong sense of injustice . . . I think that he felt he was in the right to fight back.
>
> (N: Traveller Support)

Although most of the excluded pupils mentioned were boys there was evidence of the exclusion of a few girls. Where there was exclusion it tended to be for reasons similar to those found in other research on exclusion, i.e. violence between pupils or general disruptiveness (Cullen *et al.* 1996; Lloyd 1999).

Lack of confidence by teachers

Several teachers and Traveller support teachers suggested that sometimes a lack of confidence on the part of colleagues may lead to difficulties in class.

> I think a lot of it just depends on how secure the teacher feels. And if they feel that they're in a class where they're on the borderline of being in control of that class, then anything like that is going to increase the level of insecurity and they're going to feel threatened, so they're going to see it as a behavioural issue. Whereas the teacher who feels perfectly confident in their relationship with the other children in the class, isn't going to feel threatened by that and it isn't an issue.
>
> (D: Traveller Support)

Teachers and schools may be afraid of the impact on the class or the school of the presence of Gypsy Traveller pupils:

> . . . there was a family who were known in the area, who had been made homeless and were living outside the area but because they had just lost their dad; there were nine children, it was two who were secondary age and the dad had been

killed in a terrible road accident, just months before, and had been made homeless at the same time and they were living in temporary homeless accommodation and the mother thought for stability's sake the best thing to do was to get back to the school . . . the school said no way are we letting these two in. It would undermine the entire school and the school formally believed this.

(H: Traveller Support)

The school eventually agreed a compromise arrangement of part-time attendance:

. . . they got a part-time learning support teacher just for them and they were not allowed to do anything without that teacher being with them, they weren't allowed to go the toilet, they were kept in and couldn't have lunch with the other kids.

(H: Traveller Support)

Even when teachers are positive and supportive they may sometimes feel insecure about how to approach Traveller children. One Traveller support teacher described her first meeting with a group of Gypsy Traveller pupils and feeling that her college teacher training had not prepared her for this.

. . . they were put in a little room on their own and told that a teacher was going to come and be working with them . . . I tried saying to them 'What would you like to do?' and I was trying to be really positive about it and all I got was 'No way am I going to talk to you, we don't need another teacher, we've had enough of people like you coming in, we liked our last teacher, what are you doing here?' It was so negative from them . . . in fact after a few months it was good but I did feel threatened. I felt like any minute one of them was going to throw a chair at me.

(J: Traveller Support)

Discussion

The OFSTED report in England (1996) argues that sometimes the behaviour of Gypsy Travellers can be misjudged and this is supported by our evidence. From our interviews with teachers there was also sometimes a high level of understanding and tolerance shown by some teachers towards certain types of behaviour that may be considered as part of Gypsy Traveller culture. Although the behaviour of Gypsy Traveller pupils may be perceived as a problem, often this is understood as the 'fall-out' from repeated and sustained absences. The reasons for many such absences may be from self-exclusion or exclusion as the result of racist name-calling, or because of regular absences due to travelling. It was clear that some teachers did see some Gypsy Traveller children having behaviour difficulties but many also emphasised that other children from the Gypsy Traveller community showed good behaviour and furthermore that most of the school's behaviour problems were created by other kids from the settled community.

The findings did, therefore, confirm our initial understanding that the school behaviour of some Gypsy Traveller pupils was seen as problematic by school staff. Some of the teachers who were interviewed made sense of it by contetxualising it within an understanding of the culture of Gypsy Travellers. Other teachers either did not have much knowledge of Gypsy Travellers' lives or, like the rest of the community, had partial, stereotyped or even prejudiced views. Equally a lack of knowledge, or indeed a rejection, by Gypsy Traveller pupils of the norms and values of schools was seen by staff as underpinning their actions. Staff in schools rarely reflected critically on the culture or organisation of their schools, tending, as we argued earlier, to see problems in individual terms. Traveller support staff were more aware of the interaction between the child and their culture and the norms and values of schooling.

There was a great deal of evidence from our interviews of individual teachers and schools taking action to facilitate the education of their Traveller pupils. There were several different strategies and responses discussed that accepted some of the practicalities of nomadism and worked with these, rather than against them, with variable success. Other responses may have exacerbated the social and peer group problems that may be associated with nomadism, for example when Gypsy Traveller pupils were segregated in school from other pupils.

In most schools there was a lack of awareness of the extent of name-calling or a reluctance to see it as an issue and, therefore, little attention was paid to addressing it as a school problem (Troyna and Hatcher 1992). From interviews with Gypsy Traveller parents and children it seems that much of what the school sees as indiscipline in the form of violence may be in response to name-calling – several pupils talked of the importance of fighting back when there was name-calling in the playground. Some schools are failing to make the connection between discrimination in the wider community and what happens in schools. When some teachers perceive an inappropriate or excessive concern with their rights by Gypsy Traveller pupils they may not understand that their lives may be characterised by a struggle to achieve what are seen as basic rights and that a strong response to injustice reflects a life where injustice is experienced as routine.

Kenny (1997) argues that 'Travellers do not claim to be completely different, they simply refuse to be measured by the norms of the sedentary' (p.25). Traveller support staff who were interviewed had made an effort to make sense of this to the teachers in the primary and secondary schools and attempted to mediate between the Gypsy Traveller families and the schools. For many teachers there appears to be some confusion/tension between their understandings of some behaviour as possibly culturally defined and their desire not to discriminate against their Traveller pupils. This often results in statements which deny difference and stress the particularity of the situation, which itself may lead to failure of the school to respond to the particular situation of some Traveller children, where an understanding of their cultural background and experiences could lead to a more empathetic response by the school. Sometimes an assertion that 'they are no different' or 'they are never treated differently from anyone else' may suggest a lack of recognition of the issue of difference. The recent Lawrence Inquiry has also re-emphasised the importance of the notion of institutional racism, which, as defined by the CRE, '. . . operates through the normal workings of the system rather than the conscious intent of the prejudiced individual' (Commission for Racial Equality 1985: 2).

The literature on disciplinary exclusion relates this to wider ideas of social exclusion and to the processes by which certain groups of pupils may be devalued, particularly in a climate of emphasis on formal academic achievement (Booth 1995). Other research has identified the complex ways in which race and gender stereotyping leads to the exclusion of other disadvantaged social groups, for example working-class black boys in England (CRE 1997). Blyth and Milner and others have investigated the ways in which miscommunication can lead to confrontation in school (Blyth and Milner 1996). They argue that discipline is negotiated between teachers and pupils and that this negotiation is more complex for children from minority groups. [. . .]

Although the number of Gypsy Traveller pupils in Scottish schools is not large, a discussion of teachers' views does raise some important issues about the ability of schools to respond to children who challenge the 'normality' of school attendance and behaviour. (Other children also do this, for example others with intermittent attendance such as children with chronic illness, and truants). Gypsy Traveller pupils may challenge the fundamental and often unspoken bottom line of schooling which is that you come every day and do as you are told. There have always been groups of children who challenge these rules and schools vary considerably in their ability to include them. As Slee (1996) argues, the search for equity is itself a challenge to the structure and culture of schooling. By seeing these issues in individual terms, by not recognising difference, schools may continue merely to focus on behaviour, rather than explore the institutional response of the education system to a marginalised community.

References

Blyth, E and Milner, J. (1996) Black boys excluded from school; race or masculinity issues? In Blyth, E. & Milner, J. (eds) *Exclusion from School*. London: Routledge.

Booth (1995) Mapping inclusion and exclusion: concepts for all? In Clark, C., Dyson, A. and Millward, A. (eds) *Towards Inclusive Schools*? London: David Fulton.

Braid, D. (1997) The construction of identity through narrative: folklore and the travelling people of Scotland. In Acton, T. and Mundy, G. (eds) *Romani Culture and Gypsy Identity*. Hatfield: University of Hertfordshire Press.

Cohen, L. and Manion, L. (1994) *Research Methods in Education*. (4th edn) London: Routledge.

Commission for Racial Equality (CRE) (1985) *Reactions to the Swann Report*. London: CRE.

Commission for Racial Equality (CRE) (1997) *Exclusion from School and Racial Equality. A Good Practice Guide*. London: CRE.

Crozier, J. and Anstiss, J. (1995) Out of the spotlight: girls' experience of disruption. In Lloyd-Smith, M. and Dwyfor Davies, J. (eds) *On the Margins. The Educational Experience of Problem Pupils*. Stoke on Trent: Trentham.

Cullen, M. A., Johnstone, M., Lloyd, G. and Munn, P. (1996) *Exclusion from School and Alternatives*. Three reports to the Scottish Office. Edinburgh: Moray House.

Gentleman, H. (1992) *Counting Travellers in Scotland: the 1992 picture*. Edinburgh: Scottish Office.

Jordan, E. (1996) *Education for Travellers: towards a pedagogy for the protection of diversity*. Paper presented at ATEE Annual Conference, Oslo.

Kenny, M. (1997) *The Routes of Resistance: Travellers and Second Level Schooling*. Aldershot: Ashgate.

Liegeois, J.-P. (1987) *School Provision for Gypsy and Traveller Children*. Brussels: EC Commission.

Lloyd, G. (1992) Lassies of Leith talk about bother. In Booth, T., Swann, W., Masterton, M. and Potts, P. (eds) *Curricula for Diversity in Education*. London: Routledge.

Lloyd, G. (1999) Excluded girls. In Salisbury, J. and Riddell, S. *Gender and Policy and Educational Change: shifting agendas in the UK and Europe*. London: Routledge.

Lloyd, G., Stead, J. and Jordan, E. (forthcoming) Outsiders in School. Paper in process.

Lloyd, G., Stead, J. and Jordan, E., with Norris, C. and Miller, M. (1999) *Travellers at School: the experience of parents, pupils and teachers*. Edinburgh: Moray House.

Munn, P., Johnstone, M. and Sharp, S. (1998) Is indiscipline getting worse? Scottish teachers' perceptions of indiscipline in 1990 and 1996. *Scottish Educational Review*, **30** (2), 157–172.

OFSTED (1996) *The Education of Travelling Children*. London: HMSO.

Reid, W. (1997) Scottish gypsies/travellers and the folklorists. In Acton, T. and Mundy, G. (eds) *Romani Culture and Gypsy Identity*. Hatfield: University of Hertfordshire Press.

SCF (1996) *The Right to Roam: Travellers in Scotland*. Dunfermline: Save the Children Fund.

Slec, R. (1996) Disabilities, class and poverty: school structures and policing identities. In Christiansen, C. and Rizvi, F. *Disability and the Dilemmas of Education and Justice*. Milton Keynes: Open University Press.

Troyna, B. and Hatcher, R. (1992) *Racism in Children's Lives: a study of mainly white primary schools*. London: Routledge.

Troyna, B. and Vincent, C. (1996) The ideology of expertism; the framing of special education and racial equality policies in the local state. In Christiansen, C. & Rizvi, F. *Disability and the Dilemmas of Education and Justice*. Milton Keynes: Open University Press.

Appendix

Schedules used in interviews

These schedules were used flexibly as a topic guide.

School staff

Explain what the research is about. Confidential, no one outside the research team will have access to the data, and no schools or individuals will be named in the report.

- How many Travellers attend the school?
  Number in your class?
  Breakdown of number of girls/boys
  How often do they attend?
  What time of year?

- How do you find having Travellers in your class?

- Are there any particular issues which arise when Travellers are in class?
  Are there any particular difficulties?
  Any difficulties experienced with classroom behaviour?
  Difficulties associated with learning difficulties?
  Could you tell us about peer group relationships?

- Are there any Traveller pupils whom you would describe as having behavioural difficulties?
  Could you tell us about that?
  What do you feel are the main difficulties?
  Are there any key differences between Traveller pupils who display difficult behaviour and those who do not?
  Differences between Traveller pupils and other pupils in this respect?

- Why do you think there are/were these problems?
  Intermittent nature of attendance?
  Because of differences in culture?

Curriculum does not meet Traveller pupils' needs?
Traveller pupils' difficult behaviour is different from that of their non-Traveller peers?
Tell us about parent–school communication.

- Has anything been done to address difficult behaviour by these pupils?
  What are the strategies used in class to address such behaviour?
  Same as for other pupils?
  Other in-school support?
  Out of school support?
  Have any Traveller pupils been excluded? How many?
  If so, for what reasons?
  What was the outcome?
  Do you feel any strategies employed have been effective?

- Thinking about the curriculum, do you think it addresses the educational needs of this group of pupils?
  What are the particular difficulties for this group of children in accessing the curriculum?
  If they cannot read or write, what do you do about that?
  Do you feel the curriculum is relevant for this group?
  Do the learning styles of Traveller children match those of non-Traveller children?

- Thinking about the classroom behaviour of both male and female Traveller pupils, do you feel there are any differences in the behaviour of girls and boys?
  Do they reflect those in the non-Traveller population?
  If not, what are the differences?

- What about bullying/name-calling – is this an issue for Traveller pupils?
  How do you respond to it?

- Where do you get your support from?

Traveller children / young people

Introduction – the research we're doing is about how young Travellers feel about school and how they get on at school. None of what you say will go back to the school, it's entirely confidential.

- How many schools did you attend?

- Do your school friends/teachers know you are a Traveller?
  Do you like people to know?

171

- Did you go to school all the time or were you travelling during school time at some points?
  How was it going into school, when the other pupils had been there all the time?

- Did you like going to school?
  What did you like about it?
  What subjects did you like?

- Was there anything you didn't like about school?
  What kind of things?

- What were the teachers like?
  What did you like/dislike about them?

- Did you get on with the other pupils who were in your class?

- Was there ever any name-calling?
  If so, what happened?
  What did you do?
  What did the teachers do?

- Did you ever get into any trouble? If so, how did you feel about that?
  What did the teachers do?
  How did you react?

- What age did you leave school?
  Did you ever think about staying on?

- Looking ahead, what kind of school would you like for your children?

- Is there anything else about your experience of school that we haven't covered in the questions that you would like to tell us?

Thank you for answering our questions.

Travellers are often neglected in discussions and collections about cultural diversity. Yet, as this chapter shows, a good test of a school's inclusivity is its ability to respond positively to diversity, even when this challenges common-sense notions of appropriate school behaviour. As inclusive education gains in strength and impetus, pupils from Traveller families will not necessarily conform to school norms to any greater extent, but they should no longer be characterised as on the margins of school life.

CHAPTER 15

Peer support for young people with same-sex attraction

Colm Crowley, Susan Hallam, Rom Harré and Ingrid Lunt

This chapter is an abridged version of an article that appeared in the journal Educational and Child Psychology[1] with more methodological detail than we have included here. The chapter discusses the lack of support available to lesbian, gay and bisexual young people facing challenges and hostility at school and in their personal lives. Some youth groups have been developing throughout the UK in recent years and the story of one of them is shared here. We are offered insights from the participants of a peer support project in the north of England about their aims, views and experiences, gained through an in-depth research project.

Introduction

In this chapter we set out the views and experiences of four I5- to 16-year-old teenagers (one female, three male) with same-sex sexuality on two related matters of critical importance to them: how they became sidelined and harassed at school to the extent that their studies were disrupted, and their experiences of attending a unique study club for young lesbian, gay and bisexual (LGB) people as a response. The overall purpose of this phase of the research is therefore to gain an appreciation of issues and themes of concern to today's LGB teenagers. The sub-questions of our inquiry explore: what happens from their point of view; how it feels to be them; and their perceptions of the attitudes they encounter. This represents the initial exploratory phase of a more extensive study of identity formation in adolescents with same-sex sexuality. [. . .]

With the assistance of the Young Lesbian Gay and Bisexual Peer Support Project (PSP) in central Manchester, launched two years before (1996), we were able to begin our inquiry with a teenage LGB population concerned about their education, the trained teachers who volunteer to tutor them at the project, and the project's paid youth workers and professional advisers. Young people training and volunteering as peer supporters (some of whom had a role in initiating the project, giving it its peer-led hallmark) also took part in the investigation. [. . .] It is primarily the narratives of young people who sought study support that we present here.

---

[1] For the full account see Crowley, C. *et al.* (2001) Study support for young people with same-sex attraction – views and experiences from a pioneering peer support initiative in the north of England. *Educational and Child Psychology.* **18**(1), 108–24.

Background

In Britain at the time of writing, vexing dilemmas regarding same-sex sexuality persist in education. There is a particular need, as Comely (1993) has noted, for educational psychology services to remedy their failure to address lesbian and gay issues. The present generation of teenagers has become the focus of renewed controversy. Teachers' lack of confidence in responding to the needs of pupils with same-sex sexuality seems due in part to their confusion about the extent to which the Section 28 legislation constrains them (Douglas *et al.* 1997; Douglas *et al.* 1999).

In the past decade attempts to legislate for equality in the age of consent for male same-sex relationships have foundered following emotive debate in which the prevailing views echo a legacy of prejudicial views emanating from British psychiatry and psychology. King and Bartlett (1999) argue, in a critique of their profession's attitudes and practices to date, that the history of the pathologising of same-sex sexuality over the past century has been underpinned by a negative regard derived from social and religious opposition to it, together with the unsupported assumption that sexuality could be altered. Only now, in 2001, is a large-scale systematic study to assess the psychological status, social adjustment, quality of life and mental health care needs of lesbians and gay men in Britain getting under way.

D'Augelli (1999), having undertaken substantial psychological research on adolescents with same-sex attraction in the United States, notes that current research is finding that the lesbian, gay and bisexual (LGB) teenagers of today are coming to terms with their sexual orientation much younger than earlier generations. However, there remains a dearth of research on present-day British LGB adolescents and recent studies have tended to focus specifically on issues of hostility and harassment. Important studies have been Epstein and Johnson's (1994) work on homophobic school cultures and Nayak and Kehily's (1997) study showing young men's investment in heterosexist and homophobic displays. [. . .]

Rivers' recent extended study of bullying experienced by gay men and lesbians in their school years (and its impact on later life) found that it was more severe than general bullying (Rivers 1995a, 1995b, 1996, 2000, 2001). This state of affairs would appear to be compounded by most schools' lack of policies adequate to address the particular problems of homophobic bullying (Douglas *et al.* 1997). [. . .]

Warwick, Oliver and Aggleton (2000), while acknowledging the difficulties of comparison across lesbian, gay and heterosexual populations, conclude from a review of the literature that lesbian and gay young people are far more likely to attempt suicide than young people in general. [. . .]

Coyle (1998) concludes that, although many young lesbian and gay people succeed in resourcefully creating a workable and satisfying sexual identity, nevertheless the formation and negotiation of a lesbian or gay identity poses considerable difficulties for young people in the face of generally negative social attitudes. It seems to us then, that the numerous LGB youth groups in today's Britain provide useful opportunities for young people wanting to 'be themselves' among equals. They provide an experience that contrasts with their typical experience of lack of acknowledgement of their sexual orientation by the school system, combined with negative attitudes and even harassment from their heterosexual peers and society in general.

With this in mind, one of us (CC) set out to find LGB teenagers willing to talk about their sense of who they are, and the newly set up PSP, uniquely incorporating a Study Club, seemed like an excellent place to start. [. . .] One of the aims of the PSP Study Club is 'to provide a *safe space* [our emphasis] for young LGBs to work together, do their homework and get help with their coursework and other study' (Hierons 1998: 5) by way of response to any immediate special educational needs arising for students whose schoolwork is suffering from bullying. This curriculum-based part of the programme, the study support provision delivered by a pool of 20 qualified teachers who had undergone the usual reference and police check procedures for volunteers working with young people, was designed to be complemented by a peer-led workshop-based element dealing with personal and social education with a specific emphasis on LGB issues. This dual emphasis on support with academic achievement and personal development for those young LGBs who sought it, delivered in what Winnicott (1965) might well have agreed is 'a facilitating environment', combined to make the Study Club, the first project of the PSP to be launched, in our view a particularly interesting setting in which to begin our investigation.

Methods

[…] The approach chosen for this study was one that allowed us to access people's personal meanings. Personal accounts of individuals' experiences in narrative form are therefore the primary sources of data, rather than questionnaire or pre-structured interview formats.

The participants in this phase of the ongoing study were 10 young people with same-sex sexuality and 16 professionals (youth workers and teachers) involved in the Peer Support Project. Four of these young people had used the study support provision, and it is their narratives that form the central focus of this paper. The six other young people were involved in peer support. Of the professionals, 10 were teacher volunteers, four were paid project workers and two were advisers to the project. All participants were recruited on the basis of their availability at times when the researcher could visit. They were approached in advance by the PSP organisers, and asked if they wished to take part voluntarily in the research interviews, which were held at the PSP premises. Anonymity (primarily by changing names) and confidentiality were assured; some of the participants nonetheless wished to be identified by their own names.

Data collection took place over a half-year period when I (CC), as the interviewing investigator, made some 10 visits to the project, with a follow-up visit a year later. Single in-depth interviews lasting one to two hours were undertaken with individuals and small groups and were tape-recorded. [. . .] Verbatim transcripts were taken and analysed using computer software. Fieldnotes also formed part of the analysis, which involved drawing out themes and uncovering inconsistencies and contradictions.

Findings

The PSP was recently founded as a small voluntary organisation at the instigation of the staff of part of the city's youth service, Lesbian and Gay Youth Manchester (LGYM) who had seen gaps in the statutory services. PSP aimed to provide 'support for young lesbians, gay men and bisexuals [age range 14–25] through the creation and development of a resource of young peer supporters and peer led services' (Hierons 1998: 5). PSP's first provision was a twice-monthly Study Club for teenage students whose schoolwork was suffering because of homonegative harassment. Volunteers who were qualified teachers delivered the first academic hour, to be followed by a peer-led hour featuring issues of particular importance to young LGBs, which are almost invariably missing at school.

When as the main investigator I began my series of visits to the PSP (autumn 1998) the Study Club was nearing the end of its first year of active provision. But by then, with some 20 keen teacher volunteers available, no students were coming. As this continued throughout the six months of my visits, it was not possible to observe study support in action. Ten young LGBs had used the Study Club prior to this. It was possible to contact half of them again; all readily agreed to come along to talk to me, however one later cancelled due to taking up weekend work, so four were interviewed. In addition, 10 of the teachers, six peer supporters, all four core staff members and some steering group members were interviewed. [. . .]

It is the stories of serious difficulties at school, how they led these particular four young people to attend this unique Study Club for LGBs and their reflections on the part it played in their lives that we set out here. We believe that, although the numbers involved are small, it is nevertheless important to present some examples of how the life world of these young respondents seems to them, particularly so, we feel, at the present time, when young LGBs have been the topic of so much public debate by older generations, a discourse in which their own voices have been significantly missing. Furthermore, while the numbers using this study support initiative have been less than was expected, it constitutes, in our view, a valuable instance of an attempt to respond to special educational needs that otherwise tend to be ignored. The Study Club's existence has provided an opportunity to consider the trajectory of young people aware of the implications of the disruption to their learning, moving from a position of isolation into a supportive setting with the aim of remedying the situation. Extracts from the interview narratives of Violet, Mark, Daniel (all 16) and Dave (15)[2] are therefore presented to illustrate two principal themes of concern to them: the pressure and hassles at school that disrupted their studies; and what the Study Club offered them as a response.

---

[2]   The names of all Study Club users have been changed to maintain their anonymity, although they had all said they wanted their own names to be used.

Pressure and hassles at school that disrupted studies

Mark outlines the particular challenges that young gay people have to contend with at school, certainly those who have not somehow remained 'invisible' to their peers:

> There's a lot of pressure and hassle for young gay students because, even if they're not out, teenagers tend to have this sixth sense to spot lesbians and gay men. They just home in on them and take the piss. So you tend to get a lot of hassle and a lot of disruption in lessons.

Violet tells how pivotal the issue of homosexuality is among groups of boys, and identifies the third year of secondary school (Year 9, at age 13–14) as being of particular note:

> The main insult is 'gay' – well two lads, if one touches another he goes 'oh you're gay, you're gay', and this lad'll get beaten up just for like putting his hand on his mate's arm, you know. It's so intense and it still is with some of the gangs at school. My friends have said to me 'when you're in the third year in school', which is when I got the most hassle, 'the biggest crime is to be gay'. Definitely never be a third year at high school. It's that age when they maybe first discover what homosexuality really is.

Dave is tall and played rugby at school. He says 'I started getting camp since I was about 11.' He has had much hassle in the four years since then, and has felt quite isolated. This has been in spite of the relaxed attitude he feels most of his immediate year group (the girls in particular) have about him being gay. Although he was beaten up once, Dave attributes this not so much to being thought to be gay, but rather to being on his own 'in the wrong place at the wrong time.' However, he reflects that, were he not socially isolated from other boys at school because of his sexuality, he would have the backing of a group of them as friends, functioning as a protective deterrent. Not having this calls for continual vigilance, particularly outside of school. He refers to the 'constant fear' of attack when walking home on his own. As to overt negativity about his (perceived) sexuality, he explains about the sort of direct hassle he regularly receives:

> All the grief I get is sexually oriented so it's all about anal sex and stuff like that, it's like 'Oh, you've been bummed'. I'm like 'Why do you want to know?' They're all like that. Whenever I walk down the corridor they all pin themselves down the wall. […] It's some sort of weird mind thing, boys haven't got open minds at all, the girls have.

Violet also takes the view that boys tend to be more prejudiced about sexual orientation. But she found she got more negative reaction from the girls at school.

You generally find that the boys are a lot more homophobic than the girls, but I got my main hassle from girls. Because I'd have to go in the toilets, and when I'd go in the changing rooms I'd see everyone sort of go 'aargh' and cover themselves up. It's just pathetic the way they deal with it.

The situation for her appears to have been aggravated by her older sister having 'come out' as lesbian at school before leaving:

I'd have gangs following me and there was a lot of name calling, all sort of 'lesbian ', 'leb', stuff relating to being a gay girl, nothing else like 'bitch' or 'cow' or 'slut', it was all related to me being gay. There were lots of stories going round like, 'she was staring at me in the changing rooms the other day.' Because my sister's gay as well they made up this whole story about both my parents being gay, which they're not, and how we're like a big sort of cult, a gay household. People would say things to me like 'oh, so your sister's a lesbian, has she not been like, doing stuff to you, like, abusing you?' so it was a very, very difficult thing to work round. I wasn't actually out, I wasn't particularly out. It was because I had short hair, didn't wear high heels, didn't spend time doing what average 16-year-old girls do. I was going out with a girl, who I changed the name of to the nearest male name, saying 'I'm going out with this boy from …' and because they never saw this boy or any photos, they sort of picked it up from that.

Daniel also points to his third year as being of particular significance for him, although he emphasises his growing discomfort in the prevailing majority culture rather than a sense of victimisation. Nevertheless, the impact on his education was dramatic:

I knew I was gay when I was eight but I didn't really understand what was going on. It was when I was about 11 or 12 that I realised […] what it all meant and everything. I was alright until I hit third year, that's when everything like was coming clear to me – from that day on I started missing school, going in late, missing lessons.

He tried a strategy of openness but also considered pulling out of school:

I was thinking about coming out in school or leaving school. I wasn't happy because I couldn't be myself. I thought I was putting on an act. I told all my friends and they were OK about it but I'm sure people knew I was gay because I was becoming more camp and I was actually sticking up for gay people because they'd call them queers and everything and as soon as the word gay came up it was AIDS and HIV and it was just about anal sex and I'd correct them on it and they'd all look at me as if to say like, I was gay. If they were having a go at me I'd be bitchy and answer them back. All the people who were supposed to be really hard, they'd say something and I'd just answer back to them. And they were OK about it. I was expecting them to kind of, like beat the crap out of me every time I said something, but they didn't.

A continuing preoccupation with his position as an anomaly in relation to groups of other boys at school appears to have been Daniel's principal pressure. He was comfortable with his immediate circle of friends (girls), had come out to them and found acceptance. The process of unequivocally coming out to all was not, however, straightforward and declaring his sexuality to his head of year does not appear to have elicited any significant assistance with his dilemma. The unresolved situation appears to have weighed heavily on Daniel, judging by the eventual outcome:

A couple of times I did almost come out. One time I was close but somebody just put me off in the conversation, so I didn't come out. I told the head of year and I think he told the teachers I was having lessons with. It ended up where I actually left school. I wasn't doing good in my subjects because I, like, didn't go into school at all.

Mark tells of his trajectory from being popular and included to being progressively sidelined:

I used to play football and I used to have a big group of friends [. . .] and then I started sort of being shunted – when the abuse started – like pushed to one side. [. . .] I didn't start acting, I don't think, any more effeminate.

A teacher's collusion in his marginalisation appears to have been the catalyst for a marked escalation in this process. Mark believes that her comment to the class about him, after sending him out for forgetting some books, sealed his fate as the target of a constant barrage of abusive taunts:

I've had about 10 separate people on different occasions tell me [that] the teacher said to the rest of the class 'That boy needs a good kick up his butt to get himself in gear and I know that's not the only thing he gets up his butt' and it's at that point that the bullying really started.

Apart from one frightening situation where he narrowly escaped from a group threatening him with a hot iron, the sort of hassle Mark received did not involve physical violence. It does not appear to have been any less traumatic for him however:

You have these images of someone walking across the playground and getting beaten to a pulp, but that wasn't the sort of abuse I got. It was emotional and mental abuse that I got and I don't know which is worse.

Mark's coping strategy was to try to shut it all out, but he found the constant effort of this draining:

> You tend to switch off as soon as you walk into school, because you know that if you didn't you'd end up an emotional wreck. Switching off for so long makes you very drained. I used to sleep in the car on the way home and then I used to sleep on the couch and my mum used to wake me up to have my tea and then I used to go upstairs and go to sleep and then wake up, get back in the car spend the day at school come back and sleep and that was it. I used to spend say 12 or 13 hours a day asleep. It was a lot of strain I think. [. . .] Yeh [I was] very depressed. I mean, I got panic attacks after, when I finally got out of the school environment.

It was not until he actually left school to transfer to a college that the seriousness of the situation fully sank in, Mark reflects.

Learning disrupted

All four Study Club users interviewed reported major disruption to their education as a result of the hassles they had at school. Mark explains the effect that having to switch off emotionally can have on learning:

> I sat in science once and the teacher left the room for a couple of minutes so it was 30 unsupervised children and I started getting a load of abuse from the sort of lads that sit on the back rows. I ignored them and totally switched off and went into my own little world and didn't come out of it again till 3.30 when the bell rang. So everything that anybody actually said to me that day went in one ear and came out the other, and no work got done and nothing sunk in. There were days that I know Violet has had like that, and my friend Daniel's had like that where you just switch off totally and you don't learn anything, at which point you flunk your exams.

When things got bad for Mark he started forging notes from his parents and was absent for 40 per cent of that half term. It was not until Mark had missed about three consecutive weeks that the school contacted his parents he says. When he explained to his mother what had been going on she praised him for attending as much as he had, and went with him to talk to his head of year. Mark recalls some reluctance on the school's part to involve the educational welfare officer (EWO), and when Mark suggested a strategy of directly coming out to his peers, his head of year stressed that there were pros and cons and that the decision must be his own. Mark did so at the beginning of the following term, but instead of taking the steam out of the situation, as he hoped, he explains:

> That [didn't] work because it just grew into a much bigger thing. [. . .] It got worse.

He missed 50 per cent of that half term, and finds it amazing how much absence it took before the school contacted his parents, given the events of the previous term. This time his mother took matters further and phoned Mark's head of year requesting a meeting with him and the EWO to resolve things. Mark recalls how much stress that both of his parents, too, had been under throughout this time:

> It was very emotional for both me and my Mum – my mum was in tears and I was in tears at this meeting.

The EWO immediately agreed a transfer. Aged 15, with much valuable lesson time lost and with only six months to go before his GCSEs, Mark was now faced with moving to a college. Although he does not talk of missing school in the way Mark did, Dave too experienced disruption of his work in class by the constant name calling and taunting, and could not make the progress he wanted:

> I was having a load of problems from people in the class just disrupting me all the time [. . .] just normal things like calling me names – queer and all this lot.

Violet talks of her preoccupation with the bullying preventing her from getting on with learning:

> I wasn't learning anything in school because I was too preoccupied with being bullied. I actually left school through the hassle and didn't do any kind of work. I stayed at home for two weeks.

And while Daniel experienced less dramatic hassle from his peers and had a teacher he could confide in, he was not happy at school because he could not, as he put it, be himself. He too missed a lot of school and finally stopped going altogether. Just as Mark's mother had done, Daniel's mother too asked for him to be transferred to a college before his GCSE exams. However, Daniel concludes that reluctance on his school's part to relinquish their funding for him (a consideration to which Mark also attributes his school's 'refusal' to involve the EWO until his mother later did so herself) accounted for procedural hold-ups. The delay resulted in it being 'too late to get transferred' until the following academic year. There ensued for Daniel 'just over a year of not doing any homework, or anything' until he could finally start at college. Daniel and Mark both described their parents as being supportive about their sexuality throughout their tangles with the world of education and indeed this was so with all four respondents. When Violet's situation worsened at school, her parents also attempted to intervene on her behalf. She remembers:

> I was staying at home and my parents were worried sick and kept ringing up the school saying 'Do something'.

However, Violet found the school's response ineffective:

> The deputy head rang up my Mum saying 'We've set up a support group …
> we've talked to the kids.' I went back to school and I was still getting all this
> hassle […] all that happened with this support group thing was just one lad said
> to me 'You alright?' and I was like 'Yeh, cheers.' Even if I'd said 'Oh no, I'm
> having loads of problems' […] he wouldn't have known what to do and so there
> was nothing. […] The teachers weren't really around. But it wasn't like me going
> out into the yard and getting beaten up, if it was something like that I would have
> reported it. Walking up the corridor and getting things shouted at you, or sitting
> in a classroom and getting things shouted at you, you can't really report that, you
> know. My Mum would say to me 'So what are the names of the kids who're doing
> it? 'and I'm like 'Well everyone's doing it' and she was like 'Well how can we stop
> it then? 'and I'm like 'The only way we can stop it is if you convince 700 school
> kids that being gay is OK.'

Violet's perception that it would take a whole-school approach to make a difference
seems to get to the heart of the matter. The respondents who had the most upheaval
felt badly let down by their schools; for example, two commented that had the same
hostility and harassment occurred for racial reasons their schools would have spared
no effort in cracking down on the perpetrators. In only one case do they report that a
teacher took the initiative in investigating what was going on and how they were
coping. Typically, responses came only after a dramatic level of absence, or as a result
of direct requests for help from the young people themselves or their parents. And
rather than any of them receiving any information about or referral to the Study Club
from their school or the education services, it appears to have been these young
individuals' strong will to get on with their lives and not to let their academic futures
be undermined that led each of them to make use of it.

What the Study Club offered

For Daniel, Mark and Violet, who had been regularly coming to the LGYM youth
group for some time, coming to use the newly set up PSP Study Club in the same
premises was an easy step. Daniel, for example, who had been brought by his mother
to the youth group some years before, decided to attend after some talks with one of
the youth workers there about the amount of school he'd been missing. Dave's
experience was different. He made his own way to the Study Club after he saw an
article about it in the first copy of *Gay Times* he bought in a newsagents when he was
14. But it was a friend of his, also gay, who actually first went along and checked it out
after Dave told him about it, and he then gave Dave the confidence to go.
Nevertheless, coming to the Study Club for the first time was a big step for Dave:

I didn't know anybody. Even if there was just me, two teachers and Daniel, it might sound weird, but it was a bit scary because it was actually gay people there. [. . .] In my time I've not actually been . . . the majority of people have been straight but [this was] solely for gay people. [. . .] I found out in *Gay Times* because if I need something I'll go and try and find it. It was a big step for me, it was something that made me feel good.

The Study Club had provided Dave with a good reason to move from the isolation he had been feeling into a larger world of other gay people. He did not need it once it had served as his stepping stone to the LGYM youth group that met later in the afternoon.

It was even scarier because there was loads of gay people and [. . .] I'd never seen so many in my life. It was an added bonus to know I don't have to be scared any more of being proud that I'm gay, because there's all my friends here that, if I have any trouble, they'll support me. [. . .] I started going to the youth group every Tuesday and Saturday so it was giving me a lot more courage to rise above all the stuff that's been happening to me at school for the past four years. And then I've come out, and then I've not needed the study group since. Because basically people know that I'm gay. If it happens in the classroom, I'm normally sat round with my mates, and I'll just tell the person to shut up and like, 'I don't want to know about your sex life so you don't want to know about mine,' and they'll actually stick up for me as well, they'll tell them to shut up and get on with the work. I can manage it now. I never used to be able to, because I was always the shy and intent person with no friends.

The Study Club providing a means of contact with gay peers, when young people might not be ready to go directly to the more social and boisterous setting of a youth group, was something that Paul, one of the volunteer teachers, remarked on too:

The interesting point was he didn't come to do maths, he came along so he could make contact with the group. He did all the maths and I just sat there and said 'oh yes, that's right'. And I think there's an awful lot of that.

Having got to the point of wanting to come out at school, Dave was fortunate to have been offered practical support in responding to continuing hassles by one of his teachers who had noticed. He now feels that he can get the aid of the deputy head and this particular teacher should he need to, and he attributes this helpful response to their being relatively young. It was when she started to come to the LGYM youth group regularly that Violet began to get moral support regarding the trouble she was having at school. She decided to attend the Study Club as well, simply to keep up with her schoolwork while the hassles continued:

I just came in to do my work, but I'm sure if I said 'can I talk about the problems I'm having at school?' they would have been perfectly happy to discuss it with me. I think it's very important to have a sympathetic teacher, or a gay one, if you prefer, but I didn't actually need that.

Nevertheless, Violet travelled to the PSP Study Club in preference to what was provided locally.

There was a homework club in my school as well as an after school thing [but] I wouldn't have used it [. . .] because it's still in the area. It would have been the same teachers and things and I just wanted a whole different sort of atmosphere. That's what I needed and it worked.

Daniel too was not enthusiastic about going to study support elsewhere:

I don't think I would. Because [with] the teachers who are gay, I could be myself, I could be camp or whatever. But if it was just a straight teacher I couldn't be myself. It's kind of comfortable being taught by somebody who is gay.

Daniel had been absent from school a lot and had not been doing well in his subjects. He came to the Study Club 'about two or three times and then went into college [. . .] so I thought I don't need to go anymore.' Although Daniel stopped attending, he continued to go to the youth group where he kept up the new friendships he'd made at the Study Club. Now 16, he had started work and was thinking of coming to the Study Club again:

Well, it has been a help. [. . .] I would like to give it a go because I don't want to just slack off on my education altogether, because I'm not going to stay in this job forever.

Violet enthuses about the curriculum-based support at the Study Club:

You just turn up and there's lots of teachers and they say 'what do you want to do today?' and they'll just take you in a room and teach you. I did what I had the most difficulty with and that's maths and science. I learnt a lot 'cos you tell them what you need to do, like what you're doing at school at the moment, or just anything you don't understand, I mean you can do anything. You can say 'I've got this massive piece of course work to do and I need help with it' and they'll help you, or you can say 'can you give me some revision tips?'and they'll do that. You could just even come to use the space, you know, and not even have a teacher help you. You can just come and revise or read, so it's a space to do your schoolwork and it's brilliant.

Although Mark and Violet were doing different subjects, they were both coming up to their GCSE examinations at the time they attended the Study Club. Mark recalls:

[We] comforted each other because she was going through a lot of the hassles that I went through when I was in the same situation in high school. By this time I was in college, so I managed to get through them.

Mark transferred to college with just six months to go to his GCSE exams and he wanted to make up for time lost at school by attending the Study Club:

It was all of them teachers here. They gave us a load of past exam papers to revise from and anything I was unsure of I had in a file – at high school I missed a lot [. . .] because of disruption in the lessons – and I'd say 'look, this I'm unsure about' and he'd go through it with me. [. . . It's a] bit of a success story because through the study group I got four Bs and a C.

Yet, for the teachers who volunteered, it was typically their empathy with the young LGBs' personal struggles that drew them to the project and made it all worthwhile, as Ross explains:

To a lad who was going through some chemistry work, towards the end of the session I said 'How do you cope with things at school? 'and he was quite openly able to talk to me about his bullying experiences, how he found it very difficult and how he had to leave school for a while. And I hope that … from someone who is a teacher … although I didn't go through the bullying experience at school, I coped with it in a rather different way, yet I'm someone who is sympathetic and we can talk about it, and I think that's quite important.

Interestingly, the peer-led personal, social and health education (PSHE) element that was intended to follow the first hour of academic work was not talked about by any of the above respondents, by the teachers or by the peer supporters interviewed. As three of the four respondents who had been Study Club users were already attending the LGYM youth group (which had a Saturday session in the same building beginning soon after the study club) they were already well provided for in this respect, as PSHE work is central to the ethos of this particular group. And Dave, the respondent who came initially to the study club, appears to have moved, after only one session, seamlessly into the LGYM group where he found the peer company he needed. Staff believe that the remaining six Study Club users not interviewed most likely followed a similar pattern in relation to the LGYM youth group, although this could not be verified. In any case, the intended work-shop approach to the peer support element would not have worked well with typical attendance being in ones and twos, which might explain its non-occurrence. The lack of a PSHE element does not appear to have been a deterrent to the respondents; on the contrary, they seemed satisfied to focus on their academic aims with the support of teachers who were sympathetic to their sexuality and understanding of their predicament at school. Apart from mutual support, when their attendance at the study club coincided, they seemed content to pursue their social contact and explore their LGB identities with their peers at the youth group.

Low uptake of the service and subsequent closure

In view of the consistently positive tone of the respondents' comments on what the Study Club offered, it was perplexing that there was no uptake of its services during the half-year period of my investigation. Prior to that, only 10 teenagers had used it. Teachers' impressions overall were that they had been pleased with the service, but needed only short-term help. Once the Study Club's initial high profile in the national and local media had died down, publicity presented difficulties: budgets for advertising were minimal and it was doubted whether schools had ever displayed any of the material sent to them. What is particularly striking is the absence of any referrals from the most obvious sources, schools themselves and the education services in the area. Following an evaluation (Smith 1999), it was discontinued owing to the low attendance.

Key issues as revealed in respondents' narratives:

1. All respondents report persistent and intrusive verbal abuse, sufficiently daunting to affect decisively schoolwork in the classroom. Substantial disruption of attendance also resulted for three of the four.

2. All respondents also mentioned their failure to maintain the necessary homework schedules. They did not use homework to compensate for disrupted school hours. Our conclusion must be that the form of persecution they endured had a severe effect on morale.

3. The lack of support they have generally had in school from teachers also stands out. Even when support was forthcoming it appears that it was inadequate, particularly in the time it took for those charged with the task of providing support to react.

4. Little short of a whole school approach would appear to offer a thoroughgoing solution, and none of the schools involved appear to have had one.

5. Lacking an adequate institutional response, all respondents turned to their families. However, gaining their parents' support necessitated discussing their sexuality with them, in itself a major undertaking for most young teenagers. In the case of these respondents, they were fortunate to have particularly supportive families. Had they not felt able to risk telling them the root cause of their school based problems they would have lacked this important support.

6. This study's findings prompt the speculation that there must be others in a similar school predicament who had perhaps received negative parental reactions, increasing the pressure they might be under. The self-selection of these respondents as Study Club members, at least for a while, shows that they had retained some measure of academic ambition. A supplementary study of the lives of those who receive neither parental nor study support needs to be undertaken.

We are not taking a stance of being disinterested observers in relation to these issues. We take a human rights position in relation to sexual orientation. While harassment and discrimination abound, and cause psychosocial disadvantage, it should not be necessary to demonstrate that one is being disadvantaged in order to claim the basic human right to be allowed to get on with life unhindered as a human being (Ellis 1999). [. . .]

Warwick *et al.* (2000), referring to the UN Convention on the Rights of the Child, argue in addition that 'the right to express one's views and have them considered should apply to all young people regardless *inter alia* of poverty, class, race, gender or sexuality' (p. 132) – a sentiment that underpins the collaborative approach we have taken with our respondents in providing a platform in the academic literature for their voices. To this we would add that quite simply the right to be different is at the heart of the matter for these young people, and we strongly feel that this right should be recognised and supported by all professionals working with young people.

References

Comely, L. (1993) Lesbian and gay teenagers at school: how can educational psychologists help? *Educational and Child Psychology*, **10**(3), 22–4.

Coyle, A. (1998) Developing lesbian and gay identity in adolescence. In J. Coleman and D. Roker (eds), *Teenage sexuality: health, risk and education*. Amsterdam: Harwood Academic Press.

D'Augelli, A. R. (1999) The queering of adolescence: implications for psychological researchers and practitioners. *British Psychological Society Lesbian and Gay Psychology Section Newsletter*, **3**, 3–5.

Douglas, N., Warwick, I., Kemp, S. and Whitty, G. (1997) *Playing it safe: responses of secondary school teachers to lesbian, gay and bisexual pupils, bullying, HIV and AIDS education and Section 28*. London: Health and Education Research Unit, Institute of Education, University of London.

Douglas, N., Warwick, I., Kemp, S., Whitty, G. and Aggleton, P. (1999) Homophobic bullying in secondary schools in England and Wales: teachers' experiences. *Health Education*, **99**(2), 53–60.

Ellis, S. J. (1999) Lesbian and gay issues are human rights issues: the need for a human rights approach to lesbian and gay psychology. *British Psychological Society Lesbian and Gay Psychology Section Newsletter*, **3**, 9–14.

Epstein, D. and Johnson, R. (1994) On the straight and the narrow: The heterosexual presumption, homophobias and schools. In D. Epstein (ed.) *Challenging lesbian and gay inequalities in education*. Buckingham: Open University Press.

Hierons, D. (1998) *Young lesbian, gay and bisexual peer support project: project evaluation report*. Manchester: Young Lesbian, Gay and Bisexual Peer Support Project.

King, M. and Bartlett, A. (1999) British psychiatry and homosexuality. *British Journal of Psychiatry*, **175**, 106–13.

Nayak, A. and Kehily, M. J. (1997) Masculinities and schooling: why are young men so homophobic? In D. L. Steinberg, D. Epstein and R. Johnson (eds.) *Border patrols: policing the boundaries of heterosexuality*. London: Cassell.

Rivers, I. (1995a) Mental health issues among young lesbians and gay men bullied at school. *Health and Social Care in the Community*, **3**(6), 380–3.

Rivers, I. (1995b) The victimisation of gay teenagers in schools: homophobia in education. *Pastoral Care*, **13**, 39–45.

Rivers, I. (1996) Young, gay and bullied. *Young People Now*, (January), 18–19.

Rivers, I. (2000) Social exclusion, absenteeism and sexual minority youth. *Support for Learning*, **15**(1), 13–18.

Rivers, I. (2001) The bullying of sexual minorities at school: its nature and long-term correlates. *Educational and Child Psychology*, **18**(1), 33–46.

Smith, K. (1999) *Views and Opinions of Young Lesbians, Gays and Bisexuals on the Work of the Peer Support Project*. Manchester: Young Lesbian, Gay and Bisexual Peer Support Project.

Warwick, I., Oliver, C. and Aggleton, P. (2000) Sexuality and mental health promotion: lesbian and gay young people. In P. Aggleton, J. Hurry and I. Warwick (eds.) *Young People and Mental Health*. Chichester: Wiley.

Winnicott, D. W. (1965) *The maturational processes and the facilitating environment: studies in the theory of emotional development*. London: Hogarth.

The young people represented in this chapter did not enjoy feelings of being included and valued within their schools, but they did gain positive experiences of being part of a community through peer and other support. Tackling homophobia is just as much a challenge for inclusive education as disability awareness raising and antiracist teaching. This is essential for young people's educational achievement and also, once again, for social justice.

CHAPTER 16

Inclusive curricula? Pupils on the margins of special schools

Melanie Nind and Steve Cochrane

This chapter outlines the curriculum-focused Intensive Interaction and Inclusion Project that was part of a wider inclusion project within a Local Education Authority. The authors were the project's consultant and instigator and they discuss the thinking associated with the project, reflect on its initial year in action and draw out themes of relevance for the wider inclusion debate.

Background and rationale

[. . .] The Local Education Authority in question has not proposed closure of its special schools, though it has increasingly, for many years, pursued a largely unofficial policy of mainstreaming many pupils who would otherwise have gone to special schools. A conscious choice was made to work, right from the beginning, upon increasing the inclusive capacity of the local special schools while, at the same time, working on the same task in mainstream schools. If it proved possible to develop an appropriate curriculum in the local area for pupils on the margins of special schools, who would otherwise be sent out of the region, then resources could be reallocated to schools within the education administration and further increase inclusive capacity. If energies were focused on increasing the inclusive capacity of the special schools this would involve focusing on pupils who challenge existing practice. This in turn would provide a significant stimulus for rethinking that practice. We were concerned with that which was within our sphere of influence – what goes on in classrooms – and on the potential of this for transforming thinking and therefore other practices. This was not a bold attempt at dissolving special schools; it can be viewed instead as an example of the 'reality' of 'in-between-ness' in inclusion that Corbett (1997: 55) describes, with some of the 'compromises, adjustments and individual preferences'.

Whilst retaining a mix of schools, inclusive education in the administrative region (the 'borough') is being conceptualised in terms of community, with efforts to bring together communities of schools, their participants and their families, and in terms of breaking down barriers to participation, with emphasis on more local and earlier action. Of prime concern are pupils who fall outside of the routine competence and confidence of teachers, in both mainstream and special schools, and extending teachers' competence and confidence through staff development and collaborative inquiry. [. . .] Reflecting back to Ainscow *et al.*'s (2000: 216) discussion of local education authority policies for inclusive education, inclusion is seen here as less about participation in the mainstream and more in terms of 'commitment to develop classroom practices and forms of school organisation that respond positively to pupil diversity'.

The project was integral to efforts to remodel the policy framework away from the pupil-deficit concept of 'difficulty', and move local thinking towards a social model of disability. As part of this process, we were attempting to refocus attention away from individuals and on to the contexts within which particular individual or group needs are seen as 'special', and upon the dynamics that create 'difficulty'. [. . .]

Complex needs and Intensive Interaction

The approach of Intensive Interaction formed the vehicle for staff development through collaborative enquiry. Intensive Interaction (Nind and Hewett 1988, 1994) is an interactive approach that emphasises the quality of the teaching and interactive process, and the transactional relationship between learners and their social environments. The interactive style is modelled on the nurturing style of caregiver–infant interaction (Lewis and Rosenblum 1974; Schaffer 1977) and is used with intensity and critical reflection. Practitioners of Intensive Interaction address the interactive fit between the pupils' needs and the accessibility and meaningfulness of the educational experience. They rely on teaching using an intuitive interactive style combined with reflection, in-depth observation and collaborative problem-solving, rather than on specialist 'experts' (Nind and Hewett 1998). Pupils are involved in daily short bursts of quality one-to-one interaction in which teachers employ a set of principles to guide their interactions. By enabling teachers to see their own strengths and pedagogical potential as interactive partners, it empowers them to find their own ways forward.

In terms of the borough's problem-solving framework, the empowering, social constructivist orientation of interactive approaches seemed to hold the key to the development, at a regional and school level, of not only an inclusive curriculum, but also of a more inclusive social environment. Intensive Interaction was already familiar to some of the special schools. It was chosen for the development of the special school sector because of its apparent applicability to those pupils on the autistic continuum who were providing the biggest challenges to the special school providers, and because of its philosophical closeness to other local inclusive strategies, such as nurture groups (Bennathan and Boxall 1996) and Solution Focused Thinking (Rhodes and Ajmal 1995).

The employment of an Intensive Interaction consultant also marked the beginning of a redefinition of support. Instead of being offered extra funds or staff to provide support to pupils who were challenging the limits of local special school provision, the teachers themselves were offered additional support – an offer which they readily took up. Problem-solving approaches are frequently advocated as a basis for moving towards more inclusive practices (Skrtic 1995; Ainscow 1999) and they were seen in this project as a logical way forward.

The initial aim of the Intensive Interaction project was to increase the diversity of pupils that teachers in special schools could feel confident to respond to, with appropriate teaching strategies and curricula. The means for achieving this aim involved an exploration of Intensive Interaction as a possible approach/curriculum for pupils on the margins of special schools, provision of a consultant to act as a resource for schools to use as they chose, encouragement for schools to see each other as a resource in collaborative working, and use of an action research model. [Action research is a process through which practitioners study their own practice to better understand and solve problems in context.] It was hoped that teachers would identify problems, work with each other and with the consultant as a critical friend, reflect on the problems, plan, act, evaluate and reflect and plan again.

Intensive Interaction and inclusive thinking

A dimension of our early thinking in instigating this project was the extent to, and ways in which, Intensive Interaction fits with inclusive thinking.

Using the helpful distinctions between traditional and inclusionary approaches that Thomas *et al.* (1998) adapted from Porter (1995), it became apparent that the Intensive Interaction and Inclusion Project fits particularly well with some of the inclusionary dimensions. These are, most notably, examining teaching/learning factors, collaborative problem-solving and developing strategies for teachers.

In contrast, an aspect of the project that could be regarded as more in keeping with a traditional approach was its focus on what could be said to be a 'technical intervention' if Intensive Interaction was seen as special teaching or therapy. However, the nature of Intensive Interaction as the 'technical intervention', in this instance, involves teachers in looking at their practice, examining the quality of their interactions, and reflecting on the match between what their students bring to the learning situation and the teaching and learning experiences they offer. It does not work along the lines of buying in or learning the expertise owned by another, by a 'specialist', but by enabling practitioners to see that the expertise is available to them from within their own (potential) repertoires of behaviour. It therefore has the added transformational quality of enabling practitioners to feel more competent as people, as opposed to struggling with only mechanistic formulae to help them.

Intensive Interaction is a teaching approach that is special in the sense of being geared to a specific group of learners who are usually seen as special and who are usually placed in special schools. It was developed by teachers looking to enhance their normal practice and to facilitate the development of fundamental social and communication abilities in students who experience severe and complex learning difficulties. It evolved from a very particular concern with developing an understanding and practice of good teaching for these learners and their particular needs. However, it is also firmly enmeshed with principles of good teaching *for all*. It is based on the 'intuitive pedagogy' (Carlson and Bricker 1982) of caregiver-infant interaction and therefore on good teaching *for all at the early developmental levels*. It borrows from the intuitive teaching and learning style that characterises the playful interactive process between parents and their very young children. It is this, rather than a model that the students with complex needs/learning difficulties need something fundamentally different from that which other children need, that underpins Intensive Interaction. In Intensive Interaction, the difference in approach for individuals with complex learning difficulties emerges not so much in the interactive style, but in the way that the style is applied, that is, with intensity and critical reflection. Therefore, the difference is a matter of degree rather than kind (see the discussion in the Further Education Funding Council's Tomlinson Report 1996).

There is research evidence that the interactive style that is emulated in, or characterised by, Intensive Interaction has a positive functional relationship with development. It is also characterised by a self-perpetuating momentum in a pattern of success breeding success. This ongoing pattern of development is evident both in young children who are developing normally (Lewis and Roseriblum 1974; Schaffer 1977; Kaye 1979; Lewis and Coates 1980) and in individuals of all ages who are yet to develop early social and communication abilities (Mahoney and Powell 1988; Nind 1996; Yoder 1990). The latter group, however, are less likely to experience this interactive style or teaching approach, reflecting less ease in teachers or caregivers achieving a good interactive fit, and assumptions about the need for specialist teaching and different ways of learning.

The consultant in this project faced the challenge of sharing experience and understanding of Intensive Interaction whilst resisting the model of being someone bringing a special commodity. We did not want to reinforce any feelings of helplessness among the teachers or any thoughts that pupils might be inappropriately placed with them because they needed 'someone like her', as opposed to 'someone like me'.

The project in the initial year

Four special schools were involved in the initial year of the project: two all age schools for children with moderate learning difficulties (MLD) (that we shall call Maple Leaf and Green Street), one infant/primary phase school for pupils with communication disorders (that we shall call Cherry Tree), and one all age school for children with severe and profound and multiple learning difficulties (that we shall call Waterside).

A steering group was set up to agree the terms of the project and to discuss ways in which it might operate and be evaluated. The group comprised the headteachers of the schools, key personnel from the associated support services and a parent of a child with autism from the local parents' centre. A launch, inaugurated by the Director of Education, brought together staff from three of the special schools (one chose to defer) and staff from advisory, educational psychology, parent support and speech and language therapy services. The launch session introduced the rationale and principles of both Intensive Interaction and the project itself. [. . .]

In the immediate term practitioners were encouraged to reflect on the launch session and think about: existing practice in relation to Intensive Interaction principles, where change might be needed, how dialogue and thinking might be enriched, what support might be needed, what they wanted from the project and how they might enable each other.

Identifying the problem 1: curriculum and intruders

The first burst of action came from the schools for pupils with moderate learning difficulties. These were two very different schools with a different socio-economic mix of pupils, different culture and priorities. Yet, they identified very similar problems as the starting point for the project.

The first of these, Maple Leaf, presented itself as a school with a caring ethos as its primary source of pride. The headteacher spoke passionately about the warmth of the school atmosphere, the good team spirit amongst its staff, and the growing emphasis on circle time (Mosley 1993) and therapies in the school's approach. The 'problem' identified by the senior management team as the starting point for discussion and action was the changing nature of the school population. There was a new intake of pupils who were unlike their traditional pupil group, and the head reported that the staff had felt like 'a tidal wave was coming at them'. The graphic image was one of being unable to turn back this tide and of a feeling of helplessness in the face of it. In response, the staff had sought to regain their feeling of control and effectiveness by segregating the 'tidal wave' group in a class of their own. Thus, the decision had been made to stream the key stage three group resulting in what they termed an 'MLD' and an 'SLD' group. In this way, the 'tidal wave' was being dealt with – but they were very uncertain about the future.

The pressing issue was what to do with this new, and in their terms, homogeneous group. The teachers, it was explained, were skilled at differentiating, but 'even they' could not differentiate to the extent that had been required. It was felt that the new class of 'SLD pupils' could not access the secondary school style subjects-based curriculum on offer to the traditional pupils and they needed an alternative. The idea of learning the 'specialist technique' of Intensive Interaction and using this was very appealing. This solution perhaps offered the attraction of not interfering with the thinking and activity of the rest of the school, though this was certainly not to be the case!

The secondary issue was the problem of pupils in the Year 1 class with communication difficulties, and again not typical of the school's traditional 'MLD' population. The staff involved wanted to explore whether Intensive Interaction would be an appropriate approach for these individuals.

The second school for pupils with moderate learning difficulties, Green Street, presented itself as a school with academic success as its primary source of pride. The headteacher and deputy spoke of the way the school had been turned around, from one in which the pupils had done 'colouring in' and 'feeding ducks in the park', to one where pupils achieved mainstream qualifications. Like its counterpart, this school could not be described as a learning organisation with a culture of ongoing study and reflection, but there were more educational books available here and some links with higher education institutions.

Like Maple Leaf, the Green Street management team described the challenge in terms of a changing population, with growing numbers of non-traditional pupils who did not fit the academic curriculum on offer. Once again, the 'problem pupils' were mostly found in the youngest classes and in the secondary department. Their particular concerns were what to do with pupils needing a developmental curriculum in Years 1 and 2, what to do with pupils 'with SLD' who did not fit the qualification-based curriculum in Year 10, how to run a two-tier curriculum to suit two separate kinds of pupils, and what to do about the pupils with stereotyped communications and behaviours dotted about among the other classes.

Emerging themes

The early part of the project with these schools then, revealed some interesting emerging themes. First, increasing diversity was seen in both MLD schools as a problem to be minimised, as a problem requiring an organisational response and not as a resource for learning (for pupils and teachers) (as discussed by Booth *et al*. 1997). In Ainscow's (1999: 6) terms, less familiar pupils were viewed very much through a 'normative' rather than 'transformative' lens. The task of the consultant/critical friend then became to refocus energy on difference not as deviance (Carrington 1999), but as a means of generating change in curriculum practice and questioning long-held assumptions (Barton 1997).

Second, the project's focus on 'pupils falling outside of the routine competence and confidence' of teachers clearly reflected a very real agenda in the MLD schools where there was considerable honesty about the perceived lack of confidence and expertise to cope. This may have reflected a trend in the UK in which all kinds of teachers have felt deskilled and deprofessionalised by strong interference from government in curriculum and teaching issues. Third, this unconfident response resulted in a strong desire for the staff to label the pupils who were challenging them. The language of 'severe learning difficulties', although inaccurate in many ways, was used to signify that the pupils belonged elsewhere, in a different category of provision, with a separate breed of teachers who had the specialist skills required to teach them. There was a very strong feeling of *our* pupils and *intruder* pupils.

Fourth, there was recognition that the *intruders* were part of the schools' future, and their needs would have to be addressed. There was a willingness to do this in an add-on basis, but less readiness, in the initial stages at least, to rethink the whole curriculum and approach. Before thinking about Intensive Interaction and focused support and encouragement to do otherwise, the schools were each on a journey toward a two-tier curriculum and possibly even the creation of a special school within a special school.

We see enacted here, as Ainscow *et al.* (2000) described, teachers at school and classroom level constructing their own interpretations of policies. We see also the tensions arising from different aspirations, priorities and understandings. The initial responses to increased diversity within the MLD schools illustrate the problems of separation of difference within, as well as across, schools. They highlight, too, the importance of concepts of inclusion that stress, as Barton (1997) does, 'listening to unfamiliar voices', 'being open' and 'celebrating difference', with the attitudinal aspects of moving toward inclusion permeating all policy and practice. A certain irony emerges if we understand the pupils' placement in special schools, as Clough (1988: 329) does, not in terms of their (in)ability, but the result of 'their interaction with a particular curriculum', in that the curriculum in the special schools was continuing to be the location of difficulty.

Planning and action 1: thinking through the problem together

The willingness to share the problem with someone in the role of critical friend, in the action research sense of supporter, collaborator and friendly critic, enabled the managers and teachers in the MLD schools to see their problem from different perspectives. To them, the problem was real and urgent – requiring a pragmatic solution. To the critical friend the problem was an intellectual challenge – requiring reflection and complex problem-solving. Questioning and mirroring of their thinking helped to present the problem in different ways. Was a two-tier system in the curriculum really what was wanted? What were the implications of this for the way the pupils were regarded and valued? What alternatives were there to the two-tier system? Was it really as simple as two kinds of pupil requiring two kinds of curriculum? Was it more helpful to think in terms of greater diversity of learning styles and teaching needs? How could the curriculum be structured to provide an all-encompassing framework for a diversity of pupils?

We explored the feasibility and desirability of slotting an interactive teaching approach into an otherwise unchanged curriculum. We looked at the assumptions behind different ways of working and the way pupils were constructed in each. We talked about the kind of environment in which interactive approaches need to be set. With some exceptions amongst the very young children, the pupils who were outside of the teachers' routine confidence were not lacking in fundamental communication or social abilities. We therefore departed from the original focus of Intensive Interaction itself, but we did address the kinds of thinking behind it. We also returned, repeatedly, to the issue at the core of all interactive approaches: concern with active learners and learning processes rather than with learning outcomes (Nind 2000). In this way, the project provided supported opportunities for teachers to reflect and rethink and perhaps to depart from established beliefs and current practice.

At Maple Leaf, our discussions focused on the support that teaching staff needed to develop schemes of work for the full range of their pupils in the secondary department. The schemes could not just focus on subject content if they were to be meaningful. This led us into the realms of what the teachers were actually teaching. Although working within a special school, the teachers in the secondary department identified themselves as secondary teachers and as teachers of subjects. Our discussions led us to the need for them to see themselves also as teachers of children and as teachers of learning.

Guided by a prevailing concern with the teaching and learning process, and inspired by some excellent resources (Hart 1996; Babbage *et al.* 1999; Grove and Peacey 1999), the head of department and consultant/critical friend proposed a whole-school curriculum planning framework for further development by the teaching staff. The framework in essence contained three points in a triangular image representing *subject-related* processes, *learning to learn* processes and *general* processes. Teaching staff could use this framework to develop a bank of processes to draw upon in their planning. Rather than thinking about what the pupils would produce they would think about the active processes they would be engaged with. As part of this they would think about what would help pupils to gain understandings of the subject, what would help them to become better learners, and what processes they would need to rehearse on a regular basis.

Schemes of work and individual lessons could be planned, using the framework, to achieve a balanced approach, with personalisation for individuals. For some pupils in some lessons the subject emphasis might be greater and for others the priority might be learning to learn, but, importantly, the demarcation between them would not be strong or permanent. Neither would it be based on assumptions, but rather on observation and reflection. It would allow for differentiation and diversification without exclusion, isolation and stigma. It was hoped that this could lead to more effective planning and teaching and learning experiences for all pupils. In this model, every child is viewed as a learner and, as Carrington (1999: 260) calls for, need for failure is removed. The planning framework is currently developed and being tested out in an action research style process.

At Green Street school, the constraining influence on the secondary phase curriculum was seen to be the qualification requirements rather than the curriculum subjects. Thus, the concern with outcomes was greater, with consequent understandable reluctance to switch to thinking in terms of learning processes. The problems associated with a separate qualification for one group of pupils, especially if this meant separate learning experiences, were recognised but seen as insurmountable in the short term. The impact of this on the rest of the school is currently being discussed.

Meanwhile in the primary department, an all-encompassing curriculum framework is being developed from the Foundation Stage programme. This is being developed as part of the linked early years social inclusion project. This framework is based upon a jigsaw of curriculum areas: PSHE (personal, social and health education), language/literacy, mathematical, physical, creative/aesthetic and knowledge of the world, and on models of good early years practice. In this way, interactive play is beginning to form a legitimate and integral part of the younger pupils' day. [. . .]

Identifying the problem 2: teaching and learning matters

The next schools to get involved were Cherry Tree, the school for pupils with communication disorders, and Waterside, the school for pupils with severe and profound and multiple learning difficulties. Initial identification of the problem in the action-research cycle was very different here as the sense of identity in these schools was based on meeting the needs of pupils who were beyond the routine confidence and competence of others. They already used Intensive Interaction and thus saw themselves as providing curriculum experiences well matched to the needs of pupils with extreme difficulties. They were still able to identify individual pupils who they found challenging, but this was very much within a context of them coping generally and positively with diverse needs.

Challenges at Cherry Tree and Waterside were identified in terms of how to enhance the quality of interactions and their benefits both for particular pupils and the school population generally. The thinking here reflected the kind of inclusive school culture described by Carrington (1999: 260):

> School failure will always be a reality unless the student is considered central to the learning interactions with a unique set of prior experiences that shape their perceptions. The learner, rather that the teacher/curricula/dominant culture must be considered the driver of their educational experience if the goals are engagement and success.

Through collaborative observation and feedback routines we identified some plans of action.

Planning and action 2: enhancing teaching and learning through Intensive Interaction

At Cherry Tree the plans of action involved practitioners in focusing on some matters of sensitive use of the interactive style. These included how to hold back their own behaviour ready for responsiveness and how to outweigh negative interactions with a vast number of mutually enjoyable ones. We also discussed experimenting with different venues within school for interactive sessions and allowing more time to rehearse pre-communication abilities before introducing symbols/sign/speech.

At Waterside, we focused on effective practice with pupils with whom achieving access and engagement was more challenging. We observed each other interacting with pupils with physical impairments and (multiple) sensory impairment, pupils who were very passive in school, and pupils with whom interactions had not been enjoyable. We developed a useful process of the consultant and less experienced teachers working alongside each other sharing ideas and concerns. Staff have made action plans to develop imitation of sounds into turn-taking with 'turnabouts' (Ware 1996) and generally to use each other as a resource more in collaborative partnerships. Together we have identified areas where there were tensions between the secondary style subject-based curriculum on offer and quality interactive practice. The problem of getting to know the pupils and their learning styles and preferences when they move around the staff throughout the week is also currently under reflection.

Further developments

During the next phase of the project, work has begun in mainstream schools. We will also be exploring a school accreditation framework that can recognise the achievements of schools in their development of interactive and inclusive practice. The Index for Inclusion (Booth *et al*. 2000) will be used as a stimulus for this. Greater emphasis will be placed on coordination within schools such that in-house expertise is shared and collaborative inquiry fostered (Ainscow 1999), perhaps through the adoption of coordinator roles. There will also be further work on facilitating schools working together to form a more functional and inclusive educational community (Booth *et al*. 2000).

Reflections

Reflection on the themes emerging from the project illuminates some key points. Pupils who fall outside of their traditional population may present a significant challenge to teachers and managers in special schools. Special school identity and experience does not automatically protect them from this, but the development of a curriculum framework that already allows for diversity does. The project is educational for us in demonstrating (as Belanger (2000) shows) the processes of inclusion and exclusion at work within particular school settings. A focus on pupils who fall outside of the routine competence and confidence of teachers reflects a real agenda for teachers and allows for an inclusionary approach to moving forward by addressing teaching strategies, curricular issues, and classroom environments.

The challenge of non-traditional pupils with whom teachers lack confidence may result in a strong desire to label those pupils. This categorisation helps to maintain the distinction between pupils who rightly belong and *intruder* pupils who really belong in a different category of provision, with a separate breed of teachers who have the 'specialist' skills required. This categorisation of pupils and teachers presents significant barriers to inclusive thinking and to extending the diversity of pupils with whom teachers feel competent and confident. Negative feelings about the challenge of non-traditional pupils, the history of traditional approaches to special education, and a rigid curriculum framework are associated with responding in an 'add-on' basis to the challenge. This can result in a two-tier curriculum and even special schools within (special) schools. With sustained, ongoing support for innovative thinking, teachers are more likely to rethink their whole curriculum offer and approach the challenge in an inclusive way.

It could be argued that the project was just about a supportive consultant working with staff to reflect on improving practice and that the Intensive Interaction focus was almost incidental. We do not support this view, but rather acknowledge that the Intensive Interaction element assumed greater or lesser importance at different times. Strong belief in the potential of interactive approaches to transform thinking and action, however, was always the lens through which the consultant viewed the 'problem' under inquiry. This interactive lens was also significant for many of the teachers.

The ubiquitous tendency to locate problems within the pupil rather than within the school/curriculum was a challenge for the project. This orientation increases the mystique of difficulties in learning and further undermines teachers' confidence. In contrast, we found that an interactive orientation supported a culture of readiness to address difficulties in teaching and the interactive process, rather than deficits in pupils.

Practitioners with experience of Intensive Interaction looked for answers to the challenge presented by particular pupils in the process of observation, feedback and reflection on the interaction process. They readily accepted it was their responsibility to make the adjustments to enhance the interactive match and they had created a flexible enough framework to do so. They were not immune, however, to valuing the feedback of an outside 'expert' to that of a colleague – perhaps a legacy of the situation Hart (1996) critiques, of the answer being seen as 'out there' rather than within this school and its skilled and reflective staff.

Like some of the local education administrations ('local education authorities') in Ainscow *et al.*'s (2000) study, the LEA here was concerned with developing the capacity of schools to respond to diversity before changing placement priorities. By pursuing this agenda within the special schools, some of the anxious responses to *intruder* pupils may have been played out in microcosm. This could be seen as wasted time on route to fuller participation being achieved or alternatively as valuable lessons being learnt. Whether or not the latter applies will depend in part on the eventual degree of success, of the particular and wider project, in getting practitioners within and across schools to communicate and learn from each other. It will also depend on, and tell us something about, the extent to which an underlying premise holds true, that is, that by transforming thinking surrounding matters of key detail, wider benefits will accrue.

In many respects, the project reported here falls a long way short of the kind of radical reconstruction of education called for by many inclusionists (e.g. Skrtic 1995; Lloyd 2000; Thomas and Loxley 2001). However, it makes some tentative inroads into action at the level of classrooms and the interactions that take place there, and into exploring the potential of a collaborative problem-solving approach.

References

Ainscow, M. (1999) *Understanding the Development of Inclusive Schools*. London: Falmer.

Ainscow, M., Farrell, P. and Tweddle, D. (2000) Developing policies for inclusive education: a study of the role of local education authorities. *International Journal of Inclusive Education*, **4**, 211–29.

Babbage, R., Byers, R. and Redding, H. (1999) *Approaches to Teaching and Learning: Including Pupils with Learning Difficulties*. London: David Fulton.

Barton, L. (1997) Inclusive education: romantic, subversive or realistic? *International Journal of Inclusive Education*, **1**, 231–42.

Belanger, N. (2000) Inclusion of 'pupils-who-need-extra-help': social transactions in the accessibility of resource and mainstream classrooms. *International Journal of Inclusive Education*, **4**, 231–52.

Bennathan, M. and Boxall, M. (1996) *Effective Intervention in Primary School: Nurture Groups*. London: David Fulton.

Booth, T., Ainscow, M., Black-Hawkins, K., Vaughan, M. and Shaw, L. (2000) *Index for Inclusion: Developing Learning and Participation in Schools*. Bristol: CSIE.

Booth, T., Ainscow, M. and Dyson, A. (1997) Understanding inclusion and exclusion in the English competitive education system. *International Journal of Inclusive Education*, **1**, 337–55.

Carrington, S. (1999) Inclusion needs a different school culture. *International Journal of Inclusive Education*, **3**, 257–68.

Carlson, L. and Bricker, D. D. (1982) Dyadic and contingent aspects of early communicative intervention. In D. D. Bricker (ed.) *Interventions with At-Risk and Handicapped Infants*. Baltimore: University Park Press.

Clough, P. (1988) Bridging 'mainstream' and 'special' education: a curriculum problem. *Journal of Curriculum Studies*, **20**, 327–38.

Corbett, J. (1997) Include/exclude: redefining the boundaries. *International Journal of Inclusive Education*, **1**, 55-64.

Further Education Funding Council (1996) *Inclusive Learning (The Tomlinson Report)*. London: FEFC.

Grove, N. and Peacey, N. (1999) Teaching subjects to pupils with profound and multiple learning difficulties: considerations for the new framework. *British Journal of Special Education*, **26**, 83–6.

Hart, S. (1996) *Beyond Special Needs: Enhancing Children's Learning Through Innovative Thinking*. London: Paul Chapman.

Kaye, K. (1979) Thickening the thin data: the maternal role in developing communication and language. In M. Bullowa (ed.) *Before Speech*. Cambridge: Cambridge University Press.

Lewis, M. and Coates, L. (1980) Mother–infant interaction and cognitive development at twelve weeks. *Infant Behaviour and Development*, **3**, 95–105.

Lewis, M. and Rosenblum, L. A. (eds) (1974) *The Effect of the Infant on Its Caregiver*. New York: Wiley.

Lloyd, C. (2000) Excellence for all children – false promises! *International Journal of Inclusive Education*, **4**, 133–51.

Mahoney, G. and Powell, A. (1988) Modifying parent–child interaction: enhancing the development of handicapped children. *Journal of Special Education*, **22**, 82–96.

Mosley, J. (1993) *Turn Your School Round*. Wisbech: LDA.

Nind, M. (1996) Efficacy of Intensive Interaction. *European Journal of Special Needs Education*, **11**, 48–66.

Nind, M. (2000) Teachers' understanding of interactive approaches in special education. *International Journal of Disability, Development and Education*, **47**, 183–99.

Nind, M. and Hewett, D. (1988) Interaction as curriculum: a process method in a school for pupils with severe learning difficulties. *British Journal of Special Education*, **15**, 55–7.

Nind, M. and Hewett, D. (1994) *Access to Communication: Developing the Basics of Communication with People with Severe Learning Difficulties through Intensive Interaction*. London: David Fulton.

Nind, M. and Hewett, D. (1998) Introduction: recent developments in interactive approaches. In D. Hewett and M. Nind (eds) *Interaction in Action: Reflections on the Use of Intensive Interaction*. London: David Fulton.

Porter, G. (1995) 'Organisation of Schooling: achieving success and quality through inclusion', *Prospects*, **2592**, 299–309.

Rhodes, J. and Ajmal, Y. (1995) *Solution Focused Thinking in Schools*. London: BT Press.

Schaffer, H. R. (ed.) (1977) *Studies in Mother–Infant Interaction*. London: Academic Press.

Skrtic, T. (1995) *Disability and Democracy: Reconstructing Special Education for Post-Modernity*. New York: Teachers College Press.

Thomas, G., Walker, D. and Webb, J. (1998) *The Making of the Inclusive School*. London: Routledge.

Thomas, G. and Loxley, A. (2001) *Deconstructing Special Education and Constructing Inclusion*. Buckingham: Open University Press.

Ware, J. (1996) *Creating a Responsive Environment for People with Profound and Multiple Learning Difficulties*. London: David Fulton.

Yoder, P. J. (1990) The theoretical and empirical basis of early amelioration of developmental disabilities. *Journal of Early Intervention*, **14**, 27–42.

Nind and Cochrane's experiences underline the idea that inclusion is a process, moreover a process that needs to be actively engaged with by all. As with other chapters, this one highlights the value of listening to others and gaining different perspectives. This starting point can create a context that empowers teachers to develop their practices in relation to acceptance of diversity within the classroom. Nind and Cochrane's cases are real ones and, as such, the outcomes they describe are not perfect. However, the chapter suggests that giving teachers opportunities to communicate and reflect on their own practice encourages a move away from a reliance on external 'experts' to treat 'within child deficits' and has the potential to move us towards more inclusive interactive educational systems.

CHAPTER 17

Exclusion: a silent protest

Janet Collins

In this chapter Janet Collins presents a unique consideration of a group of children who are often ignored in discussions of inclusion. These are children who, whilst being physically present in the classroom, opt out quietly through non-participatory behaviours. Collins' original analysis discusses this phenomenon in relation to truancy and social exclusion.

Introduction

Elsewhere, issues of combating social exclusion are held to be synonymous with a reduction of truancy and exclusion from schools. In the UK, for example, New Labour have expressed a commitment to reducing the number of pupils truanting or excluded from our schools. The Social Exclusion Unit's (SEU) remit is to report to the Prime Minister on how to:

> make a step-change in the scale of truancy and exclusions from school, and to find better solutions for those who have been excluded.
>
> (SEU 1998: 1)

The aim was to reduce truancy by a third by the year 2002 (SEU 1998: Annex A). As this chapter will illustrate however, the social exclusion of pupils goes way beyond simple measures of school attendance. Equally important are issues related to the motivation, engagement and active participation of pupils in school. Drawing on in-depth case studies (Collins 1994; 1996) this chapter demonstrates how attendance in school does not necessarily ensure social inclusion or a commitment to learning. In particular, it highlights the plight of children who may well be physically present in the classroom but who are unable or unwilling to participate in the learning opportunities provided there. Understanding the possible causes of this, often habitual, non-participation is an important first step towards increasing pupil participation and reducing social exclusion. Comparing the findings of research into truancy and my own work with non-participating pupils it would appear that both forms of behaviour might be influenced by similar 'individual', 'social' and 'in-school' factors. Consequently, insights gained in the study of one should help to shed light on the other. However, in-depth case studies of the kind presented in this chapter help to provide detailed analysis of the complex and interrelated factors which impact on individual pupils' behaviour. These challenge some of the sweeping and occasionally stereotypical views expressed in larger scale surveys of truancy and social exclusion.

The chapter begins with an account of the longitudinal research study on which it draws. It then identifies four non-participation or, to borrow a term from Young (1984), 'truanting in mind' behaviours. Following an exploration of the possible causes of habitual non-participation, i.e. 'individual', 'social' and 'in-school' factors, each section suggests strategies that may reduce incidence of non-participation in schools. Given that non-participation and truancy may have similar root causes the implication is that these strategies may be effective in reducing social exclusion by combating both.

The original research began in an inner city primary school in which I had previously taught. The school had a large number of pupils who were identified as having serious emotional and behavioural difficulties. Invariably the attention of teachers and support staff was focused on those pupils who exhibited loud, aggressive behaviour and who posed a potential threat to the smooth running of the school. In this climate I felt there was a danger that the social, emotional and educational needs of the relatively quiet and undemanding pupils would go undetected and ignored. Ultimately, this research grew out of this concern and a growing frustration at my inability to communicate with, and therefore teach, a group of pupils who seemed unable or unwilling to participate in the learning activities in my classroom. These pupils were physically present in the classroom and their quiet, seemingly compliant, behaviour did not present obvious problems in terms of discipline or classroom management. However, initial observations and one-to-one conversations revealed an acute lack of engagement in the learning process. These pupils appeared to be so intent on surviving in school without being noticed by teachers or peers that they paid little attention to what they should have been learning. In my opinion this coping strategy was every bit as detrimental to learning and social inclusion as physical absence or the more obvious signs of disaffection.

Beginning what was originally a three-year research project my aims were to understand the possible causes of the pupils' non-participatory behaviour and to design and implement teaching strategies that would empower the pupils to play a more active role in their education. The research focused on in-depth case studies of twelve pupils, ten girls and two boys, who were, at the beginning of the research, all in the same Year 6 class in primary school. Exhibiting quiet and non-participatory behaviour in class was the one criterion that united the group of selected pupils. In many other respects the pupils were extremely diverse. Ten of the twelve selected pupils were girls, which raised the issue of a possible link between non-participatory behaviour and gender. In terms of racial origins the group was mixed. Two pupils were of African-Caribbean origin, whilst one was of mixed race and another Asian. The case studies were constructed from observations while the pupils worked with their regular teacher during the last two years of primary school and the first year of secondary school. They also drew on a series of in-depth open-ended interviews with the pupils, their parents (or nominated significant others) and teachers. Each interview lasted between 30 minutes and an hour and was tape-recorded, transcribed and analysed following ethnographic principles. During the first two years of the study I also worked directly with the pupils as part of an intervention programme. This chapter draws on the full range of data gathered during the study. All names have been changed.

During the three years of data collection, and despite the fact that the pupils transferred from one primary school to seven secondary schools, I was able to maintain contact with ten of the twelve pupils and their families. During that time eleven of the pupils had good attendance records and Charlene was the only pupil with a record of intermittent truancy. It is perhaps indicative of the relationship between Charlene's family and the school that I was unable to obtain an interview with members of her family. I finally lost contact with Charlene altogether during the second year of the research when Charlene and her family 'disappeared' from the area without leaving a forwarding address.

Truanting in mind

Absenteeism from school is a large and very visible problem. The official figures published by the SEU are likely to be alarming for parents and teachers alike. Moreover, there is growing evidence that the official figures are a gross underestimation of the real truancy levels. Surveys involving anonymous pupil questionnaires (for example, Gray and Jesson 1990; O'Keefe 1994) suggest that the incidence of both blanket truancy and post-registration truancy are much greater than was believed by the schools or than is reflected in official figures. Whilst there is some disagreement about the actual extent of the problem there does seem to be a general agreement that truancy levels are too high and that strategies which reduce truancy are to be welcomed. One can understand the attraction for governments in being seen: to measure truancy levels; to set targets for improvement; and to be able to measure improvement in a school's performance.

What remains significantly less visible is the plight of children and young people who, despite their attendance in school, remain as disaffected and uninterested in what school has to offer them as their absent and often more vocal peers. Indeed, the current emphasis on measuring and improving school attendance masks a serious underlying issue, namely pupils' disaffection with school and lack of engagement with the learning experiences which school offers. Getting pupils into school is only the first step towards solving the problem of truancy and social exclusion. There is also a need to ensure that all pupils are active participants in the social and academic life of the school. Whilst this remains an under-researched area there is some evidence that researchers and policy makers are increasingly aware of the problem. Speaking at the TES conference in 1997 David Blunkett talked about how youngsters who are dispirited about their chances of finding employment are likely to drift away from the education process.

... we all know that the 1 in 12 who get no qualifications at all, by the time they reach 16, are primarily, but not exclusively, those who have not been attending school. It is not merely a matter of actually being there, it is sometimes 'being there but not being there', if you know what I mean.

(Blunkett 1997)

Blunkett and others recognise that school attendance does not necessarily equate with a commitment to learning. Pupils who are 'there but not there' do not actively participate in classroom activities and consequently run the risk of becoming socially excluded. They may be thought of as 'playing truant in mind whilst present in body, [seeing] neither the relevance nor the reason for all they are asked to do' (Young 1984: 12). Although they complete the minimum of work, they appear to have little interest or investment in the outcome. 'They conform, and even play the system, but many do not allow the knowledge presented to them to make any deep impact on their view of reality' (Barnes 1979: 17). Currently we have no evidence of the numbers of pupils who play truant in mind and without systematic research on a large scale the issue of 'truanting in mind' will effectively remain an invisible problem. The fact that pupils who exhibit this behaviour may not present their teachers with acute attendance and discipline problems is likely to contribute to this invisibility.

In the context of this chapter 'playing truant in mind' describes situations in which a pupil is physically present in the classroom but who, for whatever reason, does not participate in the experience which has been planned and presented by the teacher. Identifying this kind of truancy can be difficult. Pupils can truant during any activity irrespective of whether it requires observable physical action or not. However, participation, or lack of it, is more easily observable in some situations than others. For example, pupils who are required to read silently could be actively engaged or they could simply be waiting for the lesson to be over. In a classroom of sighted children those who are looking in the right direction with their eyes open are more likely to be reading than those who are not. Admittedly the child who has his or her eyes closed might be thinking about the text but they might be thinking about completely unrelated matter. What is going on in the child's mind and the extent to which the pupil has indeed read and understood the texts can only be ascertained by talking to the child and/or by assessing their ability to complete a task that requires knowledge of the text.

Elsewhere (Collins 1996: 36–47) I identified four types of withdrawal or truanting in mind behaviour. I described these as 'being invisible', 'refusing to participate', 'hesitation' and 'an inappropriate focus'. Although all the children in the study exhibited these behaviours, here they are described in relation to observations of Justina. In some many of the lessons I observed Justina would have no direct contact with the teacher. Often there was evidence to suggest that where she sat or how she behaved made her 'invisible' and minimised her contact with the teacher. Alternatively, she would be invited to participate but would 'refuse' to join in. Sometimes her refusal would be direct and possibly supported by a seemingly valid reason. On other occasions she would not acknowledge the request; she would remain still and quietly avoid making eye contact with the teacher. Whilst these behaviours were relatively easy to detect the remaining two presented more of a problem and required closer observation. In both of these situations Justina appeared to be busy, however, closer analysis revealed that she was not actively engaged in the task. When Justina 'hesitated' she appeared busy but she never really became engaged in the task and would remain on the periphery of an activity. Sometimes she actually seemed to be too afraid to join in.

> In craft, for example, Justina spent significantly more time watching her partners working than she did actively engaged in the task. Similarly, during a practical lesson Justina walked round the science lab, touching some of the equipment with the tips of her fingers but rarely carrying out the intended experiment. On both occasions she seemed reluctant to 'get her hands dirty' by handling the equipment.
>
> (Collins 1996: 43)

In both these cases it would appear that the teachers were expecting pupils to play a physical and active role in the lesson. They were expected to learn by doing. Having the experience of making a model or carrying out an experiment was deemed by the teacher to have educational value. In the case of the craft lesson Justina might have learned something from watching her peers. However, as Justina walked around the science lab on her own she never even observed someone else carry out an experiment. Consequently, it is difficult to know what science was being learned. The fact that the teacher did not comment on her behaviour might, however, have reinforced her non-participation.

The final, and to my mind the most disturbing, form of truanting in mind is where pupils have 'an inappropriate focus'. In these instances pupils are actively involved in an activity which has little or no bearing on the learning task presented by the teacher. During my observations of Justina this concerned me because in the majority of instances the teacher was either unaware of what she was doing or, worse, condoned the behaviour. The most dramatic example of an inappropriate focus occurred during a French oral lesson during which Justina did not speak a single word of French.

> Her one interaction with the teacher was conducted in English and focused on a point of detail about the setting out of her work. He seemed oblivious to her lack of participation in the oral part of the lesson. When, out of sheer frustration, I asked Justina to read what she had just written she said, 'I don't speak French because it confuses me'.
>
> (Collins 1996: 45)

Despite this refusal to speak the language Justina later described herself as being 'really pleased with myself in French. I've got really loads of ticks in my book and I am glad I know a lot about it now'. Her physical presence in the classroom and positive statements from the teacher reinforced her image of herself as a successful student. In one respect she was a model pupil. She did not cause the teacher any discipline problems. She handed her neatly completed work in on time. However, in other far more serious respects she was a failure, she had learned nothing of the spoken language. I believe this kind of behaviour may be more problematic than physical truancy. Justina's presence in the classroom did not ensure that she learned the language. However, her physical presence masked the fact that there was a serious problem.

Sadly, none of the teachers in the study appeared to notice or be alarmed by the pupils' lack of participation in curriculum activities. Moreover, even if individual teachers had noticed the truanting that went on in their lesson it would take time and energy to establish if this pattern was repeated in other lessons. I think it unlikely that teachers would easily be able to find the time or motivation to ask their colleagues about pupils like Justina who appear on the surface to be model pupils. Recognising that non-participation or truanting in mind is detrimental to learning is an important first step. Suggesting possible solutions requires an understanding of the possible causes of this behaviour.

Possible causes of truancy

As part of a two year NFER funded project Kinder *et al.* (1995) identified a number of possible causes of disaffection and truancy. This and other truancy studies (for example, Gray and Jesson 1990; Graham and Bowling 1995; Balding 1996) raise issues very similar to those raised in my own work with quiet non-participatory pupils. Thus it would seem that the causes of disaffection are similar for pupils who fail to attend school and those who 'play truant in mind'.

Kinder *et al.* (1995) organise their analysis around the three main arenas constantly highlighted by research into truancy, i.e.: *individual pathological or personality traits; family circumstances* or values and/or social factors within the non-attender's communities; and *school factors*, often located in either the curriculum or the ethos and relationships encountered there by the pupils. This chapter takes each of these in turn and compares Kinder *et al.*'s findings with those of other researchers in the field of truancy and of my own research with pupils who truant in mind.

Individual pathological or personality traits

Kinder *et al.* (1995) report that where individual characteristics were cited, these were largely viewed in terms of some kind of deficit in emotional or social health, such as lack of self-esteem, lack of social skills, lack of confidence or poor peer relationships. I also identified these factors as potential causes of truanting in mind behaviour. However, I rejected the individual deficit model implied in Kinder *et al.*'s work. Following Oliver (1988) I regarded these issues as being socially constructed and created. Thus, for example, whilst truanting in mind was associated with a lack of confidence, the extent to which a pupil feels confident varied considerably from situation to situation.

Generally speaking quiet pupils are likely to be more talkative at home and with people that they know well . . . They tend to be shy when they are being watched by others and their shyness is particularly acute when they are asked to speak in front of the class or during assemblies.

(Collins 1996: 20)

As pupils are more likely to feel confident and participate in situations in which they know people well this suggests that their confidence is socially created and constructed. Moreover, there is evidence to suggest that there is no simple causal relationship between lack of confidence and behaviour. Lacking confidence can inhibit pupils and prevent them participating. However, failure to participate can also reduce an individual's confidence.

Anxiety about talking to relative strangers can contribute to poor self-esteem, especially when individuals compare themselves with more confident friends and relatives. Quiet individuals see an ability to converse easily as a skill to be envied and an inability to 'perform' in this way can make quiet pupils feel inadequate.

(Collins 1996: 22)

The impact of non-participation is particularly acute in conversations with teachers. The discomfort of quiet pupils is often so visible that teachers become reluctant to ask them to participate in class discussions. This reinforces the pupil's truanting in mind behaviour. For example, Mandy was clearly anxious about being asked questions in class. In order to reduce her anxiety the teacher chose other more willing pupils. Thus rather than increasing Mandy's confidence and skill the teacher reduces her opportunities to practice skills which have an important educational value. Knowing that she is unlikely to be chosen to answer the teacher's questions might reduce Mandy's need to listen to the rest of the discussion. This could provide Mandy with even more opportunities to play truant in mind thus reinforcing her image of herself as an observer not a participant. I would suggest that a similar self-fulfilling prophecy is at work in the case of pupils who truant from school. Perhaps failure to attend school also reinforces pupils' negative image of themselves that makes it subsequently more difficult to attend school.

As with pupils who absent themselves from school, pupils who truant in mind also lack social skills and have difficulty in forming and sustaining relationships with their peers. Consequently, during the first year of the research I initiated a twelve-week withdrawal programme of collaborative group work. The aim of the programme was to improve the pupils' social skills and confidence and to enable them to work collaboratively with their peers. I saw this as an important aspect of my work because,

… where pupils have difficulties in peer relationships which interfere with their learning, it is important not only to help them as individuals to develop their confidence and social skills, but also to work with the class as a whole in order to ensure that they do not become the subject of teasing, ridicule or rejection.

(Beveridge 1993: 96)

The effects of the programme were encouraging and led to a development into whole class teaching the following year. Throughout these sessions all the pupils played an active role in all the activities. This subsequently led to a longer programme of work in a whole class context (for full details see Collins 1996; chapters 9 and 10).

Social factors

In terms of social factors, a profile of truants is developing. According to the research truants tend to be 'older pupils, and from poorer backgrounds' (SEU 1998, section 1.5). The parents of truants are more likely to be in low skilled than in professional or managerial jobs, and more likely to be in local authority housing than owner occupiers (Graham and Bowling 1995). In addition some studies (for example, Gray and Jesson 1990) suggest that truancy is more common in inner city areas. Given that all the children in the study lived in an area with a high level of unemployment and the majority lived in rented houses or maisonettes, this profile may be as applicable to pupils who play truant in mind as it is to those who physically absent themselves from school. However, as I found during my research, making assumptions about pupils based on where they live is over-simplistic. Angie's educated and articulate parents resented being perceived, and subsequently housed, as if they were working class by English housing authorities when they arrived in the country from the Caribbean.

Another common thread between the two forms of truanting is that, in both, significant domestic problems and inadequate parenting skills may be linked with disaffected behaviour in school. Drawing on post-Bowlby accounts of parenting (for example, Chodorow 1978; Benjamin 1990) I highlighted the possible connections between parent–child relationships and the truanting in mind behaviour witnessed in school. In essence, I argued that pupils who had experienced anxious attachments in their relationships with parents or caregivers might subsequently experience difficulties in forming relationships with teachers and pupils in school. I believe that difficult relationships in school are one of the underlying causes of truanting in mind behaviour. However, once again I believe the situation is far more complex than large-scale studies would suggest.

In a section on significant domestic problems Kinder *et al.* appear to perpetuate a view that one-parent families are, by definition, problematic. They quote, but do not challenge, the following assertion made by a respondent.

> A number of [disaffected] pupils bring huge social problems into school, they are mainly from one-parent families where carers have multiple social problems of their own, including debt, drug taking and unemployment.
>
> (Kinder *et al.* 1995: 10)

By comparison, in my research, I found no evidence to support the view that one-parent families were necessarily problematic. There were examples of good parent–child relationships within one-parent families and examples of anxious attachments within two-parent families. In addition, other researchers (for example, Collins 1991) have found no evidence to support a link between lone-parenting and delinquency. Based on this research I believe it is time to dispel rather than perpetuate the negative image of one-parent families. In particular teachers should examine the ways in which stereotypical views, which regard nuclear two-parent families as the 'norm', may exclude or marginalise fathers and lone-parents. A re-examination of the parenting role should also influence the ways in which parents are portrayed in school. It is important that textbooks and other teaching materials do not portray lone-parent families as a mutant form of the so-called 'normal' two-parent family. Similarly, teachers should be aware of how their own assumptions about parents and families could colour their expectations of the children they teach. A serious issue in the parenting debate around truancy is teachers' refusal to accept and respect the home backgrounds of the pupils they teach.

In Kinder *et al.*'s (1995) research parentally condoned absence was seen as a major problem. By comparison, during my own research I was only aware of three instances of parentally condoned absence. Twice Rasheeda took time off school to look after younger siblings, whilst Mandy's mother registered her disapproval for the school's multicultural curriculum by forbidding Mandy to attend Eid celebrations in school. As has been said before, with the exception of time off for illness, Charlene was the only pupil who was physically absent from either primary or secondary school.

With these exceptions the pupils in my research had good attendance records and parents clearly thought it was important for their children to go to school and 'get a good education'. Sadly, the parents did not seem to be particularly concerned that their children exhibited quiet and non-participatory behaviour in school. Some parents were themselves quiet pupils. Others saw it as a harmless phase that their children would grow out of. All the parents seemed convinced that regular attendance and good behaviour was all that was necessary for their children to get a good education and 'make something of their lives'. This is not surprising given the official emphasis on school attendance.

My research would seem to support the Social Exclusion Unit's assertion that family and peer pressures are important factors behind truancy.

> Parents bear the primary responsibility for ensuring that their children attend school regularly and home circumstances exert an important influence over pupils' attendance and punctuality. Poor parental supervision and lack of commitment to education are crucial factors behind truancy.
>
> (SEU 1998, section 1.8)

Poor parental supervision and lack of commitment to education may help to explain pupils' physical truancy from school. However, on the whole, pupils who truant in mind have good attendance records. Parents have clearly done their job in getting the pupils to school. In order to explain why they do not participate in school activities it is necessary to consider other, in-school factors.

School factors

The Social Exclusion Unit recognises that 'how schools operate can make a great difference in shaping whether children do in fact truant' (SEU 1998, section 1.7). In addition OFSTED (1995) found that in some schools poor attendance was centred among pupils who were weak readers and that non-attendance could also be a result of anxiety about GCSE coursework deadlines. Balding (1996) found that anxiety about bullying was frequently cited as a reason for truanting. Kinder *et al.* (1995) cites a number of in-school factors directly associated with truancy and disaffection. These related to the school itself, relationships with peers and teachers, and the curriculum. In my own work I have also identified a number of in-school factors directly associated with truanting in mind behaviour.

Unlike Kinder *et al.* I did not focus on the 'most disaffected age group'. Instead I chose to work with younger pupils, i.e. from Year 6 to Year 8. Nevertheless, some of the pupils and parents I interviewed expressed strong feelings about the curriculum offered by the school. As has already been mentioned, Mandy's mother had strong negative feelings about a multicultural curriculum that she felt was inappropriate for her daughter. For different reasons the Black and Asian parents were equally disaffected by what was on offer.

> What's used to defuse the argument is multicultural education and 'let's do some bhaji, let's cook an Indian food, I'll wear a sari today, and that's multicultural education' – that is not multicultural education, multicultural education is the culture that's multifaceted and unfortunately education in England is very one-sided, it's really a culture to satisfy whites' perspectives of Black people.
>
> (Aberash's stepfather)

According to Aberash's stepfather at least, the mismatch between the school and the individual's lived experience was not restricted to racial issues.

> Crack exists and some of the biggest runners for crack and cocaine are eleven and twelve. They are not adults. Another issue is child abuse. There is a patronising way in which we talk to kids about child abuse, yet they go home and they get abused at home. It's like I've seen teachers talking about racism to black children in a way that makes them laugh. Teachers don't come out and talk about these issues as they really are.
>
> (Aberash's stepfather)

This is not a call for teachers to accept and condone drug abuse, child abuse and racist behaviour. However, it is a genuine plea for teachers to talk about such issues in a way that is real and meaningful to the pupils for whom it may be part of their daily-lived experiences. Without this, pupils may come to regard teachers and what they teach as irrelevant.

Despite their frequent truanting in mind, few of the pupils I interviewed saw the school curriculum as irrelevant. However, all the pupils were very clear about the lessons they liked or disliked. Basically, the pupils liked lessons that were taught by good teachers, i.e. those who seemed to respect the pupils as individuals and who were always willing to provide support and help when it was needed. This would appear to support previous findings that so far as young pupils are concerned 'how children are taught matters to them more than what they are taught' (Wade and Moore 1993: 29). In considering the qualities of an effective pupil–teacher relationship, it is generally accepted that pupils learn most effectively when they feel valued and secure, trust their teachers, and both understand and accept the full range of classroom demands.

Sadly, many pupils who exhibit truanting in mind behaviour have difficulty in forming relationships with their teachers. Rasheeda admitted that there was little communication between her and her teacher.

'Cause he has to work, some work to do and I have some work to do and if I say like speak to him a lot, he says 'just carry on with your work'.

(Rasheeda, Y6 pupil)

She seemed unaware that both she and her teacher should be engaged in the same task, namely her education. The way in which pupils who truant in mind exclude themselves from learning relationships is also demonstrated by Diana's comment about what she sees as the teacher's role.

. . . when I am stuck he has to help me . . . work and everything but most of the time he's . . . he's like talking hisself like doing things on the board and things so you can't really talk to him when he is trying to learn the children.

(Diana, Y6 pupil)

In this account she effectively precludes herself from any participation in the whole class discussion for fear of disturbing the teacher. Moreover, she does not include herself in the group of pupils being taught. Little wonder that she feels free to play truant.

In terms of truanting in mind behaviour, issues of teacher expectation, feelings of security, teaching style and classroom organisation appeared to be more significant than teacher popularity or the subject being taught. Observations suggest that pupils are more likely to participate when the teacher clearly expects participation and they are explicit about the reasons for this participation. Conversely, teachers who ignore or condone truanting in mind behaviour actively discourage participation. Classroom observations, particularly during the intervention programme, suggest that, where collaborative working is supported by the teacher, pupils find it easier to talk in small group discussions rather than in whole class lessons. Consequently, there is greater participation in lessons in which the learning has been organised around small group activities. Similarly, structured but open-ended activities provide a secure environment that discourages truanting in mind. The current Government policy of encouraging more whole class discussion bodes ill for pupils who truant in mind and who might well benefit from small group activities. The needs of all pupils should be considered in discussions of classroom organisation and management.

Reducing truancy and social exclusion

There is general acceptance that physical truancy is a problem for individuals and for society. In terms of truancy in mind the first issue for pupils, parents, schools and government agencies is to recognise and accept that this may be a serious problem. However, my research suggests that not everyone understands the need for active participation. Some of the pupils, teachers and parents who participated in this study seemed to assume that physical presence in the classroom was synonymous with learning. The research discussed above suggests that this is not the case. The need for active participation in education should be recognised and made explicit to all concerned. This should be supported by research into the causes and effects of truanting in mind behaviour. Given the potential similarities between the causes of both forms of truancy this might be done in conjunction with research into physical truancy. The next step would be to devise, implement and evaluate initiatives for reducing truanting in mind behaviour.

Once the need for active participation has been established, my work with pupils who truant in mind suggests that the three strategies for reducing physical truancy identified by Kinder *et al*. (1995) are likely to be effective for both groups of truants.

In terms of reducing truancy in mind the strategy of *maintaining and monitoring attendance* would have to be interpreted in terms of organising and managing the classroom in such a way as to maximise participation. This would require careful observations and monitoring of the four types of truanting in mind behaviour identified above. In secondary schools and large primary schools where pupils are taught by a number of different teachers there would have to be school-wide monitoring of non-participation and some means of sharing knowledge of pupil behaviour.

Experience of working with quiet pupils highlights the need to *provide direct support for the emotional and behavioural needs* of those who play truant in mind. Once again, this begins with the recognition that, despite their good attendance records, these pupils do in fact have emotional and behavioural needs that are not being met. In addition to improving relationships in school there is a need to provide time to listen to pupils. I feel strongly that all professionals who work with children and young people should be trained to identify the signs of abuse or other forms of acute distress and be able to contact appropriate specialist support.

Where, as was the case in the school where I began my research, there is parental disaffection about the curriculum offered by the school, *offering alternative curriculum experiences* would be a good way to reduce truanting in mind behaviour. However, such a curriculum would have to take account of and respect the reality of the pupils' daily-lived experiences.

In conclusion, it could be argued that this small-scale qualitative research contributes to an understanding of social exclusion in a number of ways. First, it suggests a refocusing of attention from simple measures of attendance to more subtle measures of participation in school. Second, it challenges some of the more general and stereotypical views expressed in large-scale research into absenteeism. Finally, based on the possible causes of truancy, it suggests possible strategies for increasing participation and reducing social exclusion for a potentially vulnerable and largely ignored group of pupils. What is required now is further research into the phenomenon of truanting in mind. Particularly useful would be empirical research into the long-term effects of truanting in mind and the effect of interventions. Sadly, given that these pupils do not demand attention I fear that their silent protest will remain unheard.

References

Balding, J. (1996) *Young People in 1995*. Exeter: University of Exeter: Schools Health Unit.

Barnes, D. (1979 first pub. 1976) *From Communication to Curriculum*. Middlesex: Penguin.

Benjamin, J. (1990 first pub. 1988) *The Bonds of Love*. London: Virago.

Beveridge, S. (1993) *Special Educational Needs in Schools*. London: Routledge.

Blunkett, D. (1997) TES Conference.

Chodorow, N. (1978) *The Reproduction of Mothering*. London: University of California Press.

Collins, S. (1991) Transition from lone-parent family to step-family. In Hardey, M. and Crow, G. (eds) *Lone Parenthood*. London: Harvester Wheatsheaf.

Collins, J. (1994) *The Silent Minority: developing talk in the primary classroom*. Unpublished PhD thesis: University of Sheffield.

Collins, J. (1996) *The Quiet Child*. London: Cassell.

Graham, J. and Bowling, B. (1995) *Young People and Crime*. London: Home Office research studies, 145.

Gray, J. and Jesson, D. (1990) *Truancy in Secondary Schools Amongst Fifth Year Pupils*. University of Sheffield: QQSE Research Group.

Kinder, K., Harland, J., Wilkin, A. and Wakefield, A. (1995) *Three to Remember: strategies for disaffected pupils*. Slough: NFER.

Office for Standards in Education (1995) *Access, Achievement and Attendance in Secondary Schools* (Report No. 16/95). London: OFSTED.

O'Keefe, D. G. (1994) *Truancy in English Secondary Schools*. London: HMSO.

Oliver, M. (1988) The social and political context of education policy. In Barton, L. (ed.) *The Politics of Special Education*. London: The Falmer Press.

Social Exclusion Unit (1998) *Truancy and Social Exclusion*. Report. London: Social
    Exclusion Unit.

Wade, B. and Moore, M. (1993) *Experiencing Special Needs*. Buckingham: Open
    University Press.

Young, D. (1984) *Knowing How and Knowing That*. London: Birkbeck College.

Collins applies ideas for reducing truanting to children who opt out, quietly, within the classroom. There are clear parallels between her ideas and the development of an inclusive pedagogy. She proposes that active participation in learning is essential and, further, that attending to the social aspects of the classroom, such as the pupil–teacher relationship or the use of small group activities, acts to increase pupil participation. Being physically present is not synonymous with learning, although this belief was held by several of the participants in her study. Learning happens within a social context and pupils need to be supported in their engagement with this social context.

Part 4

Inside classrooms

CHAPTER 18

Learning without limits

Susan Hart

This chapter shares some of what was learnt from a research project in which a team of researchers and teachers sought to understand the distinctive features of teaching that does not rely on the concept of fixed ability. The key ideas were developed collaboratively through exploring and comparing the similarities and differences across nine teachers' very different, individual ways of working. They are illustrated through the distinctive features of the thinking and practice of one member of the team, Julie, who works as a history teacher in a secondary school. The chapter offers an alternative model of practice that does not rely on the ability grouping and categorising that research has shown has damaged so many young people and their life chances.

Beginnings of a project

Over the years since comprehensive reorganisation, many teachers committed to the comprehensive ideal have rejected ideas of fixed ability and developed their practice to reflect their beliefs. They share the view, so powerfully expressed recently by Clyde Chitty (2002) that 'comprehensive reform has no meaning unless it challenges the fallacy of fixed ability or potential in education. It should aim to dismantle all the structures rooted in that fallacy that act as barriers to effective learning while, at the same time, it should facilitate practices that enable everyone to enjoy a full education'. However, while such teachers have, individually, developed their practices in line with their ideals, the distinctive features of teaching approaches based on a more optimistic view of human educability have never been articulated in such a way as to present a convincing and practicable alternative to ability-based teaching.

Meanwhile, long-discredited ideas about IQ and fixed ability continue to have currency in schools. Indeed, the thrust of government initiatives to raise standards over the past decade has been to place more, rather than less, emphasis on the need to differentiate by ability. These developments have reinforced the belief that it is essential to categorise – and group – pupils by ability in order to provide challenging teaching for all young people and to raise standards. Ofsted inspectors are briefed to check that teaching is differentiated for 'more able', 'average' and 'less able' pupils. Teachers are expected to make explicit in their schemes of work how this differentiation is achieved. The new emphasis upon target-setting and value-added measures of effectiveness means that from the earliest stages of education teachers are required to make explicit predictions about future levels of achievement.

In all of these developments, what exactly is meant by 'ability' goes largely unexamined. One view is that 'ability' is synonymous with 'attainment'; to say someone is 'less able' is simply to say something about how their current abilities to do certain things compare with others of the same age. Another view is that 'less able' implies something stable and relatively unalterable about underlying cognitive capacities, allowing predictions about future potential to be legitimately made. Current reform initiatives do not explicitly state that 'ability' means 'fixed ability'. Nevertheless, as Gillborn and Youdell (2000) point out, constantly requiring teachers to predict future performance can only be justified if it is underpinned by the assumption that current differences in children's learning reflect stable, measurable and relatively unalterable differences of potential.

This chapter describes the outcomes of a project intended to explore and elaborate models of teaching which do not rely on the notion of fixed or inherent ability. The project, which draws on the work of nine teachers, was initiated by researchers at the University of Cambridge School of Education, who felt that there was an urgent need to challenge the ideas about ability underlying the government improvement agenda. This follows decades of research testifying to the injustices and damaging effects of ability labelling (Hart 1998). The projects' name, *Learning Without Limits*, was inspired by a powerful passage in Stephen Jay Gould's *The Mismeasure of Man* which seemed to capture our central concerns:

> We pass through this world but once. Few tragedies can be more extensive than the stunting of life, few injustices deeper than the denial of an opportunity to strive or even to hope by a limit imposed from without but falsely identified as lying within.
>
> (Gould 1981: 29)

The team realised that it would not be sufficient simply to re-open well-rehearsed debates about the impact of ability labelling on young people's education and life chances. We would need to propose an alternative to ability-based pedagogy underpinned by a more optimistic view of human educability. We needed to show how teachers can cater for diversity within their classrooms without assuming that students can legitimately be grouped into the 'more able', 'average' and 'less able'. This would allow us, we hoped, to propose an alternative improvement agenda backed up by evidence.

About the research

The project began by advertising nation-wide for teachers who shared the aims and values of the project. The response reinforced our conviction that there were many educators 'out there' all over the country who shared our concerns. Fifty teachers sent for information about the project, and 22 applied, explaining why they wanted to participate. We were deeply moved by some of the personal experiences described in those application forms, including one from a teacher who, aged 16, had been devastated to be told by her head teacher that it would be 'a waste of everybody's time' for her to stay on in the sixth form. We held 17 interviews, and a team of four primary and five secondary teachers covering a range of very different teaching contexts was established.

Over the following year we spent many hours in these teachers' classrooms, observing and interviewing both teachers and pupils. We also met to share our thinking and develop the research collectively. In constant collaboration with the teachers, we gradually built up individual accounts of the key constructs at the heart of each teacher's thinking, and an understanding of how these constructs worked together to create a distinctive pedagogy. We then summarised these and looked for common themes and differences, to try to identify the key concepts and practices that are distinctive of teaching that does not rely on ideas of fixed or inherent ability. From this collective analysis, we have identified one core principle, which acts as the inspiration and driving force at the heart of these teachers' practice. In addition, we have identified three core ideas that describe the mechanisms through which the principle is translated into practice in the classroom to create a distinctive and practicable pedagogy. This principle and its associated ideas are illuminated in the distinctive features of one teacher's work.

The principle of transformability

Julie is the head of Humanities in a secondary school serving a predominantly white, rural community. Her antipathy to ability labelling goes back to her own school days when she noticed the damage that can be done. She determined to create, in her own classroom, an environment where young people's learning powers would not be limited or demeaned by such labels. When she applied to become a head of department, she chose a school where she would have freedom to organise groups and develop her teaching in accordance with her values. In her application she explained her feelings on labelling some young people as 'less able':

Less able to succeed in a rigidly structured testing system maybe, but not less able to develop into thoughtful, talented human beings with a great deal to offer society. It would seem reasonable to assume that as the human intellect and potential is so diverse, the way children and teenagers express their intellectual and creative capacity will also be equally as diverse. [. . .] Stories of students who achieved little at school but went on to great success in all walks of life should not surprise us. Millionaires who cannot even sign their name are a rare and probably somewhat exaggerated example, but the concept is clear. Not everybody is able to demonstrate their unique talents in the current rigid education system. Once such people leave the establishments that labelled them 'failures', they can draw on their untapped skills. Others, however, robbed of self-esteem and confidence struggle to make a go of their lives.

Looking at this now, we can see how it links to the core principle we call 'transformability'. Julie rejects ability labels because she knows that existing ability hierarchies are predicated upon particular systems of education, curriculum and pedagogy which do not provide adequate opportunity or flexibility for all to succeed. There is nothing natural or inevitable about the existing education system, any more than there is anything natural and inevitable about the attainment or ability hierarchies that it produces. Ability labels lead us to expect a stable relationship between present and future – that future attainments will broadly reflect existing patterns. But this will be so only if everything continues unchanged – if nothing is done to unlock some of the 'rigidities' that constrain learning. The driving force underlying Julie's work is a passionate conviction that she does have significant power to change current practices in a direction that she believes will be more enabling for young people.

Julie sees considerable scope for enhancing learning by freeing it from the limits imposed by organisational practices such as streaming and setting. These not only damage self-esteem, but lock young people into boxes that determine and justify the provision subsequently made for them. Julie sympathises with those who give up because they feel that they have been written off. 'It's hard to keep trying, isn't it,' she says, 'when you are told you are being entered for an exam where you can only get a D?' Her resistance to streaming, setting and attainment-based grouping in the classroom is not just in the interests of those who find themselves in the lower groups and sets. Her experience has led her to conclusions similar to those recently reported by Boaler *et al.* (2000), who, when investigating mathematics teaching found that teachers working with top sets often did not recognise or address the students' difficulties, while students, feeling under pressure to perform, were afraid to admit when they didn't understand.

Julie strives to increase flexibility and create space for individuality and creativity to flourish through offering a wide variety of learning opportunities with open access for everybody, though this work is inevitably constrained by the rigidities of examinations. She sees herself as actively working to create better learning opportunities for young people. So, when she looks to the future, she expects to see significant changes – not continuity – in young people's attitudes, responses and attainments, as a consequence of the learning environment becoming more supportive and enabling. With ability-based teaching, children's futures as learners are already to some degree laid down. Teachers see their task as one of ensuring that each child reaches his or her presumed 'potential'. In contrast, for Julie the future is in the making in the present. What will happen next depends upon what is done now. There is scope for all young people to become better learners if conditions are enabling and learning can be freed from some prevailing constraints. The exact nature and extent of future improvement cannot be known in advance, so the future is necessarily open and unpredictable. Julie is inspired by the sense that the making of the future is at least in part in her hands, that through her practice she can help to make the everyday experience of education more enriching and life-enhancing. Through the choices she makes, Julie works to *transform* both current patterns of interaction and future possibilities for learning by opening up opportunities that might otherwise have remained closed, and by taking concerted action to release learning from limits that might otherwise constrain future development.

This core principle of transformability is at work in everything that Julie does: her questioning, expectations, the tasks she sets, the environment she constructs, her interactions, assessments and feedback to pupils. She understands that the choices she makes have profound and transforming effects upon the quality of young people's educational experiences.

Mechanisms of transformability

An example of the principle in action can be seen in Julie's early efforts to win round a particular group. Joining the school in the summer term, before she had been able to introduce any changes into the systems of grouping already in place, Julie took over a bottom-set history group. They greeted her, she recalls, 'with something like "We're the thickos, we don't do any work but we managed to give our last teacher a nervous breakdown."' Despite what was probably exaggerated bravado, she felt their remarks were highly revealing of their perceptions of themselves: 'They thought all they were good for was being pains and tried as hard as possible to fulfil that image.' Nevertheless, Julie was convinced that, in time, it would be possible to change their image of themselves, and that there were specific things she could do to enable that change to happen.

As Julie talks about how she set about trying to change the dynamics with this challenging group, she relates her choices and actions to what she thinks might be going on in students' minds. She shows that she recognises the young people as active agents who make sense of their day-to-day experience in their own terms and who act accordingly. She also understands that students' states of mind are profoundly affected by their experiences in school. She understands the subtle messages that environments, resources and practices can convey to young people about their worth and capabilities. She exploits this to help rebuild their sense that they are taken seriously as learners, that their efforts at learning are valued, and that they can derive enjoyment and satisfaction from learning. She tries to turn things around with this group by offering them experiences which gradually, incrementally, enable them to change the way that they think about themselves and what school has to offer them.

As she describes the steps she took, practically, in her own teaching, Julie emphasises the *connections* between these steps and the positive effects that she expected and hoped for in the self-image, attitudes and feelings of the students. She began by 'changing the whole image' of the room where they were working, to create a more stimulating and relaxed environment. She changed the way that desks were grouped and provided them with attractive new folders 'so that they could see that their work was going to be valued'. She also used a lot of model making in the initial stages, which they enjoyed and during which she had the opportunity to begin building relationships. Slowly things began to change.

Julie's main strategy is not to try to influence students' behaviour through exercising forms of control. Rather she tries to turn things around by connecting with their consciousness as people, by trying to understand what makes a difference to their willingness and power to make use of the resources available to them to sustain and further their own learning in school.

Co-agency – connecting teachers' power and learners' power

We call the immense potential that is opened up by connecting teachers' power and learners' power *co-agency*. Julie understands that if teachers' power is to be effective it must connect with and harness young people's own power to make a difference to their own future lives. However committed and thoughtful teachers are, they cannot make a difference unless students themselves choose to take up the invitations to learn that are extended to them. And they will not do this unless what they encounter in school connects with their own sense of who they are, what they can do and what they want for their lives. So a major priority for Julie is to try to understand school experiences from the young people's perspective.

As Julie talks about her teaching, she continually makes reference to the subjective conditions that she believes will lay the foundations for young people to become more powerful and committed learners. Young people are more likely to choose to engage and invest in school learning if they are enabled to feel competent and in control, to find learning stimulating and enjoyable, to feel safe and supported and to feel themselves an equally valued member of the school community. Julie plans tasks and activities that should enable everyone to participate and succeed; she chooses *not* to set different tasks for different groups or tables of pupils by reference to their perceived levels of achievement, as is common in ability-focused classrooms. She prefers to offer common tasks presented in ways that make them open, accessible and engaging for everybody:

> I tend to set work that everybody can engage in at one level or another, which doesn't mean that I am not aware of their difficulties, if they have any. It just means that I don't want to go round the room saying 'well you're very clever, so you can do this but you're a bit thick so I'll give you that'. Because that's what you are doing, isn't it really? And it's surprising how well students do perform at certain tasks if they are given the chance.

Julie is convinced that, whatever the good intentions, the message that young people pick up from different tasks and/or ability-based groups is that some young people are 'not good enough' to do the tasks offered to others. While it is essential that everyone has work that they can do, these differentiated approaches are not an option for her because of the negative impact they can have on people's states of mind. Sometimes she provides double-sided sheets – with the same task presented in different ways on either side – and trusts the students to choose which side they want to do. What often happens, she finds, is that 'students who you would think will struggle do both sides'. Julie vets her choices, in relation to routine tasks of planning, teaching and assessment, not just in terms of immediate learning intentions but also in terms of the anticipated effects of her chosen approaches on the states of mind that she knows will determine the quality of future learning.

Julie is also highly alert to shifting emotional states that cause young people to switch off or give up when they encounter difficulties or challenges. She makes choices that she believes will increase their sense of safety and therefore willingness to take risks in their thinking and learning. She is very careful how she responds when offering help as she knows that this will affect students' willingness to admit to difficulties and ask for help in the future. She recognises that it is much more risky to ask for help than to cover up difficulties by copying from others or going through the motions of a task in a superficial way.

She tries to reassure students that they are not being judged when they admit to difficulties, and is always prepared to explain again and again, until students are confident that they understand. She stresses how important it is 'not to make them feel stupid (by saying) something like' "What do you mean, you don't understand that? we went through it last lesson"'. She realises how easily comments and assessments of work can be read and interpreted by students as judgements on their worth and identity as people. She uses a set of stamps with different positive messages to lighten the atmosphere around the making of judgements, as well as helping (as one of her students expressed it) creating 'a friendlier feel with the teacher' than is created by grades or by comments alone.

Perhaps the most important state of mind that Julie seeks to nurture is 'feeling equal'. Often in schools what comes across to some students is that they are not valued equally. They feel second-class, and 'their work becomes second class. It's a self-fulfilling prophecy'. This sense of inequality is derived from unintentional messages that often go unnoticed by teachers. Julie tries to undo the effects of such negative messages by, for example, offering open tasks, constructed so that everyone can take part whatever their starting points. She encourages collaborative interaction, where everybody is recognised as a resource for the rest of the group. She structures tasks and activities so that everyone can become, and experience being seen as, an expert in particular areas of the curriculum that they, and not others, have chosen to research.

The ethic of 'everybody'

While Julie is very appreciative of the diversity and individuality of her students, it is noticeable that she frequently talks about them collectively. She constantly refers to what 'everybody' must have the opportunity to do, learn and experience. She expresses concern to ensure that 'nobody' is excluded or deterred from engaging in the learning activities offered to the group. She makes her choices based on what she believes will make for better learning for everybody and not just better for 'some people'.

Though students are individuals with diverse interests, backgrounds, experiences, knowledge, understandings and skills, Julie's formulation of what will enable them to become better learners – the positive states of mind and strengthened powers as active agents in their own learning – is the same for everybody. To be a powerful and effective learner, *everybody* needs to have a sense of competence and control, to feel safe enough to take risks, to experience curiosity and excitement in learning, to feel equally valued and to derive a sense of satisfaction and success. What helps to create, restore or enhance these states of mind will not necessarily always be the same for everybody, but the framework of choice-making *is* common to everybody.

We can see, then, that with ability-based teaching, teachers reference their teaching decisions to different ability groups. They set expectations, form groups, design tasks, ask questions, interact to support learning and evaluate progress, on the basis of what is considered appropriate for 'more able', 'average' and 'less able' students. Julie, in contrast, has a single, common point of reference: the potential for enhancing the exercise of student agency. Because she has a single reference point, many of these decisions can legitimately be taken collectively. Julie does not need to start out from an assumption that because students are all different she ought ideally to make her choices 30 times over, or (as a minimum) three times over to take account of the differing needs of young people of different ability.

In Julie's approach, diversity in learning experiences, opportunities and outcomes is achieved through co-agency, through what teachers and young people do *together*. Catering for diversity is not simply a task for the teacher, as in ability-based pedagogy. The technical task of *matching* tasks and learners gives way to a deeper, more complex, interactive process of *connection*, a meeting of minds, purposes and actions (co-agency) in which the teacher acts to try to enhance young people's ability and willingness to make full use of all the resources available to them to sustain and promote their own learning in school. Since young people are active agents in their own learning, when connection is successful it inevitably results in different experiences and outcomes, since everyone is unique, everyone brings and contributes something different, and makes their own meanings through active engagement in the learning opportunities provided. The teacher's task is to make the good choices, those that will enable and encourage everyone in the productive exercise of their agency, and then extend an open invitation to learn that can be accepted equally by everyone.

Trusting the learner

Such an approach rests on a basic position of trust. Julie trusts young people to find relevance and purpose in relevant and purposeful activity. She trusts them to make choices and construct their own learning within the supportive framework she provides. She trusts them to contribute to one another's learning, to take up her invitation to co-agency and to participate in the worthwhile activity of learning. This basic position of trust assumes that young people will choose to engage if the conditions are right. So when learners choose not to engage or appear to be inhibited in their learning, she tries to re-evaluate her choices and practices in order to understand what might be hindering their participation and learning.

> Sometimes you come out of the lesson and you think 'That didn't really work' or 'I must change that next time' or 'so and so is sitting in the corner there and was very quiet and didn't seem to get anything out of that'. So that is what I am always looking for. I try to think beforehand but sometimes things happen that you don't allow for, or an activity just wasn't suitable for a certain student. So you have to try to change it.

Julie realises that she cannot just rely on her own observations to make accurate judgements about how students are responding. She encourages dialogue with them in order to find out what is going on in their heads. As part of the research, Julie involved the students in some activities to explore their experiences and perceptions of themselves as learners. For the most part, she found that her trust in her students was reciprocated by a trust in her. She was deeply dismayed, however, to find that one or two students admitted to feeling uninterested or even unhappy in her history lessons. Julie comments:

> This was a complete revelation to me and my initial reaction was one of incredulous indignation – how could students possibly feel like that in my lesson? However, after this initial reaction, I began to understand that for some students the whole experience of school was uncomfortable; given a choice they would rather not be there. This made me more aware that as a teacher one should never become complacent. It is necessary to try to empathise with all students and strive to find new strategies to help them cope with the emotional nightmare of being compelled to come to school and participate in lessons.

For students whose previous experience has generated such significant barriers to learning, there is a long path to travel to undo the damage and begin to build more positive states of mind. In her response to these students' comments, Julie demonstrates her acceptance of and empathy for young people as they are, while at the same time recognising the possibility for change. Her trust sustains her effort to go on searching for ways to reach out and make connections that will free young people to learn more successfully.

Summarising key ideas

So what have we learnt from the research about the distinctive features of teaching free from the concept of ability? We have found a common belief in **transformability** that informs everything that teachers do. Transformability contrasts with the fatalism associated with ability labels. It means that things have the potential to change, and that people have the power to change things for the better by what they do in the present. Teachers understand that they must harness their own power to young people's power **(co-agency)** if they are to be successful in making a difference to future development. They do this by constantly making connections in their minds between classroom conditions and subjective states; by considering the positive and negative effects of their choices on the students' exercise of agency. Choices must be made in the interests of **everybody**, because everybody counts and everybody's learning is equally important. Moreover, what the teachers are working to achieve – at the level of subjective experience – is the same for everybody. So they do not have to start out each time from a perception of the class divided up in their minds into different groups of learners with significantly differing needs. All of this depends on a fundamental **trust** which the teachers have in their students, trust in their powers as thinkers and learners, to engage if conditions are made right and to find and create meaning. Moreover, they trust that no matter what has gone before, there is always potential for growth and change as a result of what happens in the present.

Ideas in action

To conclude, I show how these ideas come together in the construction of a single lesson. As part of a topic on medicine with her Year 10 group, Julie decided to use an extract from Chaucer as a key resource for students' enquiry into people's views of doctors and medicine in the Middle Ages. A Chaucer text may seem to be a bad choice for a class where a number of students experience considerable difficulties with literacy. But Julie felt, on balance, that a successful experience of engaging with such a difficult text might do more to reshape these young people's view of themselves as competent readers and learners than an activity that spared them the challenges of using their literacy skills. She believes that it is what teachers and learners do with a text, not inherent difficulties within the text, that determines its suitability and its potential for becoming accessible to everyone. None of the students in the class would be able to make much of this Chaucer text, if simply given it to read. Yet *everyone* can get something out of it if it is presented in such a way that they feel empowered to engage with it and are helped to construct their own meanings in relation to it.

In thinking how to achieve this, Julie projects herself into the minds of her students and tries to imagine how they will respond. She decides that the priority must be to nurture students' sense that they *will* be able to do the task, to create positive expectations of success, while at the same time helping them to recognise and use fully their resources. She decides to begin with some questions which invite students to contribute their present-day experiences of doctors. She then asks different groups to discuss briefly and report on what they already know about medical practices and how people viewed doctors and medicine in other periods of history already studied. This is intended to help build a context for reading the text, drawing attention to areas of existing knowledge that they could draw upon as points of reference in interpreting the passage. She begins to build up a narrative context for reading the text, through introducing them to the *Canterbury Tales,* via a brief, entertaining video extract to heighten interest and curiosity in the topic. By doing this, Julie hopes to relax and reassure them that this is something that they are going to enjoy and be able to do. By offering visual support as well as background information, she hopes to strengthen their ability to picture what they are reading and so assist them in making the text meaningful. She then explains the purpose of the Chaucer passage, and reads it aloud to them, to allow students to hear it and begin to make their own meanings. Students are encouraged to spot difficult words and passages in the text, and annotate their texts to explain word meanings. They then work in pairs to construct their own understandings, with the support of a series of questions. Working together means they can share ideas and explore meanings, and the mutual support gives students a chance to do things with a partner that they would not or could not do on their own. Julie monitors closely individuals' responses during the course of activities – and particularly their body language – for signs of frustration or confusion so that she can judge when best to intervene to assist their learning.

As Julie makes her choices about the lesson she is constantly thinking about their subjective experience. She anticipates barriers to learning at the level of task and text and takes steps to minimise them.

> There are students in there who have difficulty with written sources – written anything really; the language of that particular source without a lot of guidance would have just thrown them and they would have gone into panic mode and wouldn't have been able to do anything.

She does not define this reaction simply as a problem for the less confident readers and learners, but as a natural reaction for any individual – adult or child – confronted by a complex text or task.

You know that they are going to glance at it and think 'what on earth is that about?' as you know sometimes *we* (adults) can, when you see a poem or something for the first time, it takes a few readings and you feel a little bit threatened by it.

As well as providing the video introduction to heighten interest and reassure them that what they were going to do was accessible, she makes a point of acknowledging the difficulty of the source. She takes active steps to make students feel comfortable and safe by explicitly acknowledging how they might be feeling – not just legitimising their feelings but reassuring them in advance that adequate support was going to be provided. She also builds into the activity the support of collaborative working, reinforcing an ethos of collectivity: that everybody has something to contribute to and learn from one another.

Julie decides what to do on the basis of what she believes will make it more likely that everyone, rather than just some people, will feel empowered to engage in the activity. To an observer, the lesson generates a lively buzz of activity, and there is no evidence of anyone opting out or finding the text just too challenging. In her own review of the lesson, Julie comments, 'I don't think there was anybody in the room who was struggling with the work. Even if they were being prompted a little bit, they were still getting it done … The source was difficult but they managed to cope with it after we went through it and they felt quite good about that.'

Julie's account of the thinking underpinning this lesson demonstrates her understanding that learning tasks and activities are *made* accessible to everyone through judicious thought and action on the part of the teacher. Accessibility is a quality produced through choices and actions, not an objective quality inherent in the relationship between particular content and learning objectives and the characteristics of particular students. While fully cognisant of the diversity of her group, Julie makes the text, and the learning that it is intended to promote, accessible to everyone through *one* set of choices judiciously selected to support and empower everyone.

No doubt there are some teachers reading about this lesson who feel that it would be completely unsuitable for some of the young people they work with. However, what is important and distinctive about Julie's pedagogy is not tied to any particular set of choices or classroom practices but to the principles and mechanisms through which decisions are made. Julie would not choose this text as a way of developing students' skills in working with historical sources if she did not think she could make the experience of working with it empowering for everybody. With different groups of students, she might make different choices about how to include everyone, but the basic process and points of reference for decision-making would be the same.

If all young people could have the opportunity regularly and routinely to participate fully and on an equal basis in activities carefully devised in this way, such experiences could, in time, dramatically influence how they see themselves as learners, their power and desire to develop their learning in school contexts. And if teachers like Julie join forces with one another to share and expand their repertoires and to make the experience of learning without limits more widely available across the education system, they will be able to bring closer to reality their vision of making the experience of education more enriching and life-enhancing for everybody.

An alternative improvement agenda?

We believe that transformability-based teaching could play a central and critical role in the construction of an alternative improvement agenda, based around a critique of intelligence testing and ability labelling. While the project started out from a critique of current reform initiatives, there clearly is overlap between our values and some of those underpinning the standards agenda. There is common concern that the talents and capabilities of many young people remain untapped throughout their compulsory education. There is a common wish to challenge assumptions that not much can be expected of young people from disadvantaged backgrounds, and a common commitment to concerted action to reduce class-based discrepancies of achievement (*TES* 2002).

The current programme of reforms rightly recognises the power that schools and teachers have to influence young people's development. The ideas in this chapter offer a readily sustainable and self-generating approach rooted in teachers' own values, commitments and aspirations. Improvement does not have to be imposed on teachers, and superimposed on existing teaching by managers or inspectors, because the driving force comes from teachers' passions and sense of social justice; teachers' desire and ability to make a difference *are* what makes teaching worthwhile.

Acknowledgements

I would like to thank all the members of the Learning Without Limits research team for their contribution to the ideas in this chapter: Narinder Brach, Claire Conway, Annabelle Dixon, Mary Jane Drummond, Nicky Madigan, Julie Marshall, Donald McIntyre, Alison Peacock, Anne Reay, Yahi Tahibet, Non Worrall and Patrick Yarker. I would also like to thank Julie Marshall, Annabelle Dixon, Mary Jane Drummond and Donald McIntyre for reading and commenting on early drafts.

References

Boaler, J., Wiliam, D. and Brown, M. (2000) Students' experiences of ability grouping – disaffection, polarisation and the construction of failure. *British Educational Research Journal*, **26**(5), 631–48.

Chitty, C. (2002) Selection by specialisation. In Chitty, C. and Simon, B. (eds) *Promoting Comprehensive Education in the 21st Century*. Stoke on Trent: Trentham Books.

Gillborn, D. and Youdell, D. (2000) *Rationing Education: Policy, Practice, Reform and Equity*. Buckingham: Open University Press.

Gould, S. J. (1981) *The Mismeasure of Man. New* York: Norton.

Hart, S. (1998) A sorry tail: ability, pedagogy and educational reform. *British Journal of Educational Studies*, **46**(2), 153–68.

Times Educational Supplement (TES) 4 January 2002.

We were pleased to be able to commission this chapter and inspired when we read it. For us, it illustrates how inclusive education is less about differentiating educational experiences to meet different needs, and more about challenging traditional practices and discourses to make education meaningful for everyone. The chapter is challenging to our thinking, yet entirely practical for professionals wanting to draw on its wisdom.

CHAPTER 19

From 'curriculum access' to 'reflective, reciprocal learning'

Susan F. Simmons

Susan Simmons describes her action research project aimed at facilitating inclusion in mathematics through the use of audio recordings. She narrates her journey from thinking about this as a curriculum access issue to understanding it as a matter for researcher, teachers and students learning from and with each other. She has not used real names to preserve the anonymity of all those involved.

Introduction

In this chapter I tell part of the stories of three students who tried using audio materials to enhance and complement their mathematical learning. They are three of over 50 taking part in the project, which was inspired by my experience in the 1970s of teaching mathematics in a school for children with visual impairment (VI). Those who had recently lost sight or whose vision was deteriorating experienced frustration due to limited access to print information. Some students found their anxiety lessened by listening to the same mathematical information on audio recordings as they were attempting to read in print or Braille.

In the research on which this chapter is based the students were contributors as well as recipients. I provided opportunities for them to access and learn mathematics more easily. They gave me ideas for improving recordings and taught me which equipment was appropriate and whether and how they felt using audio materials was an asset. I refer to the interchange of knowledge, skills and feelings that took place as 'reciprocal learning'. The students' active role extended into supporting each other's learning through developing and sharing self-help recordings in which they could listen to strategies as well as answers. This was part of a two-year Millennium-funded project entitled CHAMPE (Community Helped Audio Mathematics for Participation and Equity), which evolved during the study. However, the majority of students were not given the opportunity to pursue their preferred way of learning in class owing to barriers that were largely put up by others.

Initially I needed to get to know the present-day 'reality' of the world within mainstream classrooms. Hart (2000) sums up my starting point and how the research evolved:

> Trying to move out of our own frames of reference and view the situation through the child's eyes . . . It may help us to see our original concern in a new way...
>
> (p.14)

Mohammed

I first met Mohammed in his primary school. He was registered as partially sighted and English was his additional language. Like other eleven-year-olds, he was apprehensive about moving into a school with 960 students aged 11–16. These feelings must have been fuelled by remarks by adults about his partial sight and the size of the building compared with his present, compact, primary school. Mohammed had attained an above average level in Key Stage 2 national tests (SATs) in mathematics but he was reported to be experiencing difficulties in this subject. I was unsure whether he was referred to me because problems were anticipated in secondary school, due to fragmented knowledge attributed to his impaired vision, and the only way I could find out about this was from Mohammed himself.

I also needed to talk with the staff. The SENCO and maths teacher thought that audio materials might appeal to more pupils than Mohammed and they agreed that I should speak to the whole staff and to Mohammed's class, to introduce myself and explain the purpose of the investigation. Mohammed approved of what I proposed to say. The future seemed promising. When I arrived for the staff briefing, however, I was informed that an announcement had been inserted in the weekly bulletin instead. I was not given a chance to talk at a full or departmental staff meeting. Even the most thorough planning had not ensured a trouble-free start. This was the first of a series of incidents that tested Mohammed's and my ability to accommodate to working conditions that neither of us could control.

No one could have forecast the events that followed. I stressed to Mohammed's class that he was contributing to research. In the second lesson he used a tape recorder until an invasion of wasps. Everyone had to vacate the room. This happened again in the next lesson. Whilst waiting to move to another room, several students asked if they could use audiotapes. I had purchased three recorders so that I could respond to feedback from users but I could not offer the opportunity to all individuals who expressed interest. This was one of the incidents that influenced my thinking and ultimately led to expanding the target population away from just those with VI.

The Mathematics Level by Level scheme had just been introduced into the school to replace SMILE. Apart from Mohammed's teacher, members of the mathematics department were not interested in the investigation. I assumed that they were overwhelmed by the demands of implementing the National Numeracy Strategy (NNS) guidelines recently recommended for year 7 and establishing a new scheme. By the end of the first term worksheets were being reduced in size to save money on photocopying. As Mohammed needed print enlarged 141 per cent, audio recordings became essential.

Expectations were high for Mohammed based on his formal test results. He was started on level 4 of the scheme. During room changes, his worksheets and written work had been mislaid. At this early stage he was struggling to match the speed and progress of his peers. The stress of an imminent Ofsted inspection started to prove too much for some members of the staff. Mohammed's teacher was frequently absent. Cover teachers took the class but continuity was lost.

During a casual conversation Mohammed mentioned that other pupils were 'jealous' of him and he was worried that they might damage equipment. He was desperate not to appear different in the classroom. He would volunteer answers in lessons and was alert and interested but gradually his attitude changed. He resorted to avoidance strategies; his learning was 'jammed' (Claxton 1984). He gave the impression of working hard by writing continuously but he had given up trying to answer questions, he was just copying down what he could see or hear. He did not possess the prerequisite knowledge and understanding to tackle topics set. He wedged himself against a wall, in the classroom, at the end of a long row of tables, giving the message that he wanted to avoid attention. His individual support teacher (IST) was distressed by his rejection of support.

What happened to Mohammed gives support to Ollerton and Watson's (2001) claim that 'the provision of starting points is not enough provision on its own to ensure that everyone participates' (p.38). Without easy access to essential knowledge and 'tools' together with confidence to use them, frustration and disillusionment are likely outcomes. When Mohammed was attempting 'drawing conclusions from pie charts' his lack of understanding, and missing knowledge, about division and angles made the task impossible. As Ernest (1991: 238) concluded '. . . ability to proceed with new work is very often dependent on sufficient understanding of one or two pieces of work which has gone before'.

Mohammed became increasingly defensive and his feelings affected his ability to enjoy life outside as well as inside the classroom. The incident that eventually decided his future and mine was a departmental decision to withdraw him from a lesson to do typing in the Learning Support room so that his IST could assist a year 11 student at the same time. In another mathematics lesson, Mohammed had to share support with a student who demanded a disproportionate amount of attention owing to behavioural problems. There was a shortage of mathematics teachers in most schools. I was tempted to offer to officially support Mohammed but I knew that combining the role of an 'outside researcher' with another role prescribed by a school can cause confusion and political dilemmas. Also I was wary of detracting from my longer-term intention to train people in schools to take over responsibility for production and use of audio materials. The only way forward appeared to be to assist Mohammed out of the classroom.

Mohammed's conscientious, caring IST expressed her concerns about the workload which the audiotapes might add to ('What I'm still not clear about is how much work is entailed for us, as Mohammed gets going. Is it that we would be making the tapes up ourselves?') I was anxious not to make more demands on her. She was undergoing health checks; she had no free time. Finally she went on long-term sick leave and Mohammed felt unable to confide in anyone in the school.

I sought permission to contact Mohammed's parents and through visiting his home I gained greater understanding of the implications of his cultural background. He was the eldest son and expected to achieve academically and accept responsibilities within the home. He spoke English more fluently than either of his parents. I realised he was fearful of failing his family and he was not using audio equipment that I had lent in case the younger children misused it. Neither Mohammed nor his parents wanted to inform the school about the 'peer pressure' he experienced or the 'inadequate support' that was causing problems.

Learning from each other

During one-to-one withdrawal sessions a reciprocal learning relationship began to develop. I gained insight into Mohammed's mathematical understanding and background. He experimented with the equipment and use of audio recordings and was delighted to spot errors and suggest ideas for improvements. I devised ways to develop memory, listening skills and 'showing working' skills.

Initially, Mohammed's typical, agitated response when he was listening to a topic beyond comprehension was: 'What's he talking about... I didn't understand it properly cos he was chatting a whole load of mathematics language that I ain't even heard before, cos I wasn't taught that stuff...'. He learnt to criticise constructively. He was willing to do this when listening to a disembodied voice but it took time before he overcame the courtesy instilled into him at home that prevented him from questioning recordings when he recognised my voice. I learnt from his emotional reactions and muddled thinking how problematic mathematical terms can be for a student with poor vision and English as an additional language. Together we scripted and recorded an audio dictionary with strategies explained before answers. This provided a justifiable reason for thinking and conversing mathematically. This method of working was productive but it was learning in isolation. By the end of the first term there was even less prospect of the audio process being allowed to happen in the classroom.

As a practitioner involved in inclusion for over twenty years, and having prepared thoroughly for the main research, I had presumed that I could predict and prevent crises arising. After the first six months I felt a failure. I was yet to be reassured by Mercer's (1995: 2) words that 'failures are as important for our understanding as the successes'. During the next two years I realised how much I had learnt from Mohammed during those traumatic few months. I was fortunate to receive support from my family, supervisors and a friend with a flair for scripting strategies for finding solutions to mathematical problems and acting as a confidante. I wished that Mohammed could have found similar support, but with no prospect of change I reluctantly ended my research in this school. I continued to communicate from home by mail and telephone until Mohammed had taken his end-of-year examinations.

The situation deteriorated to such a degree that Mohammed moved to a special school. The comprehensive school was put 'in special measures' following an Ofsted inspection. I felt this was some evidence that Mohammed and I had not over-reacted to barriers erected against us. An opportunity that seemed to promise so much for Mohammed and research was closed. His school did not offer an environment in which the project I proposed could survive, let alone thrive. I had to look for an alternative host organisation.

Opportunity opened for Derek

I contacted a comprehensive school in south London and the Head asked me to work for a trial period with Derek, who was in Year 8. Derek's statement of special educational needs specified that he was visually impaired and dyslexic. He was in the 'lowest' mathematics set taught by Ms A. (also his Head of Year), who suggested withdrawing him for a few sessions to introduce the audio items to him, before bringing these into the classroom.

I had been given a second chance to discover mathematics and wanted to offer Derek a similar opportunity. In order to avoid forming preconceived ideas about him, I delayed looking at his record file. I used my role as an 'outsider' and Derek's strengths and forceful personality to gain his interest in contributing to research. He quickly mastered the recorder, finding tones at beginnings of questions, and his interest and ability in talking about mathematics showed more understanding than his written work. I realised that the eye injury he sustained early in life was not the main factor affecting his ability to fulfil his potential in mathematics. I gradually learnt from him how misreading words and numbers and having memory difficulties can affect confidence and consequently learning. He marvelled at being able to work independently by listening without constantly requesting help to read text. It was several weeks before his specialist teacher for dyslexia agreed that he should not miss a mathematics lesson each week for extra literacy.

Derek wanted details about how the blind student, whom I supported for seven years, studied for A level mathematics in mainstream. He was intrigued to hear about the blind Australian who trained his own narrators whilst obtaining his doctorate in mathematics. I showed him some Braille equipment. His comments indicated an inquiring mind and willingness to question. He held strong views on equal opportunity and when the time came insisted on 'E' for 'Equity' being included in the name of the project CHAMPE. Suddenly he began to talk freely and openly about his own sight and his experiences and feelings. For example, in his homework he had been unable to read the word 'enough', he thought it was a new mathematical term. He missed out that question. Glasses helped him to see work on the board but did not solve his print disability problem. The initial one-to-one sessions opened the door to an ongoing, two-year reciprocal learning relationship that positively affected our production and use of audio materials.

At the end of the trial period the Head had no hesitation in offering to host a project and support further research in classrooms. Derek was placed in Mr D's 'middle band' set, in which students followed SMP individual programs. Mr D. warmly welcomed me into his classroom and with Derek's agreement invited me to explain my role and the aim of the investigation. No student commented or asked questions. Mr D. arranged times for planning and evaluation meetings during his non-contact periods.

In September 1999, Derek was assigned to a different teacher. After several weeks he reluctantly admitted that he was having access difficulties again. In his new position as a Deputy Head of Mathematics, Mr D. resolved the situation. He moved Derek and two other students, who had opted for audio for formal tests, into his set but it took several weeks. Mr D. remained the sole mathematics teacher who regarded audio means and my presence as an advantage in the classroom. He was respected by the thirty students in his set: most of them were keen to benefit from his ability to make maths interesting and academically appropriate, and to allow time to get to know them as individuals. An exciting positive phase followed with good communication leading to constructive planning and collaborative action. The students, seemingly, followed Mr D's example and respected the rights of the audio users to learn in the way they chose. My role changed. I went into lessons if requested or when I needed to know which topics to record next. I was able to concentrate on production of recordings and ensure that they were ready for listeners to use in the classroom.

Opportunity threatened

Mr D. kept me updated on the outstanding progress Derek was making, so it came as a shock when Derek casually told me that he had decided to cease using audio in lessons. He described taunts from peers. Mr D. was unaware of this problem and agreed that I should spend more time in the classroom to observe unobtrusively. It was a 'covert', cleverly disguised operation. Physical gestures were directed at Derek and his friend John, when Mr D. was writing on the board or helping other students. Derek had opted out of the small group intent on disturbing lessons. During a meeting with the Head, he eventually revealed the history behind this incident. One of the girls in his set had been 'better at maths' than him in primary but now he was obtaining higher marks and receiving praise. Derek asked to try and resolve the problem without adult intervention. He commented, 'We are an easy target at the back; if you think about it we are still a separate class', and suggested that he and John sit at the front. Mr D. had arranged seating so that I could easily help audio users but he readily agreed to their idea. Allowing ourselves to listen and learn from students and take action in response enabled a potentially disastrous outcome to be averted. There was no recurrence of peer pressure in this classroom.

Derek and John worked together outside school and Mr D. allowed them to develop a reciprocal learning relationship in the classroom. John assisted Derek to access print text displayed on the board or unavailable on audio recordings and Derek reciprocated by helping John with mathematics and audio equipment. Similarly Norma, who lacked confidence in reading, formed productive learning liaisons with several other students that enabled her to progress in mathematics.

After lengthy negotiations with the Qualifications and Curriculum Authority (QCA) I received permission to audio record the national test (SATs) papers, with the proviso that I could not open them earlier than 24 hours before tests. Derek was delighted to obtain a higher grade than expected. He described how use of audio materials helped him '. . . when you're under pressure you just can't read the questions. If you listen to the tapes it helps, just to flick through it . . . sometimes I just listened to the tape and looked at the diagrams . . .'

Derek's attitude towards mathematics and school life had changed. His learning went beyond mathematics. He commented 'There are great demands on teachers, if you can't read, they have to come over and specially read it to you and leave everyone else, so it ain't fair, but if you have the tape thing you can do it on your own.' He was made a school prefect and he emerged as the leading protagonist of use of audio materials to assist mathematical learning. His determination not to be diverted from being allowed to use an audio medium eventually led to students without visual impairment, or any other official disability label, having a chance to try helping themselves in this way.

Stephen following in Derek's footsteps

When I first met Stephen he was reluctant to talk about maths. He felt that he was failing in this subject and seemed to be blaming himself. He was registered visually impaired but had no statement of SEN or individual support and there was no adviser for VI in the borough. I raised the issue of access denied to him owing to displays in red in textbooks, for marking and on the board. Glasses did not offer a solution. Reports from the ophthalmic consultant, the school and myself led to Stephen being prioritised for a statement that he should have received at the start of his education. When I asked Stephen some months later how he had managed in the classroom he replied 'I used to get all my mates to help me out and read things for me off the board . . . I think they got a bit annoyed sometimes, like they were getting a bit behind with their own work. So in the end, I used to let them do their work and when they'd finished I asked if anyone would help me do as much as I could of my work'.

When his year 8 maths groups were reorganised for the new term Stephen still had no statement or support. Mr N. described him as a diligent, hardworking student, too able for his set, and he transferred to Ms P's class. There were 31 students, space was limited but I was welcomed into the classroom. Ms P. consulted Stephen before agreeing that I spoke about the research to the whole group. Two students asked for more details after the lesson. Ms P. arranged secure, accessible storage for equipment and expected Stephen to collect and return items. She took responsibility for his learning and, like Mr D., mastered the art of 'verbalisation' for board work. She asked Stephen about appropriate ways of incorporating audio materials in lessons. She was a Head of Year but made time to plan and evaluate, initially, weekly. I was given lesson materials at least a week in advance. I was able to provide recordings ready for the start of lessons. This collaborative way of working was ideal and supported findings that:

> There is much evidence to suggest that effective learning takes place when lessons are structured and well prepared . . . There is a growing conviction that the opinions of pupils are key factors in the planning and organisation of what goes on in classrooms.
>
> (Hopkins *et al.* 1996: 42)

Towards the end of the summer term Ms P. told me that she thought 'Stephen seems to be enjoying it, I have asked to keep the group for next year . . . if you've got those two or three who need extra time, it's much better for them I feel, to be in there, than if they were in the next set down where you've got twenty who need extra help . . .' Everyone was surprised when the mathematics sets were changed again for September and Stephen was, as he described it, 'moved down' to Mr N's group. When this happened he seemed almost relieved and said that he had found the speed of work and silence in Ms P's set stressful. He preferred background noise 'like at home'. I believe that this incident re-established Stephen's fears of failing in mathematics, when he was beginning to build up confidence through use of audio recordings for access. Neither Ms P. nor I had enough power to alter the decision.

In Mr N's class, students were allowed to talk more freely and some took advantage of this. Students willingly assisted Stephen to access information from print that I had not been requested to audio record. Stephen won their respect through being uncomplaining and willing to talk about the implications of his visual disability. Mr N. preferred informal meetings in the staffroom and not to have anyone else in the classroom, but, he said '. . . as long as the overall effect is positive, as it seems to be, I'm not grumbling'. I did not manage, though, to establish a collaborative working relationship with Mr N.; it was mainly one-way communication.

Stephen was one of ten students promised that if they opted to use audio in lessons they could use this method for SATs. They were assigned to five different classrooms instead of two as I had recommended. I was frustrated by being unable to provide effective support, until I realised that through random visiting, I was getting to know 'reality' within each environment. For example, equipment remained locked away, batteries were flat and students were being praised for not needing to listen to recordings. No requests for recordings or support were placed in my pigeonhole designated for the purpose. Verbally, people were extolling the process, but in practice there was a mismatch between words and actions. The students got the message that they pleased their teachers by rejecting audio means. Their enthusiasm changed to disengagement. Stephen reverted to relying on his 'mates', because the audio recordings I made based on schemes of work were different from print copy utilised in lessons. I sought advice from the Head and Head of Mathematics. There seemed no alternative to supporting only Stephen in the classroom. I never knew whether this was explained to the other students as promised.

I cannot claim to know the motivation of the people who closed opportunity for nine out of ten students. No mathematics teachers were encouraging students to use audio materials. I gradually got to know the history and politics of this department and realised that the resistance to innovation was not a personal criticism of my attempted intrusion into what I felt was a community, isolated from other subjects. This was reassuring for me but I was powerless to change the status quo for students.

I was in the classroom with Stephen for part of lessons, three times each week for a year. I learnt how students can be affected when they are in disabling environments where reciprocal learning is not supported and their voices are ignored. Stephen's description of his brief period of full participation in mathematics was: '. . . the tapes came in quite handy, most of the work was on tapes . . . I could start my work first as well and I had time to do it . . . I never used to have to ask my mates anything then, I could just listen . . .' Through coping with incidents that occurred, Stephen acquired interpersonal skills and self-confidence that he later applied when working with younger students in the enabling environment of the Main School library.

CHAMPE: Community Helped Audio Mathematics for Participation and Equity

I was motivated by the requests of students in Mohammed's school to apply for funds to buy more audio items that had proved suitable in mainstream classrooms. I proposed a project that would enable students to help themselves practise and revise mathematical topics independently by using audio materials but it was not intended to take over teaching. One aim of CHAMPE was to offer students opportunity to acquire experience and skills in listening and using audio equipment, that they could then transfer into classrooms. It was at this stage, when I started writing scripts for self-help recordings, that I appreciated and applied my learning from Mohammed.

Two conditions of the funding award were that it should be an extra-curricular activity, with the theme of working across the generations. CHAMPE was launched as a lunchtime club and I turned to the older generation for 'community help'. An unanticipated problem arose, however, when the combination of mathematics and technology proved too daunting for many of them. They were unused to being asked to contribute to either research or education. They had been excluded at the other end of the age spectrum. Several spoke about 'fear' of mathematics and feelings of 'shame' (Biddy 2002) and inadequacy in this subject, that was rooted in their past. Nonetheless, in June 1999 I formed a narrating service of seven volunteers who assisted with script writing and recording and made changes in response to feedback from users. This was distance, rather than direct, reciprocal learning.

Offering students an option to attend CHAMPE on a casual basis caused a dilemma. They required reliable, regular assistance but I could not ask adults to voluntarily give up their time if students chose not to come. The issue was resolved through discussions about consideration for others. Agreed procedures were put into practice.

Members of CHAMPE were encouraged to request topics and suggest ideas for improvement but they offered little input at first. Changing from 'orders' to 'options' was too sudden. They were overwhelmed by too much choice; I was expecting them to try a different medium, make decisions about maths, suggest how to run CHAMPE and forego their free time without any tangible reward. Most participants who ceased attending the club gave the reason that they did not want to give up their free time. Those who continued to attend were delighted when their ideas were implemented. They seemed surprised that they could influence what happened.

Changing from club to library

The Head supported CHAMPE in practice as well as in words. The club was transferred from a classroom to the school library and embraced enthusiastically by the Senior Librarian and the Media Resource Officer. I incorporated their ideas of awarding and designing certificates that students could submit for their national record of achievement. Recordings were loaned under the same conditions as books.

Stephen and his friend Jeremy obtained a mathematics assistant's certificate that qualified them to mentor other learners in mathematics. Through this learning they realised the amount of thinking, knowledge and skill necessary to script and narrate high quality recordings. Initially they tended to instruct and give answers rather then share their learning when passing on knowledge. Were they modelling their interpretation of teaching maths on their own experiences?

I emphasised the importance of interpersonal skills during the decision-making to reorganise CHAMPE. Jeremy gained confidence to make verbal contributions through Stephen's willingness and ability to voice his views and Stephen gained mathematical knowledge and became interested in computer skills through his friend's involvement. Oliver (1992: 111) contends that 'to achieve social change (transformation) . . . the main technique for empowerment will be encouragement of reciprocity' and this supports my own thinking. Moreover, Hewett and Nind (1998: 3) contend that, for reciprocity to develop, both 'giver' and 'receiver' must '. . . want to communicate . . .'. The students' desire to communicate seemed to have been damaged through frequently failing in mathematics, but in these enabling environments reciprocal learning between adults and peers stood a chance of developing. I was hopeful that more students might experience enjoyment and gain sufficient self-esteem to 'want to communicate'.

A turning point came soon after the club was opened as a loaning library. There was no adult school coordinator and I could not attend a session. Stephen immediately suggested that he and Jeremy took charge. I had organised the filing cabinet so that access to materials was easy for anyone with partial sight or using a wheelchair, and Braille labels could be added. The boys enjoyed taking responsibility and were keen to continue the arrangement. The librarian proposed that CHAMPE should become a student-owned and run project.

Daniel offered to assist with technology and Teresa asked if she and her friend could train to be assistants. This was the beginning of a creative and modernising phase. They suggested making maths more fun and enjoyable and invited anyone to come and listen to the recordings. The stigma that CHAMPE was only for low attainers in mathematics and students with special needs was finally removed. It evolved as an inclusive club/library open to all. Daniel moved it into the future, by mastering and writing programs to transfer material from tapes to CDs and creating an interactive website for the intranet. It seemed that when students chose to participate without inducement, their commitment was more likely to withstand trials and tribulations encountered, but merely offering opportunity did not guarantee that this happened.

The innovative aspect of the audio recordings was that students without impairments were required to use materials produced for students with impairments; most users were unaware of this. Reciprocal learning flourished in the supportive, social environment of the main school library. Why could this not have been replicated in classrooms?

Barriers

Much has been written about 'barriers' to inclusive learning (Ainscow 1999; Allan 1999; Ballard 1999; Booth *et al.* 2002; Mittler 2000; Potts 2000). The type of barriers to reciprocal learning that were encountered in this project depended on how people in positions of power chose to use or misuse their power. Despite seeking to understand I often did not get to know the real reasons why people erected barriers. Why did heads of mathematics resist innovation and devote their efforts to retaining the status quo? Maybe they, as maths educators, were 'still haunted . . . by the repressive basis of the tradition they are trying to liberalise' (Winter 1992: 81). Why did a network manager not listen to a student encountering technological problems while striving to contribute to educational research? Why did some adults raise students' expectations but then take no action to enable them to experience positive outcomes? Why did all publishers, except one, apply copyright conditions so rigorously for audio reproduction, that they restricted who could use the recordings? Why was print disability receiving little attention in mathematics? Some adults intentionally or unintentionally undermined students. They seemed to have conflicting, hidden agendas. The majority of students who contributed to this research already associated failure with mathematics. In most cases their new-found confidence and enjoyment through using audio means was too fragile to withstand further set-backs.

The most powerful tool for all those claiming to be 'superior' was 'language'. This was true in mathematics: 'When mystification makes mathematics inaccessible entitlement to its power is denied' (Burton 1994:127), but also in other aspects of the research. In this investigation there were moments when I felt devalued as an individual, purely through my inability to converse in and understand technical terminology in the ever-changing world of computers. Through experiencing these feelings, I could empathise with students. I was aware of their self-esteem and confidence seeping away as they struggled with the mathematical vocabulary of the NNS, which seemed to create more barriers to learning.

Another barrier was the pressure of time. Teaching to the next test and covering topics within a set time was not conducive to enabling reciprocal learning, founded on mutual trust and frequent communication to facilitate collaborative action. With most students in secondary schools I had too little time to achieve this type of working relationship.

As the investigation progressed, I searched constantly to open 'doors of opportunity' to enable reciprocal learning to develop. Whether or not this was successful depended on how participants reacted to the barriers they faced. For example, 'peer pressure' had a negative outcome for Mohammed and he had inadequate support when he needed it, whereas Derek received appropriate support from influential people as needed. The outcome was positive for him and those working with him. Much depended, too, on environmental factors and I believe that by adopting the Reggio Emilia approach (Filippini 1990), and creating environments in which reciprocal learning is understood, encouraged and valued, there might be a way of preventing barriers to inclusive learning. Could this happen for mathematics, in secondary, mainstream classrooms?

Conclusion

I started by accommodating to restrictive conditions and learning to relinquish control and ended by acting as a 'change agent' (Jelly *et al.* 2000). I took every opportunity to get people to listen, learn and respond appropriately to the opinion of all individuals, especially students, even if they regarded them as inferior in the field in which they thought of themselves as 'experts'. I refused payment from schools, to allow me to follow this route but I took the precaution of remaining a member of a professional union. I was fortunate that I could draw on my experiences as a practitioner in the 'power' areas of this research and received support from my family, supervisors and a confidante throughout its unpredictable path with its high and low points. I found the research experience and the students' contributions remarkable. I explored the emerging concept of reciprocal learning, both as a pedagogic relationship facilitative of inclusion and as a method for practitioner research. Thus, research that was originally formulated in terms of issues of access became reconceived in terms of reflective, reciprocal learning.

References

Ainscow, M. (1999) *Understanding the Development of Inclusive School*, London: Falmer Press.

Allan, J. (1999) *Actively Seeking Inclusion: Pupils with Special Needs in Mainstream Schools*. London: Falmer Press.

Ballard, K. (1999) Concluding thoughts, in Ballard, K. (ed) *Inclusive Education: International Voices on Disability and Justice*. London: Falmer Press.

Booth, T., Swann, W., Masterton, M. and Potts, P. (1992) *Learning for All: Curricula for Diversity in Education* (Open University Reader 1). London: Routledge.

Booth, T., Swann, W., Masterton, M. and Potts, P. (1992) *Learning for All: Policies for Diversity in Education* (Open University Reader 2). London: Routledge.

Biddy, T. (2002) Shame: an emotional response to doing mathematics as an adult and a teacher. *British Educational Research Journal*, **28**(5), 705–21.

Burton, L. (2001) Mathematics? No Thanks – Choosing and then Rejecting Mathematics, in Key Stage 3 Mathematics Teachers: the Current Situation, Initiatives and Visions CME Conference, Open University.

Claxton, C. (1984) *Live and Learn*. Buckingham: Open University Press.

Ernest, P. (1991) *The Philosophy of Mathematics Education*. London: Falmer Press.

Filippini, T. (1990) The Reggio Emilia approach. Paper presented at the annual meeting of the National Association for the Education of Young Children, Washington DC.

Hart, S. (2000) *Thinking through Teaching*. London: David Fulton.

Hewett, D. and Nind, M. (eds) (1998) *Interaction in Action*. London: David Fulton.

Hopkins, D., West, M. and Ainscow, M. (1996) *Improving the Quality of Education for All: Progress and Challenge*. London: David Fulton.

Jelly, M., Fuller, A. and Byers, R. (2000) *Involving Pupils in Practice: Promoting Partnerships with Pupils with Special Needs*. London: David Fulton.

Mercer, N. (1995) *The Guided Construction of Knowledge*. Clevedon: Multilingual Matters

Mittler, P. (2000) Profile, in Clough, P. and Corbett, J. (eds) *Theories of Inclusive Education*. London: Paul Chapman Publishing Ltd.

Oliver, M. (1992) Changing the Social Relations of Research Production? *Disability, Handicap & Society*, **7**(2), 101–14.

Potts, P. (2000) Profile, in Clough, P. and Corbett, J. (eds) *Theories of Inclusive Education*. London: Paul Chapman Publishing Ltd.

Ollerton, M. and Watson, A. (2001) *Inclusive Mathematics*. London: Continuum.

Winter, R. (1992) Mathophobia, Pythagoras and Roller Skating. In Nickson, M. and Lerman, S. (eds) *The Social Context of Mathematics Education*. London: South Bank Press.

There are echoes in this chapter of the cries from other authors that we must listen to, and act for and with learners and those experiencing marginalisation. Susan Simmons, like Susan Hart, shows here how much there is to be learnt from students and what a rich resource they can be in the drive for inclusive education. The other powerful message, of course, is that we must be prepared to release and utilise this resource and to be open to learning from each other.

CHAPTER 20

Gender, 'special educational needs' and inclusion

Shereen Benjamin

In this chapter Shereen Benjamin shows that it is nonsensical to isolate special education needs from other aspects of diversity. With particular reference to gender and SEN she shows how the two social constructs interact and limit the ways in which pupils see themselves and are seen by others. She goes on to show that, by giving careful consideration to their processes and cultures, schools can generate conditions of greater equality in the drive towards inclusion.

Introduction

Two distinct strands run through many of the current debates on inclusion in education, and these are reflected in policy, practice and provision. The first strand increasingly addresses 'inclusion' as though it refers almost exclusively to educational provision for children considered to have 'special educational needs' (SEN). This strand is underpinned by particular understandings of perceived academic ability. The second strand, often referred to as 'social inclusion', addresses aspects of educational provision in relation to structural and systemic 'differences': principally those of gender/sexuality, social class and ethnicity. The separation of these two strands, however, has led to incomplete analyses of the complexities of school life, and can contribute to an erroneous assumption that SEN can somehow be separated from other axes of difference. If we want to understand processes of inclusion and exclusion in schooling, we have to look at the intersection of multiple axes of difference – for example what it means to be a girl from a minority ethnic group who experiences difficulties with literacy. This chapter looks at how the understandings of perceived academic ability that underpin SEN interact with differences of gender/sexuality in the schooling experiences of children and young people. It also takes account of how this interaction is further nuanced by social class and by ethnicity.

Statistical evidence gives a clear indication of the fact that provision for children and young people considered to have SEN is a gendered phenomenon. A recent survey of SEN provision in wealthy Organisation for Economic Co-operation and Development (OECD) countries found that boys are consistently over-represented amongst those pupils considered to need specialist educational provision, both in special schools and in special classes in mainstream schools (OECD 2000). This chapter starts with a brief review of this, and other, statistical evidence. But to begin to unravel the stories behind those statistics, we need to look at the links between SEN, and masculinities and femininities – what it means to be a boy or a girl – in schools and classrooms. The bulk of the chapter is given over to an exploration of how masculinities and femininities interact with understandings of 'ability', as well as with understandings around ethnicity and social class, in the complex processes through which boys and girls come to be identified as having SEN. It goes on to consider how schools and teachers can act on such understandings as they strive towards inclusion. The chapter draws on research evidence in the form of interviews and observations with children, parents/carers and teachers in primary, secondary and special schools.

Gender and SEN: What do the statistics tell us?

To almost any SEN practitioner, the answer to this question – of what the statistics tell us – is a very obvious one. Certainly, those of us who have worked in specialist schools and other settings for any length of time have become very used to seeing girls outnumbered by boys in most of our classes. The figures confirm this. In 2000, the OECD conducted a major survey into SEN provision in its member countries (OECD 2000). The findings on gender were fairly consistent across all the countries surveyed. Girls accounted for between 30 per cent and 40 per cent of special school pupils, with boys being a significant majority: in the UK 32.2 per cent of special school pupils were girls as against 67.8 per cent boys. The gender ratios in special classes in mainstream schools were very similar. When it came to the gender ratios of pupils with SEN in mainstream classes, the UK figure was again 32.2 per cent girls to 67.8 per cent boys, though the proportion in some countries evened out slightly, and in France came close to an even balance at 48.4 per cent girls to 51.6 per cent boys.

When we examine the statistics further, other interesting variations come to light. In 1996, a team of researchers in England noted that the over-representation of boys in special schools and units 'is especially marked in schools for those with emotional and behavioural difficulties (6–8 times as many boys), language units (4 times) and autistic schools (2–4 times as many). Moreover, these gender disparities are strongly influenced by 'race': children of African-Caribbean origin are over-represented in special schools and those of South Asian origin under-represented' (Daniels *et al.* 1996: 1). In the case of schools for children considered to have emotional and behavioural difficulties (EBD), it is worth noting that there is considerable evidence that African-Caribbean boys of both primary and secondary school age are at greater risk of exclusion from mainstream schools (Parsons 1996; Hayden 1997; Wright *et al.* 2000; Blair 2001), and that many of these excluded children are considered to have SEN, which are subsequently met in EBD schools or units. Traditionally, pupils of Asian origin have been less at risk of exclusion: there is evidence that this remains largely true for girls of Asian origin, whilst the proportion of boys of Asian origin excluded from school is growing (Mehra 1998). Meanwhile, Scottish Office figures confirm that working-class boys are found in greater numbers in the 'less acceptable' categories of moderate learning difficulties (MLD) and EBD, whilst the non-stigmatised category of specific learning difficulties is dominated by middle-class boys (Riddell 1996).

These statistics raise a number of issues that are of interest here. First, they raise all sorts of questions about the implications of labelling, and about the particular consequences of particular labels. Whatever we may feel about the rights and wrongs of assigning children and young people to specific SEN categories, we need to look at how the consequences of assigning them are gendered. Second, they raise the question of why the gender differentials are so consistent in the participating countries, and why these differentials have endured over time. Third, and perhaps most important, they require us to consider gender, SEN, and what I call the 'multiple axes' of difference of ethnicity, social class and so on, as inter-related and interactive. If we accept that inclusion is a desirable goal in society in general and schooling in particular, the policies, practices and provision we design at all levels will have to take account of differential school effects across multiple axes of difference (Lingard *et al.* 1998).

In order to explain the over-representation of boys amongst children considered to have SEN, we need first to think about how we understand the phenomenon of educational needs. At one extreme, we could argue that SEN are entirely biologically- and physiologically-produced. We could then argue that boys are over-represented amongst those pupils considered to have SEN because they are 'naturally like that', due, perhaps, to some at present unknown aspect of male physiology. Or, at the other end of the continuum, we could argue that SEN are entirely socially-constructed, and that boys' over-representation is due, therefore, to social practices and societal inequalities. Somewhere between these two extremes is an understanding that SEN have a material, organic basis, which can sometimes be easy to discern, but are sometimes far from obvious. This material or physical origin produces a range of possibilities for an individual, which then interacts with social practices. Thus girls and boys schooled in a society with sexist assumptions are more likely to experience different responses to their behaviour and go down different educational pathways, but this is not inevitable.

This chapter will focus mainly on the 'high incidence' category of mild to moderate learning difficulties (MLD). This category is characterised by debates as to how far these perceived learning difficulties have a material, biological origin and as to what that biological origin might be. The category also presents something of a challenge to sociologists who might prefer explanations that are entirely social (Nash 2001). The understanding I am working with here is that material factors interact with social phenomena, and that, in the end, it is unproductive to try to tease out the 'real' from the socially-constructed, though it remains vital to interrogate the consequences of SEN designation.

In Norway, where 70 per cent of pupils considered to have SEN are boys, Skarbrevik (2002) argues that 'the higher incidence of boys in special education during the school years is caused by an interaction between genetic or biological factors and a pedagogy that does not match the educational needs of male students' (Skarbrevik 2002: 97). In other words, he argues that boys tend to be predisposed to have SEN, and that this combines with teachers' boy-unfriendly practice to produce an over-representation of boys amongst pupils considered to have SEN. But this is far from being a plausible explanation in a UK context. It does not give us any way of coming to understand the active participation of boys in the processes through which they come to be perceived as having SEN. Nor does it take account of gender as a lived social, and not just biological, practice. What is missing is an understanding of the interaction between discourses and discursive practices – the taken-for-granted meanings and actions – of SEN with those of masculinities. Connell (1995) notes that,

> Rather than attempting to define masculinity as an object (a natural character type, a behavioural average, a norm) we need to focus on the processes through which men and women conduct gendered lives. 'Masculinity', to the extent the term can be briefly defined at all, is simultaneously a place in gender relations, the practices through which men and women engage that place in gender, and the effect of those practices in bodily experience, personality and culture.
>
> (Connell 1995: 71)

Children with SEN conduct gendered lives, as do all children. The statistics tell us that there is a story to tell about the processes through which children considered to have SEN conduct particular versions of gendered lives. This story has two aspects. First, how does the gendering of school and pupil cultures produce a system through which boys are disproportionately considered to have SEN, and through which the extra resources associated with SEN are allocated disproportionately to them? Second, how does the designation as having SEN constrain or create a specific range of possibilities within which children can conduct gendered lives?

Masculinities and SEN

Ryan spent most of his primary years in a mainstream school, transferring to the special sector at the beginning of Year 5 (aged 9–10). He brought with him an unhappy history of failing to make discernible academic progress, and of failing to make friends with other children in mainstream schooling. By the end of his first half-term in a small all-age special school, he declared himself to be much happier, and began to make academic progress, albeit not at a typical rate. His mother described how she made sense of the improvements in Ryan's attitude towards schooling:

We didn't want to put Ryan into a special school, but now that he's here, our family life, well, our family life has changed beyond recognition, he's like a changed boy... In [mainstream] school, all he could think about was playtime, it was a complete nightmare for him, you know, he couldn't make the football team, let's face it, he couldn't begin to even kick the ball or even know which goalpost to aim for, and his playtimes were a complete nightmare, so he never wanted to go to school. It wasn't even that they bullied him, the teachers there were very good, they didn't allow bullying, it was just, I don't know, in the atmosphere somehow, between the children . . . He obviously wasn't a clever boy, not in the usual sense of the word, and the boys were either clever or good at football, it had to be one or the other, and poor Ryan, well, he just didn't fit in. There was another child in his class, she was a sweet little thing, Ryan used to like her, they sat on the same table, and they both went to [the Learning Support Unit] together, and she used to play with the little infants at playtime, but Ryan could hardly do that, could he, a boy his size? So it really dented his confidence, but now that he's here [in the special school] he's much better, he even tells me he joins in with football at dinner time sometimes.

(Interview, Greyhound School)

It is no coincidence that Ryan's mother attributes Ryan's more positive attitude largely to his inclusion in playground football. Sport in general, and football in particular, is one of the foremost sites for the production of masculinities in schools in the UK. It is on the football field (or, in most urban schools, the allotted corner of the tarmac playground) that boys struggle over their hold on dominant versions of masculinity (Renold 1997; Benjamin 1998; Gard 2001; Skelton 2001). The version of masculinity being struggled over is one of physical strength and skill, where that physical strength is associated with the considerable material rewards of top footballers, with the ability to win fights, and with heterosexual prowess and attractiveness to girls (Epstein and Johnson 1998; Benjamin 2001). As Thorne (1993) and others have noted, failure to excel in playground football is associated, for even very young boys, with 'gayness', and seen as the antithesis of successful masculinity. This failure is particularly marked for boys with SEN. Thorne observed that very successful boys – those who have many resources 'in the bank' on which to draw – can afford to be least invested in continual demonstrations of 'macho' masculinity, since their hold on success is secure. The opposite is true for many boys with SEN. Like Ryan, they cannot lay claim to many of the traditional markers of success. A group of boys in Year 6 at Ryan's special school described the importance of football:

The boys talked at length about the material rewards of 'winning'. Alex described the opulent lifestyle that he saw as the justifiable reward for success on the football pitch, contrasting this with the abject poverty of 'failure'. There was, for him, no intermediate position. For all three of the boys, the 'winner' indeed gained everything – money, acclaim and security – while the 'loser' was left with nothing . . . Inclusion was a priority mentioned by all the boys. Conflating football success, financial success and inclusion, Joe remarked that 'If you score the most goals, everyone will want you to be in their team, and you'll earn loads of money and have a big house and car'. Respect was also part of the overall picture. Ennis said that, 'When you're the best in the team no one will laugh at you and call you names and say you're rubbish . . . Because they'll want to be your friends'.

(Benjamin 1997: 58)

The point here is that a constellation of practices around gender and SEN have made success in football, linked to very absolute notions of 'winning and losing', particularly desirable to these boys. They are boys for whom other markers of success have proved inaccessible: they have failed to make the normative academic progress required of primary school pupils, and their experience has all too often been of formal and informal exclusion from classroom and playground activities. Football is one of the few activities that they can make theirs, and that can allow them to dream of current and future success. The flip side of their investment in football is that the 'cultural package' that goes with it is also associated with aggression, homophobia and heterosexism (Epstein 1997; Kenway and Fitzclarence 1997). This can lead to a cycle in which boys' investment in football leads to or reinforces their disconnection from schoolwork, and channels them towards disruptive behaviour. Such attitudes and behaviour in turn reinforce their designation within SEN discourses, which may in turn have the unintended effect of re-inscribing them as academic 'failures'.

Femininities and SEN

Femininities produce a very different set of possibilities for girls with SEN. At present, a critical literature that specifically addresses 'femininities' has not been as fully developed as has the range of critical literature on masculinities, and this is particularly true of work in the field of education and schooling. The work that does exist points to the way in which femininity has been theorised as 'that which is different from masculinity which assumes femininity as a given' (Skeggs 1997: 20). Nonetheless, it is possible to draw out from the literature models of femininities that might help us understand something of the gendered lives of girls with SEN.

Whilst it would be inappropriate to argue for the existence of dominant femininities, there are clearly some femininities that are more associated with power than others. Recent work on children as consumers (Kenway and Bullen 2001) indicates the existence of feisty, in-your-face femininities, associated with heterosexual attractiveness and the desire to consume the 'right' goods and wear the 'right' brands: in schools, this type of femininity can encompass academic achievement, since better-than-average academic performance is also associated with choices and material success in adult life (NACETT 2000). Alongside this version is a more traditional version of femininity – the decades-old stereotypical 'dumb blonde' of popular culture – where heterosexual attractiveness connotes not so much a positive life choice, but the perpetual vulnerability of needing care and protection (Walkerdine 1997; Benjamin 2002). The 'dumb blonde' is an easily recognisable stereotype, and one that draws heavily on discourses of social class as well as 'race' to position some girls and women as inherently and essentially childlike, appealing (to men), and lacking in intellectual ability of all kinds.

'Cleverness', for girls, has tended to be seen as something struggled for: where the achievements of boys who do well tend to be attributed to 'natural' brilliance, the achievements of girls have been attributed to their capacity for hard work, born out of a desire to please (Walkerdine 1988; Rossiter 1994), and out of physical inability to access, or disinclination towards, heterosexual attractiveness. Girls at the margins of SEN can blend into the normative range of the class by positioning themselves as hardworking and diligent, and their difficulties may escape 'official' detection. But girls whose difficulties are more severe may find their room for manoeuvre severely constrained by the expectation that they will remain rather endearingly vulnerable.

> I sit with the science group. Anna is struggling . . . She asks if I will help her, and to refuse seems inhumane. She doesn't seem to like writing. She wants me to point to each word as she copies it. I get the impression that she doesn't actually need this amount of help, but it's a way of securing and retaining my attention. Every time I turn to Joe and Kofi, who are sitting next to her, she stops work. They, also, are doing very little. I try to help Joe to write a draft of his conclusion. All he then has to do is copy it out, but he doesn't do this. Instead, he starts to tease Anna. He makes fun of her, talking in a voice that is clearly supposed to be an imitation of the younger-than-eight-sounding way in which she speaks. Kofi tells him to leave Anna alone . . . I try to reconnect him with his work, but he is not having this. He calls Anna 'Sabrina the teenage witch' and she retaliates by saying that she really *will* be a witch when she grows up, and will turn him into a frog. She turns to me and asks if this is indeed a possibility – can one realistically hope to become a witch? Her question is transparently coquettish.
>
> (Fieldnotes, Year 3, Bankside Primary)

Both Anna and Joe have been identified as having MLD. In the above extract, Anna is positioning herself squarely within a discourse of rather charming, ultra-childlike vulnerability, securing the adult help that will enable her to complete her work but also re-inscribing herself as needy of help. There is a tendency for SEN discourses in school to draw upon what has been called the 'charity/tragedy model of disability' (Barton and Oliver 1997; Allan 1999; Thomas and Loxley 2001). The charity/tragedy model, which originated in the nineteenth century but continues to influence perceptions and practices today, positions people with disabilities as the helpless objects of pity, concern and charity, and is used to legitimate their control by non-disabled people. Likewise, SEN discourses can position particular children as the passive recipients of care and control (Tomlinson 1982), though this may not be the explicit intention of the educational professionals who work with them. As Riddell notes, 'there are clear connections between the child-centred approach in special educational needs and the individual tragedy discourse identified by disability theorists' (Riddell 1996: 4).

It is interesting to think about how class and 'race', as well as gender and SEN, are played out in the vignette. Anna had turned on me such a look of pathetic helplessness when I sat at her table that I could not do anything other than pay attention to what she was saying and doing. She was able to keep my attention focused on her through strategies that made her seem younger and less able to manage than was really the case: a conundrum of independence made to look like dependence, and activity made to look like passivity. The classed and raced stereotype of the 'dumb blonde' was a position made readily available to Anna who happens to be blonde, working class, and small for her age. Joe and Kofi aided and abetted her in this strategy. Kofi took up a 'gentlemanly' role in relation to Joe's teasing, positioning himself as Anna's protector. Joe's teasing worked to distance him from the model of needy, vulnerable child, enabling him to resist the position of 'helpee', and also drew attention to Anna's production of herself as needy and ultra-childlike. In parodying Anna's 'babyish' voice, he made the strategy look ridiculous, and also made me want to protect Anna from him, further inscribing Anna and myself within a helper/helped relationship. When my strategy for putting an end to the teasing was unsuccessful, Anna made use of a very different kind of feminine archetype – that of the witch – that Joe had introduced into the encounter. In momentarily abandoning the dumb blonde in favour of the mysterious and powerful figure of the witch, Anna threatened to strip Joe of his masculine power by turning him into a frog. But this re-positioning was short-lived, and she threw herself straight back into neediness and vulnerability, by asking me, with what seemed like deliberate childlike 'charm', whether she could really be a witch.

Something paradoxical is going on. If girls can be much more readily recognised as vulnerable and needy, and SEN discourses draw on vulnerability and neediness, why is it that girls are less likely to be identified as having SEN? Perhaps the answer to this lies partly in the fact that SEN discourses draw partly on the (feminised) notions of care and concern for the helpless, but also on the masculine notions of imposing control through a technical, managerial apparatus. Girls' expertise seems to lie in securing informal help: which can mean they access the help they need without recourse to the official channels of SEN identification and assessment, but could also mean that their difficulties 'may remain undiagnosed and invisible' (Riddell 1996), and that their access to SEN resources is unduly limited. Once identified as having SEN, however, girls find themselves all-too easily inscribed within traditional discourses of vapid and vulnerable femininities.

Addressing disparities in gender and SEN

In their study of differential SEN provision in mainstream primary schools, Daniels *et al.* note that,

> Boys' learning seems to be more teacher-dependent than girls', and boys have various anti-learning behaviours. Girls, on the other hand, have a capacity collectively to 'keep out' of SEN provision by generally supporting each other's learning, not demanding too much of the teacher's time, and giving each other appropriate help.
>
> (Daniels *et al.* 1996: 3)

Daniels and colleagues go on to recommend that mainstream schools should address the disparity in SEN provision through objective assessment criteria, resulting in equal provision for equal levels of educational need. This is fine, as far as it goes. But it does raise questions about how to prioritise educational needs that cannot be measured in the same currencies. How, for example, would we quantify the needs of a child with global learning difficulties, whose proficiency at reading is roughly that expected of a child four years younger, in comparison with a child who has, say, an autistic spectrum disorder, who is able to decipher print but has not yet developed the skills of making sense of what s/he reads? Perhaps it is more useful to keep in mind the necessity of equal provision across both genders, and to develop assessment and allocation systems accordingly, but in the context of attention to the gendered nature of school, classroom and playground cultures.

This is a long-term agenda, and, whilst the development of appropriate tools and strategies for the management of SEN is important, so, too, is an understanding of the implications of masculinities and femininities in the construction of SEN. Raphael Reed (1998: 72) critiques the tendency of school effectiveness and school improvement literature to demonise the 'under-achieving boy', and argues that, instead, what is needed is a reformulation of social justice ideals that will include 'a critical focus on gendered actions and school cultures alongside a continuing debate on the nature of the curriculum'. This critical focus has to take into account the reality that SEN are produced in relation to a school system in which testing, and the achievement of externally-determined 'expected levels' (DfEE 1999), have already, to some extent, positioned children with SEN as academic failures.

This kind of critical focus can be hard to operationalise in the current climate of accountability through test results and league tables, but it is not impossible. Hilltop Junior School in the Midlands, and George Holt Primary in London (not their real names) are high-achieving schools that prioritise inclusion in their development plans. George Holt is specifically resourced by its LEA to provide places for up to 12 children who have been identified as having EBD and who have been excluded from other primary schools[1]. The head teachers of both schools are passionate about a range of social justice issues, and maintain a belief in the possibility of addressing social inequalities through schooling. Both head teachers are committed to the inclusion of children for whom schooling has been a struggle, and they both share the view that this can be done without compromising 'standards'. Indeed, both schools are characterised by an orientation towards 'high standards', broadly conceived beyond the requirements of test results and performance management.

> Jack and Daisy are sitting on the same table, not next to each other, but near. Meg [the teacher] tells the class they can start. I'm not at all surprised when Jack's first response is to walk over to the waste-paper bin and spend ages sharpening his pencil. Daisy is alternately staring into space and swinging on her chair. The other children on the table – two girls and a boy – don't appear to be bothered by this, but get started on their own work. I begin to wonder whether Meg will have to intervene. One of the girls on the table nudges the boy, and indicates towards Jack. The boy gets up, goes over to where Jack is sharpening and re-sharpening his pencil, and offers to lend him one of his. Jack accepts, and returns to the table, where the boy shows him what to do. The two girls, who have been working together, lean over to help Daisy.

> (Fieldnotes, Year 5, Hilltop)

This incident, which I witnessed during my first classroom observation, turned out to be typical. Daisy and Jack are children who might, until recently, have found themselves in schools for children with MLD. They stand out fairly sharply in this mainstream classroom, as children for whom the ordinary work of the class is a struggle, and they are not always able to make sense of what is going on in the classroom. The class's literacy and numeracy targets, which are written on the board at the front of the classroom, are not accessible to Daisy and Jack, immediately positioning them as vulnerable. In many ways this is a constant conundrum in schools, since the curriculum necessarily contains activities and concepts that cannot be made meaningful to everyone. At Hilltop, this is a problem that is addressed head-on through flexible grouping policies that sometimes set children according to academic proficiency for discrete activities, and sometimes require them to work in mixed-proficiency groups. In the incident described above, and in many others I saw at Hilltop, both girls *and* boys appeared to be acting in the ways noted by Daniels *et al.*: the giving and receiving of help seemed to be taken for granted.

Hilltop emphasises education as a collective project, and a team enterprise, as does George Holt. Whilst neither school can completely resist 'the allure of competitive success in education which derives from [a] masculine world-view' (Potts 1997: 185), they are able

1 The data from George Holt Primary School were gathered as part of the Inclusion in Schools Project, funded by the Open University. I am grateful to project co-directors Janet Collins, Kathy Hall, Melanie Nind and Kieron Sheehy for permission to use these data here.

to mediate this through a very active construction of themselves as learning communities. George Holt has three 'golden rules': high standards, teamwork and celebrating success. Because these three rules operate very much as an integrated whole, they go some way towards re-configuring what counts as success: they carry with them the notion that individual success counts for much more when it is shared by the community, and that if an individual within the community 'team' is prevented from being successful, then the community is the poorer. I videotaped some Year 6 lessons at George Holt, and was struck, watching the videos, by the amount of 'helping' – the pursuit of shared, collaborative success – that went on, almost unseen, and again taken for granted.

> Ken tells the children to get into groups of four. There is instant noise and movement, as children negotiate their groupings. I zoom in on Stephen, who remains sitting, cross-legged, looking up and around him with a look of utter bewilderment on his face. I am somewhat surprised when Jermaine goes over to him, invites him to stand up, then puts an arm around Stephen's shoulder and negotiates for them both to join two girls. I wouldn't have been surprised if one of the high-status boys, or a girl, had looked after Stephen in this way. But I would have thought that Jermaine, who always seems to have an insecure grip on both academic and micro-cultural success, and who often acts 'macho', would have been resistant to grouping himself with a boy with SEN and two girls.

> (Fieldnotes, Year 6, George Holt)

George Holt Primary and Hilltop Junior both have robust SEN policies and procedures, with assessment criteria that are rigorously applied. This goes some way to ensuring gender parity in the allocation of SEN provision. Crucially, though, both schools address, on an ongoing basis, what Corbett (1999) has called 'deep culture', and this is what seems to make the difference in both schools. What they are doing is freeing up room for manoeuvre by both girls and boys: when 'help' is recast as shared pursuit of success, boys can take up helping and helped roles without consequent loss of masculine status, and girls who are struggling can access help without needing to position themselves as overly vulnerable or ultra-childlike. This is not to claim that either school has found the perfect solution. But both schools show us that, by paying attention to the gendering of SEN provision and to the gendered lives of children considered to have SEN, it is possible to address disparities in provision and generate conditions of greater equality in the drive towards inclusion.

Conclusion

Issues of gender are at the core of policy, practice and provision in relation to SEN, though they may not always be seen as such. Though the gendering of SEN provision is a crucial component in our (often unspoken) understanding of inclusion, it has been all too common for discussion of the intersection between SEN and gender to be limited to the popular notion of boys' 'underachievement'. This chapter has focused on the classroom experiences of girls and boys: it has explored both the ways in which assessment and common-sense understandings contribute to boys' over-representation amongst children considered to have SEN, and the differential implications and consequences of this over-representation. In drawing attention to masculinities and femininities as organising categories of analysis, I have shown how common-sense understandings and their gendered implications for SEN policy, practice and provision are played out in classrooms.

Studies of gender and SEN in the schools detailed in this chapter indicate that the reasons for, and implications of, gendered inequality are not amenable to easy resolution through simple, single solution 'quick fixes'. In two of the case-study schools, the inequalities and disparities generated for and by SEN provision were tackled head-on, through strategies that permeated the cultures of the two schools. Both schools were committed to high standards and inclusion, within an environment that encompassed – but was not determined by – standard measures of academic achievement. Neither school reduced the complexities of creating an inclusive learning community to the managerial level of targets set and met: rather, they both paid attention to the ways in which girls and boys lead gendered lives, and to the ways in which those gendered lives are nuanced by issues of perceived academic ability as well as by other indices of 'difference'. The experiences of the two schools suggest that change can be made at local (school and classroom) level when staff develop an understanding of how gender and SEN shape children's classroom lives, and when they are committed to opening up room for manoeuvre for girls and boys across the perceived 'ability' spectrum.

References

Allan, J. (1999) *Actively Seeking Inclusion: Pupils with special needs in mainstream schools*. London: Falmer Press.

Barton, L. and Oliver, M. (eds) (1997) *Disability Studies: Past, present and future*. Leeds: Disability Press.

Benjamin, S. (1997) *Fantasy Football League: Boys in a special (SEN) school constructing and reconstructing masculinities*. London: Institute of Education.

Benjamin, S. (1998) Fantasy Football League: boys learning to 'do boy' in a special (SEN) school classroom. In Walford, G. and Massey, A. (eds) *Children Learning in Context*. Stamford, Conn.: JAI Press Inc.

Benjamin, S. (2001) Challenging Masculinities: disability and achievement in testing times. *Gender and Education*, **13**(1), 39–55.

Benjamin, S. (2002) *The Micropolitics of Inclusive Education: An ethnography*. Buckingham: Open University Press.

Blair, M. (2001) *Why Pick on Me? School exclusion and black youth*. Stoke-on-Trent: Trentham.

Connell, R. W. (1995) *Masculinities*. Cambridge: Polity Press.

Corbett, J. (1999) Inclusivity and School Culture: the case of special education. In Prosser, J. (ed.) *School Culture*. London: Paul Chapman.

Daniels, H. *et al.* (1996) *Gender and Special Needs Provision in Mainstream Schooling*. Swindon: Economic and Social Research Council.

DfEE (1999) *National Learning Targets for England for 2002*. London: Department for Education and Employment.

Epstein, D. (1997) Boyz' Own Stories: masculinities and sexualities in schools. *Gender and Education*, **9**(l), 105–115.

Epstein, D. and Johnson, R. (1998) *Schooling Sexualities*. Buckingham: Open University Press.

Gard, M. (2001) I like smashing people and I like getting smashed myself: addressing issues of masculinity in physical education and sport. In Martino, W. and Meyenn, B. (eds) *What About the Boys? Issues of masculinity in schools*. Buckingham: Open University Press.

Hayden, C. (1997) *Children Excluded from Primary School*. Buckingham: Open University Press.

Kenway, J. and Bullen, E. (2001) *Consuming Children: Education, entertainment, advertising*. Milton Keynes: Open University Press.

Kenway, J. and Fitzclarence, L. (1997) Masculinity, Violence and Schooling: challenging 'poisonous pedagogies. *Gender and Education*, **9**(1), 117–33.

Lingard, B., Ladwig, J. and Luke, A. (1998) School Effects in Postmodern Conditions. In Slee, R., Weiner, G. and Tomlinson, S. (eds) *School Effectiveness for Whom? Challenges to the school effectiveness and school improvement movements*. London: Falmer Press.

Mehra, H. (1998) The permanent exclusion of Asian pupils in secondary schools in central Birmingham. *Multi-Cultural Teaching*, **17**(1), 42–8.

NACETT (2000) Aiming Higher: NACETT's report on the National Learning Targets for England and advice on targets beyond 2002. Sudbury: National Advisory Council for Education and Training Targets.

Nash, R. (2001) Class, 'Ability' and Attainment: A problem for the sociology of education. *British Journal of Sociology of Education*, **22**(2), 189–203.

OECD (2000) *Special Needs Education: Statistics and indicators*. Paris: Organisation for Economic Co-operation and Development: Centre for Educational Research and Innovation.

Parsons, C. (1996) Permanent Exclusions from Schools in the 1990s: trends, causes and responses. *Children and Society*, **10**(3), 255–68.

Potts, P. (1997) Gender and membership of the mainstream. *International Journal of Inclusive Education*, **91**(2), 175–187.

Raphael Reed, L. (1998) 'Zero Tolerance': gender performance and school failure. In Epstein, D., Elwood, J., Hey, V. and Maw, J. (eds) *Failing Boys? Issues in gender and achievement*. Buckingham: Open University Press.

Renold, E. (1997) 'All they've got on their brains is football': sport, masculinity and the gendered practices of playground relations. *Sport, Education and Society*, **2**(1), 5–23.

Riddell, S. (1996) Gender and Special Educational Needs. In Lloyd, G. (ed.) *'Knitting Progress Unsatisfactory': Gender and special issues in education*. Edinburgh: Moray House Institute of Education.

Rossiter, A. B. (1994) Chips, Coke and Rock-'n'-Roll: children's mediation of an invitation to a first dance party. *Feminist Review*, **46**, 1–20.

Skarbrevik, K. J. (2002) Gender Differences Among Students Found Eligible for Special Education. *European Journal of Special Needs Education*, **17**(2), 97–107.

Skeggs, B. (1997) *Formations of Class and Gender*. London: Sage.

Skelton, C. (2001) *Schooling the Boys: Masculinities and primary education*. Buckingham: Open University Press.

Thomas, G. and Loxley, A. (2001) *Deconstructing Special Education and Constructing Inclusion*. Buckingham: Open University Press.

Thorne, B. (1993) *Gender Play: Girls and boys in school*. New Brunswick, N.J.: Rutgers University Press.

Tomlinson, S. (1982) *A Sociology of Special Education*. London: Routledge and Kegan Paul.

Walkerdine, V. (1988) *The Mastery of Reason*. London: Routledge and Kegan Paul.

Walkerdine, V. (1997) *Daddy's girl: young girls and popular culture*. Basingstoke and London: Macmillan.

Wright, C. *et al*. (2000) *'Race', Class and Gender in Exclusion from School*. London: Falmer Press.

Like many of the chapters, this one addresses the minutiae of what goes on in schools and classrooms. It is unusual, however, in that Shereen Benjamin applies a sociological lens to the practices and processes she sees and describes. Such sociological approaches have been, and continue to be, crucial in the process of understanding the power dimensions at work in schools and to offering a critique of everyday practice.

Part 5

Beyond classrooms

CHAPTER 21

Bridges to literacy

Eve Gregory

In this chapter, Eve Gregory examines the experience of literacy that children from a wide range of backgrounds bring with them into school. She looks at the different values placed on those experiences and shows how the western model of literacy learning has dominated what schools view as 'good practice'. She shows how schools can use their growing awareness of the multiple pathways to literacy taken by children from different cultural backgrounds to broaden and enhance school-based literacy schemes. Once schools are aware of how children acquire literacy at home, then they can build bridges between themselves and the diverse communities from which their pupils are drawn.

Introduction

Although Shabbir's parents' own reading is now limited to the occasional newspaper, they pay for him to attend Bengali classes six times a week. His mother proudly pulls down a new satchel containing carefully covered books and a new pencil-case from a similar high cupboard to that in Nazma's house. By comparison, practice in English is very brief:

> He often brings home his reading book, but when he doesn't know a word, I tell him to ask the teacher . . . Look, he has more sense than I do (said laughing as he corrects an English word his mother has read) . . . Let's leave it, leave it to the teacher, who can help the child more, because it's too hard for us.
>
> (Gregory 1996a: 37)

What might family involvement in early literacy mean for parents who do not feel able to initiate their children into the types of reading which count in the eyes of the school? This question is important in Britain since the New Labour Government's promise to raise significantly literacy standards at age 11 will make particular and new demands upon all parents. Voluntary home/school 'partnership in reading' schemes are likely to be replaced by the introduction of compulsory home/school 'contracts' whereby parents will now be officially obliged to engage in specific homework activities with their children. The urgency behind these stems largely from the publication of results of national attainment tests in literacy, numeracy and science at age 11 (SATs) from 1993 which, for the first time, have given written confirmation of young children's performance and have highlighted considerable differences in their achievement in poorer and wealthier areas. The form and content of new home/school agreements or 'contracts' will, therefore, be crucial if real advances in economically disadvantaged areas are to be made.

The interaction between 6-year-old Shabbir and his mother, above, begins to reveal the complexity of what family involvement in early literacy actually means. Can we say that providing access to literacy in Bengali counts as 'involvement' or not? Are her reasons for leaving English literacy to the teacher in school justified? Can she be expected to help her son (the eldest child) with his English reading homework when she, herself, is unable to read or understand the text? Paradoxically, what Shabbir's mother views as active involvement in her son's reading development (like many other families, she pays for his Bengali classes) is unlikely to count as such by the school. The same may also apply to monolingual English families whose involvement in their children's literacy may take very different forms from those currently recognised by the teachers in school.

A number of questions will need to be considered before official contracts for family involvement in literacy are introduced. Will only 'school literacy' count as valid or will children be recognised as members of different groups and communities with a variety of different literacies? Who will count as valid mediators of literacy in children's lives and in what contexts? Will the syncretism of home and school literacies be recognised as valid in the classroom? This chapter sets out to examine assumptions made by the currently accepted paradigm of family involvement in early literacy and then goes on to suggest a set of alternative principles and their implications for future practice.

Family involvement in early literacy: the current paradigm

Over the past two decades numerous studies from the English-speaking world point to the advantages for young children of family involvement in their literacy development. However, their emphasis has always been firmly and almost exclusively upon *parents* working with children *in specific ways* and often using particular school-sanctioned materials. Current models of *parental involvement in reading* in the UK are generally based on the following assumptions:

Assumption 1: *Parents need to perform school-devised activities using school materials and teaching methods. Successful parental involvement means that school reading and learning practices should be transmitted from school to home. Existing home and community practices are consequently unimportant for involvement.*

A number of studies in the UK point to the successful transmission of reading practices from school to home (see Hannon (1995) for a summary of these). Studies on the lack of parental involvement by lower social class parents during the 1970s (Newson and Newson 1977) coupled with evidence of unsatisfactory reading standards by their children (DES 1975) were also used to support a transmissionist argument: that improved performance might be achieved through involvement in school practices. A number of research studies and practical classroom projects detail particularly the improved achievements of children from lower social class backgrounds when their parents learn and take over school practices (Hewison and Tizard 1980; Tizard *et al.* 1982; Hannon and Weinberger 1994). The assumption that only school reading practices count as valid is also furthered by research suggesting that a certain type of reading will be important to which 'non-school-oriented' families may not have access at home (see Assumption 4).

A transmissionist model is also informed by a number of 'family literacy' programmes taking place in the USA. These aim to target the poor literacy skills of both parent and child and often comprise workshops where parents practise how to read with their children (summarised in Nickse 1993). Nevertheless, these have been countered by considerable evidence from longitudinal ethnographic studies detailing the *different* but nevertheless extensive literacy practices taking place in non-school-oriented families of both American (Heath 1983; Anderson and Stokes 1984) and immigrant origin (see Assumption 2 below). Arguing against a transmissionist approach, Auerbach (1989) has proposed a socio-contextual model where teachers ask: 'What strengths exist in the family and how can schools build upon them?' Some studies detail practical projects conducted jointly by university and school staff which attempt this (Moll *et al.* 1992; Gallimore and Goldenberg 1993). Similar projects are still unusual in the UK partly owing to the lack of tradition of collaborative work between anthropologists or other university-based staff and teachers and partly owing to a lack of funding for longitudinal ethnographic studies. However, evidence emerging from studies on the Gujarati-speaking community in Leicester (Martin-Jones *et al.* 1996) and the Cantonese-speaking communities in Northampton and Reading (Edwards 1995; Gregory 1996a) shows a similar variety and wealth of practices with the difference that even *very young children* are participating in extensive formal literacy classes outside the mainstream school. The assumption, therefore, that the school has nothing to learn from these and that only school practices are valid for home reading programmes must be seriously questioned.

Assumption 2: *The same home reading programmes are suitable whatever linguistic background, monolingual or bilingual, children may come from. Parents should be capable of helping their children to complete work whether or not they read English.*

Researchers in the UK have generally shown a reluctance to recognise cultural differences in the learning practices of minority group families. A number of factors might be responsible for this. Since the debate on linguistic and cognitive 'deficit' or 'difference' (Bernstein 1971; Labov 1972), researchers and teachers have been anxious to emphasise *similarities* rather than differences in language use in the homes of different social classes (Wells 1981; Tizard and Hughes 1984). A second reason may well stem from the strong British tradition of *child-centredness* in early-years education which is focused on the child as *individual* rather than a member of a cultural or ethnic group. Finally, recent government policy in the UK stresses the need to promote a 'common culture' (Tate 1995) which will iron out cultural differences between groups. This aim is practically reinforced by the English national curriculum (DfE 1995), which fails to acknowledge the learning practices of different minority groups. 'Equality of opportunity', a promise which is made in the Education Act of 1988, is currently interpreted as 'the same' provision. In practice, this means that families not benefiting from the 'equal opportunity' provided are viewed in terms of linguistic, cognitive or cultural deficit. Such a narrow definition of culture ignores the multiple pathways to literacy shown by both adults and children from minority groups in western societies (Baynham 1995; Luke and Kale 1997).

As a consequence, teachers in the UK are unable to draw upon the large body of studies on the literacy and learning practices of different cultural groups as are their colleagues in the USA. Here teachers benefit from a tradition of research investigating continuities and discontinuities of home and school learning practices (Scollon and Scollon 1981; Heath 1983; Duranti and Ochs 1996) as well as work available on the learning styles of different cultural groups and the effect of the knowledge of these on teaching styles (Michaels 1986). Nevertheless, some recent studies in the UK are beginning to reveal the rich variety of literacy practices of minority groups which may remain unknown to their children's teachers (Martin-Jones *et al.* 1996; Gregory 1996a).

Assumption 3: *Home reading programmes are for parental involvement not wider family or community participation.*

Current home reading programmes assume *parental* involvement rather than involvement by the wider family or community in young children's reading. However, the role of siblings in children's learning has been the subject of various research studies; some reveal how young children learn social and emotional skills (Dunn 1989) and cognitive skills (Cicerelli 1976) from older siblings. Others show how in non-western societies older siblings are often culture brokers who may be as influential or more influential than parents in socialising young children (Whiting and Edwards 1988; Rogoff 1990). Recent studies are beginning to highlight the special role which may be played by older siblings in linguistic minority families where parents do not speak the new language (Tharp and Gallimore 1988; Zukow 1989; McQuillan and Tse 1995) and to suggest that the ways in which children learn from older siblings in the home environment may have implications for school learning. The role played by grandparents in home literacy teaching may also be significant in closely-knit families (Padmore 1994; Williams 1997), likewise other family members, such as uncles, aunts and older cousins or friends in the widest sense. These studies problematise the notion that parents will be the exclusive caregivers and 'teachers' in families of all backgrounds.

Assumption 4: *The story-reading practice between parent and young child as it takes place in western school-oriented homes provides 'enjoyment' and 'fun' and is the most valuable preparation for children's early literacy development. Although children may participate in other practices at home and in the community, these do not initiate children into crucial patterns for school success.*

Official education reports since the 1970s have little doubt as to the precise material and form necessary for these early reading experiences:

> . . . the best way to prepare the very young child for reading is to hold him on your lap and read aloud to him stories he likes, over and over again . . . We believe that a priority need is . . . to help parents recognize the value of sharing the experience of books with their children.
>
> (DES 1975: 7.2)

The official view that 'Babies need books' and that it is the duty of parents to provide these has changed little in later decades; during the 1980s the directive states clearly that 'parents should read books with children from their earliest days, read aloud to them and talk about the stories they have enjoyed together' (DES/Welsh Office 1989: 2.3) and we read that parents of the very youngest children should support learning through 'reading and sharing books'(SCAA 1996: 7).

These official directives are drawn from findings from a number of longitudinal studies which show how a familiarity with written narrative and story-reading promotes cognitive and linguistic growth as well as preparing children for school literacy (Dombey 1983; Fox 1988). Others go further to suggest that the early reading difficulties experienced by some children may result generally from their narrative inexperience (Wells 1987) or, more specifically, through their lack of knowledge of when and how to provide 'what' explanations when required (Heath 1983). Studies on the type of reading taking place during Qur'anic classes (Wagner 1994) are not generally viewed as relevant to the British school context. However, whilst not denying the importance of experience of written narrative as a preparation for school, some researchers point to additional factors for early reading success, especially in socially disadvantaged areas. Tizard *et al.* (1988) maintain that children's knowledge of the alphabet at school entry is an important determinant for achievement at age 7 and Gregory (1993) argues that early success hinges on a child's ability to work out the cultural rules of classroom reading lessons.

A result of the current paradigm of *parental involvement in early literacy* means that it is generally assumed that all children should enter school in possession of the same 'cultural capital' (Bourdieu 1977) of the English language, culture and learning styles, represented by a familiarity with written stories imparted by the parent at home. Little attention has been given to families who do not share these ways of life. Yet paradoxically, it is precisely those parents whom the government wants most to become involved in school learning. Paradoxically also, it is likely to be these parents who view formal English teaching to be the role of the teacher in school. This may be particularly true for newly arrived immigrant families. A survey conducted in 1991 by the University of Lancaster, 'Bangladeshi Parents and Education in Tower Hamlets' (Tomlinson and Hutchinson 1991), conducted with 53 families, found that although 93 per cent of the parents they interviewed reported receiving books home from school, only 40 per cent of mothers and 50 per cent of fathers said they felt able to use these with their children. Their reasons for not doing so fell into two categories:

1 an inability to speak English: 'My English is not good enough . . . We can't do this, it is too difficult.' (p. 21)
2 the belief that it is the teacher's job to teach the children to read in English – especially knowing how little English they spoke (71 per cent judged their oral English to be either non-existent or poor and only 33 per cent claimed they were able to read or write in English as opposed to 80 per cent who were literate in Bengali).

One reason explaining the lack of involvement by parents may have been the stress placed upon *parents reading to children* which has meant that children are likely to take home books which depend upon the ability of the parent to understand and read the English text to the child. Coupled with the assumption that everyone should understand both the theory and practice of story-reading, teachers may well be asking many monolingual English and limited English speaking parents to do the impossible without actually explaining how and why they should do it. It is, therefore, understandable that parents may feel both disempowered and resentful of what is requested of them (Gregory *et al*. 1993).

In what ways might this discussion inform future literacy contracts? The second part of this chapter outlines key principles behind an alternative paradigm of family involvement in literacy and their implications for practitioners in devising home/school literacy programmes.

Recognising differences: some key principles

The second part of this chapter outlines principles and practical implications for future family literacy involvement which stress the recognition of *diversity and contrasts* through experience of a number of different reading practices (involving different purposes, materials and methods), taking place with a variety of *guiding lights* (Padmore 1994) or *mediators* of literacy and a *dynamism and syncretism* of home and school learning practices. Evidence upon which these principles are based is drawn from development projects and research studies taking place in the USA (Heath 1983; Moll *et al*. 1992; Au 1993; Duranti and Ochs 1996; Volk 1997), Australia (Freebody *et al*. 1995; Cairney and Ruge 1998) and particularly from an ongoing research and development project taking place in Spitalfields, East London (Gregory *et al.* 1996; Gregory and Williams 2000). Each of the above projects provides detailed insights into the literacy practices taking place in different communities of economically disadvantaged groups together with accounts of classroom practice showing ways in which family involvement might take this knowledge as a starting-point. Data from the Spitalfields project is used to illustrate the practical implications of each principle below.

Principle 1: *Recognise and acknowledge the variety of literacies and 'funds of knowledge' in the lives of children and their families as practised through home and community activities.*

Hasna:	. . . I didn't read *Winnie-the-Pooh* or *The Jungle Book* or anything like that. You know, if I speak to a lot of my white friends, they were really into *Winnie-the-Pooh*. It was an integral part of their bed-time stories. You know, the concept of a bed-time story didn't exist in my family.
Interviewer:	Would you have Bengali stories read to you?
Hasna:	No. It depends on the dynamics of your family unit. Some families do, some don't. It's got nothing to do with the nationality of a family. And I didn't have any *Winnie-the-Pooh* stories or their Bengali equivalent. So Enid Blyton I read . . .

(Hasna, aged 23, who grew up and was educated in Spitalfields, East London and who has since gained a higher degree from London University)

The absence of bedtime story-reading is a common factor uniting participants in ethnographic studies on economically disadvantaged communities across the USA (Heath 1983; Anderson and Stokes 1984; Duranti and Ochs 1996), Australia (Freebody *et al.* 1995; Cairney and Rouge 1998) and the UK (Minns 1990; Gregory 1996b). Nevertheless, families in all these studies took part in a wide range of reading practices. Table 22.1 reveals the scope and nature of reading in the lives of thirteen 5-year-old children (six monolingual English and seven bilingual Bangladeshi British children) in two adjacent schools in Spitalfields, East London. These show clearly how the nature of the reading activities differed in the groups as well as between both groups and the school.

However, in spite of differences between the monolingual English and the Bangladeshi British community, there were a number of common factors. Significantly, both groups of children spent considerably longer engaged in 'non-homework' reading activities at home and in the community than in work specifically sent from school. Both viewed reading primarily as a group rather than an individual activity (this was particularly so for the Bangladeshi British children). Both viewed formal 'homework' (community language or religious class or work sent from school) as a serious activity which involved repetition, practice and (for the Bangladeshi British children) a test before it was judged to have been satisfactorily carried out.

Insight into the literacy practices of individual school communities is important for practitioners if a principal aim is to build upon the strengths of families rather than exploit their weaknesses. Evidence from the Spitalfields project shows that, for this community, 'school-type reading' and *homework* are serious rather than 'fun'. This has been reflected by readers from different generations: 'I used my reading for learning. I went to evening classes. Then I had to pass exams for gardening . . .' (Annie, 82); '. . . I worked out that if you read a lot of books it improves your learning anyway. And it did . . .' (Hasna, 23).

Recognition of home and community literacies means deciding whether a variety of literacy materials in different languages, which are available to children, will be considered 'valid' or will be used in home or school reading programmes. Further, it means looking carefully at the availability and cost of certain reading materials, whether or not families prefer to buy or borrow, as well as examining how far both content and language are accessible to parents with limited skills in written English. It also means examining different learning styles and patterns of interaction used as families 'teach' young children. Some parents in the Spitalfields project looked back on very different methods from those used currently in English schools: 'The teacher would show us how to write letters and make sounds. We also had a private tutor and he would guide our hand with his to help our handwriting . . .' (Louthfer's mother in Gregory 1996a: 40).

Finally, and highlighted by the experience of Louthfer's mother, it means understanding that *parents* may not always consider themselves equipped to teach their children this particular skill and prefer to look to other mediators of literacy in the community for guidance and help.

Principle 2: *Understand and support the value of different mediators of literacy or 'guiding lights' in children's literacy development.*

> Like many of the children he (Louthfer) rocks to and fro to the sound of the voices. Children do this because they are encouraged to develop a harmonious voice; they are told Allah listens to His servants and is pleased if time is taken to make the verse sound meaningful. The old man's wife takes the children who have already started the Qur'an into a separate room, so she can hear the recitations clearly. She comments, 'English is very important for this life. But Arabic is required for the life hereafter, which is eternal. Therefore, it must be given greatest importance . . . Or else, how can our children know?'
>
> (Gregory 1996a: 41)

In contrast with the current emphasis on the responsibility of the *parent* as story-provider and reader, childhood initiation into literacy may be seen by many families as a *collaborative group activity* whereby the cultural knowledge of generations is passed on through a whole variety of mediators and methods. Mediators may be within the

Table 22.1 Children's out of school literacy activities

(a) Bangladeshi British children

Type of practice	Context	Participants	Purpose	Scope	Materials	Role of child
Qur'anic class	Formal: in classrooms or someone's living room	Group of up to 30 mixed age-range	Religious: to read and learn the Qur'an	Approx. 7 hours per week	Raiel (wooden book stand). Preparatory primers or Qur'an	Child listens and repeats (individually or as a group). Practises and is tested
Bengali class	Formal: in classrooms or someone's living room	Group of mixed age-range. Can be children of one family up to group of 30	Cultural: to learn to read, understand and write standard Bengali	Approx. 6 hours per week	Primers, exercise books, pens	Child listens and repeats (individually or as a group). Practises and is tested
Reading with older siblings	Informal: at home	Dyad: child and older sibling	'Homework': to learn to speak and read English	Approx. 3 hours per week	English school books	Child repeats, echoes, predicts and finally answers comprehension questions
Videos/Television	Informal: at home	Family group	Pleasure/ entertainment		TV in English. Videos (often in Hindi)	Child watches and listens. Often listens to and joins in discussions. Sings songs from films.

Table 22.1 Children's out of school literacy activities (continued)

(b) English monolingual children

Type of practice	Context	Participants	Purpose	Scope	Materials	Role of child
Playing school	Informal: at home	Group or individual	Play		Blackboard, books, writing materials	Child imitates teacher and/or pupils
PACT (parents and children together: home reading scheme)	Informal: at home	Dyad: parent/child	Homework: to improve child's reading		School reading book	Child reads and is corrected by parents using 'scaffolding' or 'modelling' strategies
Comics, fiction, non-fiction	Informal: at home	Individual or dyad (parent or grand-parent/child)	Pleasure		Variety of comics, fiction, non-fiction books	Child as 'expert' with comics or books; as interested learner reading adult non-fiction, magazines, etc.
Drama class	Formal	Group	Pleasure and to learn skill	2 hours per week	Books: poetry and plays	Child performs in group; recites as individual
Computers	Informal	Individual or in dyad with friend or sibling	Pleasure		Computer games	Child as expert
Video/Television	Informal	Family group or entertainment	Pleasure/ entertainment		TV/videos	Child as questioner

Source: Gregory and Williams 1998

family as grandparents (Padmore 1994; Luke and Kale 1997; Williams 1997) or siblings (Volk 1997; Gregory 1997); or in the wider community as friends (Long 1997) or aunts (Duranti and Ochs 1996), clubs and libraries (Gregory 1999) or religious and community classes (Wagner 1994).

Mediators in the community

Perhaps the most significant mediator of childhood literacy in the outside school lives of both young Bangladeshi British and older Jewish participants in the Spitalfields project was their community and religious classes. For the former group, this meant up to twelve hours per week spent at Bengali and/or Qur'anic classes. Although the role of religious classes on the literacy development of children has generally received little attention, studies undertaken (see Zinsser 1986 and Gregory 1994) detail ways in which children learn to read different scripts using a variety of methods plus a set of procedural rules (Street and Street 1995) on how to behave during literacy events.

Methods of teaching during classes conform strictly to the pattern 'Demonstration, Practice, Test'. A typical excerpt shows what this might look like in practice as five-year-old Shuma reads at her Qur'anic class, which takes place at her neighbour's house:

Teacher:	Read this, Shuma.
Shuma:	Alif, bah, tah, sayh, hae …
Teacher:	What was that? Say it again.
Shuma:	Alif, bah, tah, sayh, jim.
Teacher:	Um, that's it, now carry on.
Shuma:	Jim – jim, hae, kae, d- (hesitates),
Teacher:	Dal – dal, *remember it and repeat*.
Shuma:	Dal, zal, rae, zae, sin, shin, swad, dwad,
Teacher:	(nods), What's next?' Thoy, zoy,
Shuma:	Zoy, thoy,
Teacher:	No, no, *listen carefully*. Thoy, zoy,
Shuma:	(repeats)
Teacher:	Okay. Say it again from the beginning …

(Gregory *et al*. 1996: Appendix 2)

Similar patterns of interaction occur during Bengali classes, drama, choral and other music lessons where accuracy is considered important. By contrast, some community mediators, such as librarians and other social club leaders, may allow autonomy and encourage work in pairs where individuals, themselves, take the initiative. Such work corresponds more closely to reading which may take place with mediators other than parents at home.

Mediators of literacy at home

Various studies show young children reading with different family members who may have more time or may be better able to initiate children into school reading practices. Although an under-researched group, we know that grandparents play an important role in handing down cultural and linguistic knowledge of both the family and community through literacy practices (Luke and Kale 1997; Williams 1997). Friends at home may also be important for children entering a new linguistic community (Long 1997). For first and second generation immigrants, older siblings are likely to become crucial mediators of literacy who play a substitute but very different role from that which parents may take in monolingual households. The Spitalfields project highlights ways in which siblings engage in extensive *homework activities* with young children (Gregory 1998). Teaching strategies are characterised by a finely-tuned 'scaffolding' which is only very gradually removed. This scaffolding syncretises strategies learned during Qur'anic and English classes. The older child at first allows repetition or echoing of one word (gave/gave; her/her; fishy/fishy; gifts/gifts) resulting in a very high number of fast and smooth exchanges; this 'scaffold' is gradually removed to allow prediction and text-based questions built more upon school-based strategies.

Teachers devising home/school agreements will need to consider carefully whether and in what ways homework schemes will take account of existing mediators of literacies in children's lives. If the role of older siblings is to be recognised, should they be asked to adopt school teaching strategies or remain as cultural and linguistic 'bridges' between children's different lives? How far do children's clubs and activities 'count' as valid *homework* if it is out of control of the school? What might be the role of *homework clubs* as a literacy domain?

Principle 3: *Recognise the syncretism between home/community and school learning in classrooms and school homework clubs.*

> I went to drama club . . . It was brilliant . . . It was the beginning . . . 'cos I went into entertainment. One of our teachers is a famous producer now . . . I did my first play when I was 10 and a half. It was called *The Italian Straw Hat*. It's a very old Italian play. I'd been there only three months and I was saying 'I can do that. No problem …'
> (Andrew, now aged 40, reflecting on living in Spitalfields as a child, in Gregory 1999)

Clubs, community classes, libraries and siblings are all recalled by participants in the Spitalfields research as 'bridges' between home and school learning. Interaction between siblings in linguistic minority families reveals a syncretism whereby familiar strategies from both community and school reading classes are blended to form a dynamic literacy practice presently regarded as *homework* by the children. Studies from the USA (Au 1993; Heath 1983; Moll *et al*. 1992) and Australia (Cairney and Ruge 1998) show how home/school literacy schemes are most successful when teachers are knowledgeable about the strengths of their communities and encourage a syncretism of practices in their classrooms. In a study of innovative home/school partnerships in four multi-ethnic schools in Australia, Cairney and Ruge (1998) discuss the role of children themselves as mediators between home and school. Bruner (1986) has referred to the 'joint culture creation' needed for learning which recognises that every classroom community will be different and, as a consequence, every homework scheme will reflect this difference. Teachers in Britain might well consider the role of homework clubs in literacy development. Are they viewed as creating a dynamic new culture of learning which syncretises home/school practices rather than seeking to recreate the established practices of classrooms? A practical classroom project describing one school's approach to family literacy involvement can be found in Gregory (1996b).

Summary and conclusion

> One also hears the claim, 'All children should be treated alike. There should be no discrimination.' It must be conceded that to overlook individual differences and cultural differences and to treat everyone as though they were the same, does, indeed, involve a lack of discrimination. Think about it. It certainly is not in the child's interest.
>
> (Duquette 1992: 14)

The term 'equality of opportunity' is at the core of the Education Reform Act passed in Britain in 1988 and is central to the various documents emerging from it. It is reflected in the National Curriculum Council's initial promise (NCC 1988: 4) that it 'will be taking account of ethnic and cultural diversity and ensuring that the curriculum provides equal opportunities for all pupils, regardless of ethnic origin or gender'. The question addressed in this chapter has been: 'In what ways might equality of opportunity be provided for pupils whose parents are not familiar with school literacy practices?' Do we start by 'teaching' parents school literacy 'rules' (e.g. storybook-sharing etc.) or do we begin by learning about children's existing outside-school literacy knowledge and skills? Obviously, it is crucial that all young children become members of school literacies as early as possible; but may it be that these are best introduced explicitly by teachers within the culture of each individual classroom?

Seminal work during the early 1980s in Liberia was revolutionary in showing through tests how cognitive skills are clearly linked to a familiarity with specific cultural practices (Scribner and Cole 1981). This chapter argues that if real equality is to be promoted, we surely need to know which cultural practices young children know about both before and outside school. An approach which takes this knowledge by practitioners as a starting-point means reinterpreting family involvement in early literacy to take account of existing literacy knowledge in families, to recognise the vital role played by other mediators of literacy than parents and to be excited by the syncretism as children blend languages and literacies from home, community and school. Only then can we lay some claim to attempting to provide the equality which has been promised.

Acknowledgements

This research was supported by the Economic and Social Research Council, 1994–1995 (R000 22 1186) and a Leverhulme Research Fellowship in 1997. I should like to acknowledge the help of Ann Williams and Nasima Rashid, research officers on the ESRC project for the data collected as well as the families and teachers participating in the Spitalfields project.

References

Anderson, A. B. and Stokes, S. J. (1984) Social and institutional influences on the development and practice of literacy. In Goelman, H., Oberg, A. and Smith, F. (eds) *Awakening to Literacy*. London: Heinemann Educational.

Au, K. (1993) *Literacy Instruction in Multicultural Settings*. Fort Worth: Harcourt Brace.

Auerbach, E. R. (1989) Toward a social contextual approach to family literacy. *Harvard Educational Review*, **59** (2) 165–81.

Baynham, M. (1995) *Literacy Practices: Investigating literacy in social contexts*. London: Longman.

Bernstein, B. (1971) A socio-linguistic approach to socialisation with some reference to educability. In Hymes, D. and Gumperz, J. (eds) *Directions in Sociolinguistics*. New York: Rinehart & Winston.

Bourdieu, P. (1977) *Outline of a Theory of Practice*. Cambridge: Cambridge University Press.

Bruner, J. (1986) *Actual Minds, Possible Worlds*. Cambridge, MA: Harvard University Press.

Cairney, T. and Rouge, J. (1998) *Community Literacy Practices and Schooling: Toward effective support for students*. University of Western Sydney Nepean, Department of Employment, Education, Training and Youth Affairs.

Cicerelli, V. G. (1976) Mother–child and sibling–sibling interactions on a problem solving task. *Child Development*, **47**, 588–96.

Department for Education (DfE) (1995) *English in the National Curriculum*. London: HMSO.

Department of Education and Science (DES) (1975) *A Language for Life: Report of the committee of inquiry appointed by the Secretary of State for Education and Science under the chairmanship of Sir Alan Bullock*. London: HMSO (The Bullock Report).

Department of Education and Science (DES)/Welsh Office (1989) *English for Ages 5–16. Proposals of the Secretary of State for Education and Science and the Secretary of State for Wales*. London: Central Office of Information (The Cox Report).

Dombey, H. (1983) Learning the language of books. In Meek, M. (ed.) *Opening Moves*. Bedford Way Papers 17. Institute of Education, University of London.

Dunn, J. (1989) The family as an educational environment in the pre-school years. In Desforges, C. W. (ed.) *Early Childhood Education*. The British Journal of Educational Psychology Monograph Series no. 4, Scottish Academic Press.

Duquette, G. (1992) The home culture of minority children in the assessment and development of their first language. *Language, Culture and Curriculum*, **51**, 11–23.

Duranti, A. and Ochs, E. (1996) Syncretic literacy in a Samoan American family. In Resnick, L., Saijo, R. and Pontecorvo, C. (eds) *Discourse, Tools and Reasoning*. Berlin: Springer Verlag

Edwards, V. (1995) *Reading in Multilingual Classrooms*. Reading and Language Information Centre. Reading: University of Reading.

Fox, C. (1988) Poppies will make them grant. In Meek, M. and Mills, C. (eds) *Language and Literacy in the Primary School*. Lewes: Falmer Press.

Freebody, P., Ludwig, C. and Gunn, S. (1995) *Everyday Literacy Practices In and Out of Schools in Low Socio-Economic Status Urban Communities: A descriptive and interpretive research program*. Unpublished draft report.

Gallimore, R. and Goldenberg, C. (1993) Activity settings of early literacy: Home and school factors in children's emergent literacy. In Forman, E., Minick, N. and Stone, C. A. (eds) *Contexts for Learning*. New York: Oxford University Press.

Gregory, E. (1993) What counts as reading in the early years' classroom? *British Journal of Educational Psychology*, **63**, 213–29.

Gregory, E. (1994) Cultural assumptions and early years pedagogy: the effect of the home culture on children's reading in school. *Language, Culture and Curriculum*, **7** (2), 1–14.

Gregory, E. (1996a) *Making Sense of a New World: Learning to read in a second language*. London: Sage/Paul Chapman.

Gregory, E. (1996b) Learning from the community: a family literacy project in East London. In Wolfendale, S. and Topping, K. (eds) *Family Involvement in Literacy: Effective partnerships in education*. London: Cassell.

Gregory, E. (ed.) (1997) *One Child, Many, Worlds: Early learning in multicultural communities*. London: David Fulton.

Gregory, E. (1998) Siblings as mediators of literacy in linguistic minority communities. *Language and Education: an international journal*, **11** (l), 33–55.

Gregory, E. (1999) Myths of illiteracy: childhood memories of reading in London's East End. *Written Language and Literacies*, **12** (1), 89–111.

Gregory, E. and Williams, A. (1998) Family literacy and children's learning strategies at home and at school. In Walford, G. and Massey, A. (eds) *Studies in Educational Ethnography,* vol. 1. Stamford, Conn.: JAI Press.

Gregory, E. and Williams, A. (2000) *City Literacies: Learning to read across languages and cultures*. London: Routledge.

Gregory, E., Lathwell, J., Mace, J. and Rashid, N. (1993) *Literacy at Home and at School*. Literacy Research Group, Goldsmiths' College.

Gregory, E., Mace, J., Rashid, N. and Williams, A. (1996) *Family Literacy History and Children's Learning Strategies at Home and in School*. ESRC Final Report R 000 221186.

Hannon, P. (1995) *Literacy, Home and School: Research and practice in teaching literacy with parents*. London: Falmer Press.

Hannon, P. and Weinberger, J. (1994) Sharing ideas about pre-literacy with parents: working with parents to involve children in reading and writing at home in Sheffield. In Dombey, H. and Meek-Spencer, M. (eds) *First Steps Together: Home–school literacy in European contexts*. Stoke-on-Trent: Trentham Books.

Heath, S. B. (1983) *Ways With Words: Language, life and work in communities and classrooms*. Cambridge: Cambridge University Press.

Hewison, J. and Tizard, J. (1980) Parental involvement and reading attainment. *British Journal of Educational Psychology*, **50**, 209–15.

Labov, W. (1972) *Sociolinguistic Patterns*. Philadelphia: University of Philadelphia.

Long, S. (1997) Friends as teachers: the impact of peer interaction on the acquisition of a new language. In Gregory, E. (ed.) *One Child, Many Worlds: Early learning in multicultural communities*. London: David Fulton.

Luke, A. and Kale, J. (1997) Learning through difference: cultural differences in early learning socialisation. In Gregory, E. (ed.) *One Child, Many Worlds: Early learning in multicultural communities*. London: David Fulton.

Martin-Jones, M., Barton, D. and Saxena, M. (1996) *Multilingual Literacy Practices*: Home, community and school. ESRC Final Report, R 000 23 3833.

McQuillan, J. and Tse, L. (1995) Child language brokering in linguistic minority communities. *Language and Education*, **9**, (3), 195–215.

Michaels, S. (1986) Narrative presentations: an oral preparation for literacy with 1st. graders. In Cook-Gumperz, J. (ed.) *The Social Construction of Literacy*. Cambridge: Cambridge University Press.

Minns, H. (1990) *Read It To Me Now!* London: Virago Press.

Moll, L., Amanti, C., Neff, D. and Gonzalez, N. (1992) Funds of knowledge for teaching: using a qualitative approach to connect homes and classrooms. *Theory into Practice,* **31** (2), 132–41.

National Curriculum Council (1988) *Introducing the National Curriculum Council.* London: National Curriculum Council.

Newson, J. and Newson, E. (1977) *Perspectives on School at Seven Years Old.* London: Allen & Unwin.

Nickse, R. (1993) A typology of family and intergenerational literacy programmes: implications for evaluation. *Viewpoints*, **15**, 34–40.

Padmore, S. (1994) Guiding lights. In Hamilton, M., Barton, D. and Ivanic, R. (eds) *Worlds of Literacy.* Clevedon: Multilingual Matters.

Rogoff, B. (1990) *Apprenticeship in Thinking: Cognitive development in social contexts.* Oxford: Oxford University Press.

School Curriculum and Assessment Authority (SCAA) (1996) *Desirable Outcomes for Children's Learning on Entering Compulsory Education.* London: HMSO.

Scollon, R. and Scollon, B. K. (1981) *Narrative, Literacy and Face in Interethnic Communication.* Norwood, NJ: Ablex Publications.

Scribner, S. and Cole, M. (1981) *The Psychology of Literacy.* Cambridge, MA.: Harvard University Press.

Street, B. and Street, J. (1995) The schooling of literacy. In Murphy, P., Selinger, M., Bourne, J. and Briggs, M. (eds) *Subject Learning in the Primary Curriculum.* London: Routledge.

Tate, N. (1995) Summing up speech at the International Conference on Teaching English as an Additional Language (SCAA) London, April 1995.

Tharp, R. and Gallimore, R. (1988) *Rousing Minds to Life: Teaching, learning and schooling in social context.* Cambridge: Cambridge University Press.

Tizard, B. and Hughes, M. (1984) *Young Children Learning.* London: Fontana.

Tizard, J., Schofield, W. and Hewison, J. (1982) Collaboration between teachers and parents in assisting children's reading. *British Journal of Educational Psychology*, **52**, 1-15.

Tizard, B., Blatchford, P., Burke, J., Farquhar, C. and Plewis, I. (1988) *Young Children at School in the Inner-City.* London: Lawrence Erlbaum Ass.

Tomlinson, S. and Hutchinson, S. (1991) *Bangladeshi Parents and Education in Tower Hamlets.* Research Report. Advisory Centre for Education, University of Lancaster.

Volk, D. (1997) Continuities and Discontinuities: teaching and learning in the home and school of a Puerto-Rican five-year-old. In Gregory, E. (ed.) *One Child, Many Worlds: Early learning in multicultural communities.* London: David Fulton.

Wagner, D.A. (1994) *Literacy, Culture and Development: Becoming literate in Morocco.* Cambridge: Cambridge University Press.

Wells, G. (1981) *Learning Through Interaction.* Cambridge: Cambridge University Press.

Wells, G. (1987) *The Meaning Makers.* London: Hodder & Stoughton.

Whiting, B. and Edwards, C. (1988) *Children of Different Worlds: The formation of social behaviour.* Cambridge, MA.: Harvard University Press.

Williams, A. (1997) Investigating literacy in London: three generations of readers in an East End family. In Gregory, E. (ed.) *One Child, Many Worlds: Early learning In multicultural communities*. London: David Fulton.

Zinsser, S. (1986) For the Bible tells me so: teaching children in a fundamentalist church. In Schieffelin, B. and Gilmore, P. (eds) *The Acquisition of Literacy: Ethnographic pespectives*. Norwood, NJ.: Ablex Publications.

Zukow, P. G. (1989) Siblings as effective socialising agents: evidence from central Mexico. In Zukow, P. G. (ed.) *Sibling Interactions Across Cultures: Theoretical and methodological issues*. New York: Springer Verlag.

Once again, we see in this chapter how respect for difference can lead to increased awareness of what homes and families can contribute to school life. Schools become more diverse and inclusive when they value and celebrate what their pupils bring with them. Again, openness to change and willingness to learn from each other lead to transformation of practice.

Index